*Could you Survive
Midsomer?*

A WINTER'S
MURDER

Could you Survive Midsomer?

A WINTER'S MURDER

Simon Brew

First published in Great Britain in 2024
by Cassell,
an imprint of Octopus Publishing Group Ltd
Carmelite House
50 Victoria Embankment
London EC4Y 0DZ
www.octopusbooks.co.uk

An Hachette UK Company
www.hachette.co.uk

Distributed in the US by
Hachette Book Group
1290 Avenue of the Americas
4th and 5th floors
New York, NY 10104

Distributed in Canada by
Canadian Manda Group
664 Annette St.
Toronto, Ontario, Canada M6S 2C8

ISBN: 978-1-788405-034

A CIP catalogue record for this book is
available from the British Library.

Printed and bound in Great Britain.

1 3 5 7 9 10 8 6 4 2

Publisher: Trevor Davies
Senior Editor: Faye Robson
Copy Editor: Laura Gladwin
Designer: Rachael Shone
Illustrator: Ruth Palmer
Senior Production Manager: Peter Hunt

MIX
Paper | Supporting
responsible forestry
FSC® C104740

CONTENTS

HOW TO PLAY

Hello, Detective. Welcome back to Midsomer.

The aim of the adventure you're about to undertake is simple: survive. Can you make it through the festive season in Midsomer, all while trying to get to the bottom of a murder case?

Depending on which path you take through the story, you'll uncover different clues and meet with different endings. You might solve parts of the case – possibly all of it. There are all sorts of secrets waiting for you, and lots of different outcomes.

All you need to remember is this: at the end of each passage of text, you'll be directed to the numbered section you need to read next. Most passages end in a choice: just follow the instructions and flick to the relevant section number (use the numbers at the top of the page to guide you) to continue your investigation. That's the easy bit. The trickier bit might be staying alive.

Once you reach the end of your adventure, go to your performance review on **pp.313–22** to see how well you did and get hints on what you missed, ready for your next crack at the case.

Stay safe out there – and we hope you make it through the villages of Midsomer in one piece . . .

1

As someone who hadn't lived in the beautiful village of Causton for long, Sara McLower was determined to play her part in making it one of the most talked-about places in the area.

Unlike many around her, who seemed to have been born, lived and died in the place, she'd chosen to come to Causton. She *wanted* to come back here. It seemed a lot safer than her previous home in the city, and she admitted that was a tiny part of her thinking too. But Causton was not, she knew, an accidental choice. She was here for a reason. Sara was in her late fifties, and was thoroughly fed up of moving around. She'd worked non-stop for decades, and bided her time before choosing the perfect house with her significant savings.

Oh, and the fact that her sister, Betty Grainger, ran the local pub? Sara loved that she was back, closer to family. Family hadn't always been easy.

Sara had quickly worked out that owning this particular property in Causton still brought with it some added expectations, especially around Halloween and Christmas. It was the first building many people saw as they drove through the area, and it set the tone for the rest of the village. After last year's power-cut incident with her festive lights, she wasn't going to let the side down today.

That's why she'd doubled her efforts this year. It didn't matter that she didn't really talk to too many people. She just needed to reconnect properly with Betty, and to be a part of the village.

The outside of the house was pretty much perfect. It'd taken a whole day at the start of the week to carve out the pumpkins and to arrange the decorations. It should have taken her less time, but she'd finally had to admit that her health was declining. Her energy levels had taken a hit, particularly this year, and she was having to carefully plan what she wanted to do and when. She'd be posting her Christmas gifts this year, rather than driving around and delivering them. Not that most of the people around here seemed to appreciate them.

Today's final job was preparing snacks. She was particularly proud of her cupcakes, which she'd been finessing that morning. It meant she'd have enviable treats for those who came knocking at the door. A Halloween to remember, she smiled, as she rearranged one of the many air fresheners and bowls of pot pourri about her home. Sara didn't just like things looking prim and proper – they had to smell that way too.

She was flagging now, though, and glad that she'd posted her letter this morning, rather than having to go out now. She looked at her watch. Just gone 5pm, and her energy levels were sapped. But, just like her sister, she knew that she needed to put on a show.

Thing is, she hated Halloween evening, in truth, but she knew she had to get through it. She took a gulp from the mug of cold-remedy drink, rinsed the cup and checked the oven was off.

Thinking she might just get an hour of rest before the procession of visitors started knocking, she cursed under her breath as the shrill sound of the electric doorbell broke the silence. One of those new-fangled things with a camera in that her nephew, Finn – Betty's son – had fitted over the summer.

She was supposed to check on the video feed on her phone really, but she struggled with technology. She and her sister were alike in that way. What's more, she was close to the door anyway. I may as well get my cupcakes and open it, she figured. I don't need to check who it is. The rain was still hammering down hard as she opened the chunky door.

It's odd what goes through your head when there's a pumpkin

being flung at speed towards your face. At least, Sara thought, she could take solace in the fact that she'd hollowed it out. It was going to be soft when it hit, wasn't it?

However, if only Sara had taken a moment to count her pumpkins this morning on her way to the post box, she'd have noticed that instead of the seven she'd put out at the front of the house, there had been eight.

It was the contents of the eighth that interfaced with her skull.

Her death wouldn't be immediate, though. She'd cling on for two weeks before her body gave up. But who would want her dead? And why?

This, Detective, is where you come in!
As a member of Causton's CID team, you're asked to represent
the department at Sara McLower's wake a few weeks later.
Soon, you're going to be choosing a path to follow through
the story, via the choices at the end of each passage. For
*now, jump to **48**, and head over to Sara's wake, one month*
later. There's a crime to solve . . .

→ *2* ←

You work through things as logically as you can: if you were Finn Grainger, where would you go? If he wanted quiet time, he could have gone just about anywhere. Your only tangible hope is that he might have gone home: well, to the Windy Dog anyway. It's there you head, parking your car at the back of the building, so as not to get in the way of some of the ongoing forensics work still taking place.

There's police tape here, of course, and you make your colleagues aware that you're about. There's no obvious sign of Finn's car, but you nonetheless decide it might be worth making your way inside the pub.

It's a shadow of the place it was the day before, as if time has stood still since last night's incident. You make your way behind the bar and into the back room. A few unopened Christmas cards are on the table, but otherwise it's quite tidy. You spot Archie's coat – or at least one of them – hung up. You can't help but feel sombre. You didn't even know him that well, and he certainly wasn't a fan of yours. Even so, he didn't deserve this.

You're lost in thought as a figure appears in the doorway. Finn Grainger. You offer an awkward hello, and he offers one in return. Whatever rage he was in, he's calmed down for now. But he's not happy.

'I want whoever did this,' he says. 'I'll help in any way I can.'

You work through what you know together, occasionally stopping as he composes himself again. The murder of Sara McLower, and her slow poisoning. The toxic reviews posted about the pub, that led to trade falling dramatically. And then, of course, the lights explosion.

'Do you think they're linked?' he asks you.

'I can't rule that out,' you admit. But in lieu of fresh information about the poisoning, and the lights, you turn to what's probably the smallest crime on that list: the reviews.

Finn pulls the reviews up on his phone, and you do the same. There's a familiar pattern to the way they appear to be written, but also, to your eyes, there are two slightly different styles here.

'Is there any way you can trace who wrote them?' he asks. 'Can't they tell you roughly where they came from, geographically?'

'You're more the tech expert than me,' you suggest. On a hunch, however, you head to the extensive terms and conditions of one of the websites. You're glad you had so much coffee today, else you'd nod off trying to read them. But you skim through until you find what you're looking for: that anyone leaving a review has to have verified they've visited the place in question, or prove they live in its geographic area.

'They're being posted from Causton?' he says.

'We can't be certain,' you admit. 'But it's possible. We could just use a computer expert around here.'

'The only one I know is Teddy Jones. He's never off the thing,' says Finn.

Alison and Bob's grandson. Of course. He does their shop deliveries for them, to make money for the latest gizmo he needs.

Thinking about it, that still doesn't make him an expert on review websites, but he's worth thinking about. You check that Finn's going to be okay – he's going back to his mother soon – and head to your car.

Time for another drive, Detective. Get moving over at **191**.

You've been seen, and whoever is in the house knows that they've been seen too. You go back to the window where you made your way in, and try to intercept them. You head around the house to relocate your route back in, navigate the bush, and you're just climbing through when you realize you've been outfoxed. Whoever it was has taken the slightly easier approach, and has gone for the front door. You might want to see them, but they're a lot less keen to see you.

The front door's easier to get out of, and they've taken advantage of that. As you make your way around to the front of the house again, you get a glimpse of the figure running away from you. They're heading across the field opposite: you can't chase them on car, and they're too far away for you on foot.

Resigned to the ear-bashing you're about to get from the Chief Inspector, you call the station and put out an alert. Not that there's going to be much they can do: whoever it was will have a solid start.

Still, you did get something out of this. You're almost certain the figure was male. Dressed all in black, and their face was covered. Wearing trainers, and standing around six foot tall. Relatively slim build. It's something.

It's a couple of hours before you're able to leave the property. The Chief Inspector was, as you predicted, not on the happy side, and your ears have been decorated with a couple of new words. A sweep of the house hasn't revealed anything of note. Just that whoever was in it appeared to be in one of the rooms at the top of the house. Were they taking stuff out, or bringing stuff in? The former, is the general consensus.

---

*There's nothing more you can do here for the minute, Detective. You'd best get back to the station before you get into even more trouble with the boss. Go to **128**.*

4

You make your way over the room to greet Betty Grainger and, with a pained expression, she attempts – and fails – to put a convincing smile on her face.

The weight of the world looks to be on her shoulders, though, and you're not surprised. Today, after all, she's had to bury her only sister. As Sara's closest surviving relative, it's Betty who's had to oversee a lot of the arrangements, all while dealing with the shock not just of Sara's death, but the manner of it as well. Nobody ever thinks they're going to die by having a brick-filled pumpkin shoved in their face, after all.

But this is a taxing day for Betty Grainger for a second reason: it's arguably the biggest day of the year for the pub and one of the most hotly anticipated days of the year for the locals: the evening the lights go on, and the festive season officially begins around these parts.

'I'm going to miss her,' she says of Sara, trying and failing to hold back a tear. 'I can't believe she's gone.'

You offer condolences.

Sara and Betty never struck you as especially close sisters, or at least they weren't for some time. Sara's return to Causton a few years ago was, Betty explains, something that closed the distance that had opened up between them. She was grateful Sara came back, especially after they lost their mother. Sara and Betty had needed each other.

You make further sympathetic overtures to Betty, but she spends more time looking into her cup of steaming herbal tea than at you. Usually, there's a bulletproof exterior to her, and she knows that she's going to find that strength again later. For the minute, she's doing her best to deal with her loss.

'I can't stop long,' she mumbles. 'Still so much to do for tonight.'

You've only been in Causton a few years yourself, but you know how big a night this evening is for the area.

'Is someone helping you set things up?' you enquire.

'Well, most of the lights were all finished last week. And I've had my boys with me today.'

Ah, her sons. Archie Grainger, who you – and everyone – knows, has recently been released from prison. Then Finbar Grainger, known to everyone as Finn, who's just returned home from university for Christmas.

She keeps her attention on the pub and its lights. 'Wish we'd had more time to test everything,' she remarks. 'No matter how early we start planning, there's always a job left that needs doing. Harder this week, of course, what with Sara dying . . .'

Tears flow. You dig out a clean tissue and hand it to Betty, and she gratefully takes it, mopping her eyes.

Even the sternest of Causton residents would have understood if she'd cancelled the lights switch-on party. But that's not Betty's way. Even when her mother owned the Windy Dog, the mantra was always the show must go on, no matter what.

Betty's attention seems to drift away as you keep talking, and you figure it's time to make tracks. 'Do come along later,' she weakly smiles, as you make your farewell.

Like you have a choice. The Chief Inspector has volunteered you and DS Lambie to attend. DS Lambie's already told you he's got a cast-iron excuse, and managed to get out of it. You know it'll just be you going along again.

Talking of the Chief Inspector, you'd best not keep her waiting any longer. You need to know what information she's got hold of.
*Go to **128**.*

→ 5 ←

You need a good reason to leave Causton in the middle of an active murder investigation, but you figure that this is it: a tangible lead on the poisoned food. You grab some of the rudimentary testing equipment from the station, and drive up to Moore Farm. You know it's going to be a six-hour round trip, but you also know you have to surprise them: if they know you're coming, you can hardly do a random test on their produce.

Traffic is not on your side, though: it takes you four hours to get there, having stood still at roadworks an hour out of Causton.

A bearded man called John hears your car approach and steps out to greet you. It's a small business without a shop to it, so he's not used to visitors. You hear his dogs barking in the background.

You introduce yourself, and he looks surprised, but not unwelcoming. He takes you into the main warehouse area, and shows you his fresh fruit and vegetables. That, and a collection of other natural products.

'Test anything you like,' he says. He's not affronted by your surprise arrival. If anything, he looks pleased of the opportunity to completely clear himself.

Which is what happens. He gives you a bag of his best plums to keep you company as you get to work. Your testing kit is basic, you're well aware of that, but after two hours in John Moore's company – and he insists on keeping old records playing on his turntable in the background – you're pretty certain he's got nothing to answer.

You, however? Well, that's different. As you step back into your car for the long drive home, it's an irate Chief Inspector who calls, and – roughly translated – wants to know 'where the hell you are,' or words to that effect.

She not very patiently explains that she has an active investigation and her lead officer has left the county on a wild goose chase.

It's an even longer journey home, too, compounded by the fact that the roadworks take twice as long to get through. When you finally arrive back in Causton, late into the evening, you glance at your phone to see a note from the boss.

This, she tells you, is no longer your case. She needs someone she can count on. And that, bluntly, isn't you.

Still, the plums were nice.

THE END

Go to p.313 to read your performance review.

Like many others in the Windy Dog, you fumble through the dark for a phone, and as fast as you can activate its torch. Within seconds, several other lights are offering at least some illumination. You pick up the faint sound of something outside, presumably people fussing over the lights. Inside, it's a case of what *isn't* happening. This hasn't happened before. This wasn't in the plan. It's a party night! The lights should be smiling over the Windy Dog now, and the queue for the bar should stretch to the front door.

Instead, there's a strange stillness, save for local resident Jack Linus yelling across the pub to Betty that she should have put a few more coins in the meter. About in line with the standard of most of Jack's jokes, that.

You flash your light towards the bar where Betty Grainger, usually the life and soul of the place, looks crestfallen. She's just standing there for a minute, not doing anything. Frozen.

One or two patrons take the opportunity to knock back their drinks, but if they were thinking of ordering another, one look at Betty is enough to dissuade them.

'Where's the fuse box?' you ask, your voice rising above the muted mumblings. Betty doesn't move at first. 'It doesn't matter,' she mutters. 'None of it matters anymore.'

'It's back here,' says a voice from the back. Finn Grainger. 'Can you give me a hand with it?'

---

*Does he really need a hand with a fuse box? Finn is quite capable
of sorting that himself. Maybe you're best staying put at **53**.
No: you need to get the lights back on, and fast.
Give Finn a hand at **27**.*

7

Sara McLower's car had been missing for a little while now, and it was surprising it hadn't been discovered before. Mind you, it wasn't the most reliable of vehicles, even when it was out and about. It seemed to spend half its time in for repair.

Her murder, anyway, looked uncomplicated. Checks were made as to the location of her vehicle, but no joy . . . at least, until now.

It's 40 minutes along narrow country lanes to even get close to where it's ended up, a good way out of Causton. After you've driven to the outskirts of Northfield Wood, you park up next to DS Lambie's vehicle. He got here first. Still, it's a 15-minute walk to get to the car itself, and it's DS Lambie who has to point it out to you. Someone made quite the effort to hide it, driving over the tree-lined hills. Surely someone saw or heard something?

Or maybe not. It's daytime now, early afternoon on a Friday, and the place feels secluded and empty. The morning dog walkers are long gone. In fact, it's thanks to a dog walker the car was found at all. They let their hound off its lead this morning, and it ran off. It took them a good hour or two to find the dog, and in turn they discovered the car. Obscured by a thick bush, you have to look twice yourself to spot it. It could have remained undiscovered for weeks further.

'He's a good dog,' explains Derek James, still looking a little exhausted from his long search for his pet. He knows you're not really supposed to let dogs off leads, given some of the things that go on here, and he looks slightly contrite. You decide to turn a blind eye.

'Charlie . . . that's the name of the dog . . . it took me ages to find him, then he just started going mad and barking loudly at the bush when he saw me. He's not done that before, but I guess we've not really walked up here the last few weeks, what with all the rain.'

You note that Charlie looks a little groggy.

'Is he okay?' you politely enquire.

'He was okay before,' Derek notes. 'He must have eaten something.'

'You keep talking to him and his dog, I'll check the car out,' D S Lambie says to you, as he heads towards the bush and pulls back the foliage.

'Tell me what happened,' you ask Derek, turning your attention back to him.

'Well, just what I said. Charlie started barking, and so I took a look. I recognized it fairly quickly as Sara's car, and then called you.'

'How did you know it was hers?'

'I just remember her from the Windy Dog. She drove down there sometimes. We're the only two teetotallers there, I think, and you know how everyone tries to park at the front down there. We've parked near each other a few times.'

The dog suddenly starts whining.

'Does he do that a lot?'

'No,' says a worried Derek James. He turns his attention to his pet, as you suddenly hear a thump from the car. But what do you do here?

The car! The thump! That's DS Lambie – surely
*he needs your help! Head to **184**.*
What on earth is wrong with the dog all of a sudden? Is there
*something off? **178** is where you need to go to prioritize that.*

You arrive a minute after Finn Grainger has entered the shop, and he's at the counter, demanding to see Teddy. 'Is something going on?' you ask.

Finn looks surprised to see you. Somehow – somehow! – he hadn't noticed you'd been following him. There's a career in hot pursuit for you yet, Detective.

'I just want to see Teddy.'

Behind the counter, Alison Jones looks puzzled and a little flustered. She looks unwell, too.

'His brother's died,' you tell her, appreciating it doesn't really explain why he wants to see Teddy in the first place.

Alison looks shocked and saddened. She calls in Bob, who's working away in the storage garage next door. She breaks the news to him, as Teddy Jones finally appears from the upstairs of the shop, where you suspect he's been playing video games, or whatever it is teenagers do in their bedrooms.

'Your father,' snarls Finn. 'Where's your father?'

His father?

What on earth is going on here?
*Your inclination is to let this play out: go to **106**.*

⇻ 9 ⇺

Hamilton Grainger turns back the way he came. You figure his vehicle is close, but not too close. You didn't see it pull up, but you did hear the noise of it arriving.

You step into Hamilton Grainger's path.

'Don't do this, Detective. I don't want to hurt you.'

'I can't let you go.'

'Detective, don't do this.'

'You know I have to stop you. You know you're a wanted man.'

'Detective.'

'I need you to stop now, or I have to call this in.'

'We had a deal. If you reach for a phone, it's the last thing you'll ever do.'

'Mr Grainger, stop.'

He looks at you.

You reach for your phone.

It's the last thing you ever do . . .

THE END

Go to p.313 to read your performance review.

⇻ 10 ⇺

You ask to look at the security tapes, and are guided to a tiny room at the back of the storage garage. A bit blink and you'll miss it, in fact. You wouldn't like to be rude and suggest they were pushed for space here, but you find yourself leaning on the toilet as you look at the antiquated-looking system. 'If you know how to work it! Don't ask me for help there!' chuckles Bob, as he points the equipment out.

There's a small screen attached to the system, and you press the power button. It flickers into life, and to your surprise, there's actually a live feed from the camera just inside the door to the garage. You admit to yourself you're surprised that it's still operational. You note that the extension lead to the electrical socket seems to be groaning with plugs. How has the place not overloaded?

In terms of the recordings, though, you're not hopeful. You cautiously put one of the stack of VHS tapes in the machine and, on the bright side, it works. When you press play, you do get footage from the security camera with a time stamp in the corner of the screen. Less impressively, the tape has clearly been used lots and lots of times, and there's significant wear in the picture quality. You can make things out, but not very clearly.

You look at your watch: you reckon you can give this half an hour or so, and so you press the fast-forward button to speed things up. After five minutes, you swap tapes. 'How far back do these go?' you ask Bob. 'Well, there's a few tapes, but only when I remember to change them.'

There's no eureka moment with these tapes, though, and there are better ways you can spend your time. If nothing else, it's confirmed that security is not top priority at Jones's Store.

But why would it be? Who would steal off these two? You ponder that as Bob puts in a fresh tape, and makes a show of putting it on to record. He'd hate you to think he's not security conscious.

You decide to investigate the produce Sara bought instead.
Go to **95.**

⇾ *11* ⇽

No chances here: the sheet of paper you're looking at through the clear plastic evidence bag looks harmless enough, but it feels unusual. You spend five minutes bidding farewell to Irene Whitley. Well, ten, once you've made her another cup of the powdery gunk she still insists on calling coffee.

You get to the station and the Chief Inspector is waiting. The pair of you put on gloves and take the sheet of paper out of the bag. You remove the piece of tape that's valiantly keeping it sealed, and open it out.

Just a simple piece of paper with a single message, scrawled in pencil: 'Tell them nothing, or you know what'll happen.'

Oh no. You've left her there by herself. The two of you look at each other, panicked. 'I'll get a unit there right away.'

She goes off to do that, and you get Irene Whitley on the phone. She answers quickly, but the tone of her voice is different.

'What do you know?' you ask her. 'What do you know about Hamilton Grainger?'

'N–nothing,' she says. 'Nothing at all.'

'But you said he comes to Causton . . . that he's been round the place?'

'I didn't,' she says. 'I don't know anything.'

You're puzzled, and there's silence for a moment. The Chief Inspector comes in and says a unit is 15 minutes away. You indicate that you're talking to Irene. She didn't realize you were on the phone.

Fifteen minutes is all the person sitting next to Irene Whitley, listening to the call, needs. As it happens, they've gathered what they needed, and made their exit in less than ten.

When a unit arrives, they find a very spooked Irene Whitley, refusing to say anything about the last half hour. Something has clearly scared her here, and someone has also clearly been alerted to the fact that you may have been on to them.

You don't know for sure that it was Hamilton Grainger, either. But you do know that whoever it was has slipped away from Causton by the time you all fully realize what's happened.

With their departure, sadly, goes any realistic chance of solving what's been going on . . .

THE END

Go to p.313 to read your performance review.

→*12*←

You love chatting to Irene Whitley, one of the people who was the most welcoming to you when you first moved to the area. Her health has been declining over the last year, and she doesn't get out of the house very often now. When she does, she's the absolute heartbeat of the room. She's brilliantly eccentric, and the world's a better place for her.

You pull up outside her small terraced house on the edge of the village and navigate her copious collection of garden ornaments, as if half the garden gnomes of Causton had emigrated to her garden.

You ring the bell, and it takes some time for her to answer. But eventually she buzzes you in.

'You want a coffee?' she beams, as she sees you. 'You'll have to get it yourself!'

She laughs, and it's infectious. 'No, thanks,' you reply. 'But I'll get you one.' You spend the next five minutes boiling a kettle, and empty a gruesome-looking sachet of powder that's supposed to result in a cappuccino into a mug. It should have taken you two minutes, but you spilled the chocolate topping.

You sit down and get chatting, and it doesn't take long for the conversation to turn to Sara. The pair had been friends since school, and had kept in touch when Sara moved away from the area. Nobody, not even Betty, was happier than Irene when Sara then bought the house she did and moved back.

You decide it's best to get to the point, and tell her about the letter Sara had sent to Betty.

'That good-for-nothing brother of theirs,' says Irene, her mood sharpening. 'I think of the life Betty and Sara would have had if he hadn't caused them so many problems.'

'Did you know him?'

'Did I ever. He knows Sara told me everything. He was always wary of me.'

'When did you last see him?'

'He's around here more often than you'd think. But he won't give me any trouble. I've got that man's number.'

'He won't mess with you?'

'No. It's not a saying,' she says. 'I've actually got his number.'

Wait: what's she telling you?

He's around the area? Where can you find him?
Ask her that at **139**.
His number? You need to know more about that, surely.
Try **170**.

13

You sense Betty Grainger might just be trying to end the conversation, and there are few things that make you more suspicious than that. You weren't voted the most irritating person in your graduating class at training for nothing.

You decide not to take the hint, and leave Finn to whatever he's up to. Instead, you're going to prod at Betty a little.

'Are you telling me everything? Is everything okay?' you probe. Betty's a little irritated that you're still continuing to talk to her, but trying gamely to put her happy face on.

'Brothers being brothers,' she smiles, but with a slightly firmer tone this time.

'When did Finn get back?' you enquire.

'Two days ago,' she bluntly replies. Her answers are getting much shorter now. You're almost inclined to make your questions true or false.

'Were you expecting him?'

'His term at university isn't due to finish until next week.'

You've always sensed that Archie is the slightly favoured child – a reason it must have stung so much when he got sent away – and there's a crackle of tension here. You increasingly feel it, but see that the clock is edging towards 7.30pm. That's lights-on time, as you well know.

'Was Archie not pleased to see him?'

Steel suddenly coats Betty Grainger's eyes. 'My Archie has done nothing wrong,' she bites. 'Nothing. Now, Detective, I've been working my backside off for the last week to make sure it all goes well tonight. Can I please get on with switching the lights on?'

There's only so much you want to push her: she did bury her sister this morning. You pause. Her demeanour softens, and she's back in control of herself. But you definitely saw it: a flash of something there, and the sense that it's not been happy families here today.

Still, she's right: the villagers won't be happy if the lights don't go on, so you bid her a temporary farewell and let her get on with her business. You pick up your drink and step away from the bar.

It's time to head to the switch-on over at **162**.

⇒ *14* ⇐

Instinct kicks in as you close the distance between you and the vehicle as fast as you can. You head to the passenger-side door and look in, to be greeted by DS Lambie doubled up, in the grip of some kind of haze. He's disorientated and struggling. When he looks in your direction, his eyes look bloodshot, watering. You're not sure he's worked out you're even there. He's certainly not talking.

'You need to get out of there,' you tell him, sternly. Your voice re-centres him, and he nods, knowing he's in trouble if he doesn't struggle through some kind of escape.

In the background, you can just about hear the whines of the dog and Derek James getting slightly more flustered. 'Detective,' he calls. But your focus needs to be here.

'After three,' you say to DS Lambie. 'One, two . . .'

Not waiting for three, you drag his arm with all the strength you have. He lurches in your direction as you do so, and somehow, between the two of you, he manages to clamber out of the vehicle.

'Keep going,' you yell at him, as he just about finds the strength to claw further away. You move back from the area of the car, and yell to Derek James to move too. Something about the car is very wrong.

DS Lambie gasps in fresh air, as greedily as he can. You take a few minutes as you all reset. Your own throat still doesn't feel right, but the further you all move from the car, the better things seem to be. Even the dog has stopped whining.

'What happened?' you say, as DS Lambie regains his composure. It takes him several minutes to build up to a comprehensible answer.

'I–I don't know. I was okay right up to the bit when I opened the car door.'

'Was it locked?'

'No,' he says. 'I was surprised when it opened and, I don't know, it's hard to describe. It was like a cloud of something just came out of it . . .'

'Something you saw? Smoke?'

'No. Nothing you could see. It was, well, *something*. I got into the car and within seconds knew I was in trouble.'

You look back at it. Whatever it was that had built up in Sara McLower's vehicle has now been released into the atmosphere. The car door remains wide open, so hopefully whatever it was will have diluted safely when met with fresh air.

But there are questions here. The car obviously needs investigating, but is it safe for you to do so? Plus, Derek James: did he see anything?

You notice DS Lambie starting to shake a little and call for assistance, that's job one. But what's job two?

Do you talk to Derek James while DS Lambie recovers?
Go to **63**.
Or does DS Lambie need your attention here, at **91**?

⇀ *15* ↽

It's tempting to go after the car, but you realize your responsibilities lie here. There's an injured man on the floor, in a life or death situation, and lots of loose ends that need attending to.

You're still interested in the suspicious car, of course. But instead of driving after it, you send a message to your colleagues offering a description of the car and hope that someone spots it. You know this is a very, very long shot, and so it proves: the limited police resources available this evening end up concentrated on the Windy Dog, and nobody reports a sighting of the vehicle as they make their way around Causton.

You walk back briskly to where Archie Grainger is still getting treatment from his brother, just in time for the ambulance to arrive, along with the first few uniformed officers.

The paramedics quickly get to work trying to stabilize Archie, transporting him into the vehicle and making haste towards Causton General Hospital. He's got a long night ahead of him, and it's going to be a battle to get through it. You talk to the uniform officers, who start collecting names and details from the people who were in and around the pub, and start letting them go home.

Not a minute after the ambulance departs – with Finn Grainger accompanying his brother – a vehicle you recognize oh-so-well pulls onto the car park. The Chief Inspector. You breathe an inward sigh of relief that you opted not to leave the scene. You can't imagine she'd have been best pleased if she realized you had. You quickly fill her in on everything, including the car, and she commends you on making the right decision.

A shellshocked Betty Grainger, who opted not to go in the ambulance, comes outside to get some fresh air as her customers start to make their way back home. You sort her a chair from some of the outside tables. Understandably, she doesn't quite know what to make of it all.

'Do you need a lift to the hospital?' the Chief Inspector offers, assuming that she'll want to be with her son.

'Y–yes, please,' Betty replies, her voice trembling. 'I don't really feel I'm up to driving, if that's okay.'

It's no bother, of course. The hospital will take around 20 minutes to get to from here with clear roads, and the Chief Inspector will want to head there anyway to talk to Finn. Finn has promised to call if there's any news, but you feel like it might be a bit of a wait until you hear anything else.

A forensics team arrives, and they'll be working here most of the night. Betty goes inside, gets her coat and locks up what she can. When she returns, you're getting everything straight with the Chief Inspector for the inevitable paperwork. She approaches as you briefly summarize the power cut, the emergency care given to Archie, and the car you saw too.

'S–say that again,' says Betty, with a voice that suggests her night has just got even worse.

You and the Chief Inspector exchange a glance. You describe the power cut. 'No,' she says. 'The car.'

You reiterate the description.

'I should have guessed,' Betty sighs. 'I should have guessed.' She pauses. 'This is my brother's work.'

Wait! Guessed what? Ask her! Go to **156.**
Or: what else does she know? You've got a minute with
her here. Maybe she has something else she wants
to say . . . go to **121.**

✦ *16* ✦

The Chief Inspector had once taken you aside and advised you to err on the side of caution when you find yourself metaphorically cornered. While small villages and rural areas are generally peaceful and calm places, you can't be too careful. It's an oft-repeated mantra over at the station. Along with a reminder to pay your fair share of the biscuits fund.

That's what you remind yourself – about caution, not biscuits – as you stay still, keep quiet and feel for your phone. You can't be absolutely sure that somebody else is here, but you definitely heard *something*. You figure that if you heard something, there's a very good chance that if there *is* someone else here, they heard you too.

With that in mind, you keep still and quiet, take out your phone and message for some help, hoping someone is close.

A few minutes of absolute silence. You keep on top of your breathing, you keep yourself calm, you wait. Treat it like a stakeout, you tell yourself. Have patience. Help is coming.

Luck's on your side this time: it turns out that DS Lambie is not too far away – well, more likely sitting at the station desiring a baked product – and he gets in his car and heads towards Sara McLower's house. At speed, too.

He messages to tell you he's moving, and your heart skips a beat when your phone vibrates. You'd switched the ringer off at the wake, but not to silent. You curse yourself under your breath. But again, silence.

It's punctured by the rumble of an approaching car engine outside, as DS Lambie arrives at the front door. You take a deep breath, and exit the property, cautious to look around as you do. No movement.

You've never been so pleased to see DS Lambie's face, even if it doesn't look best pleased to be stood out in the cold.

After conferring at the front of the house for a few minutes, you decide to do one last quick look around, with DS Lambie in tow. After a few minutes, with no sign of anyone, the pair of you knock this on the head and get back to the station. It's warmer there, and the Chief Inspector will be waiting. Hopefully, not in too bad a mood.

Go to **128**.

→ *17* ←

'I need to open it,' you say to Catherine Smart. 'I need to know what we're dealing with.'

Her eyes roll, and you know she could put in a call to the Chief Inspector to stop you. But she gets it. She was a detective like you before she specialized in her forensics work. She sees both sides, and knows full well that you don't as a rule get in the way of a determined detective following a lead: you find a way to safely support them.

She hands you a safety mask and insists you head to the middle of the car park, away from anyone else. You have no idea what you're about to expose yourself to, and you need to be sure you don't endanger anyone else.

You nod in agreement, take a mask and find the most open spot on the spacious car park. Catherine Smart keeps her distance, but dons a mask as well to be on the safe side. She's watching your movements like a hawk.

You look at the container, and keep it within the sealed plastic bag for the moment. You start to apply some force to the lid. It's still rigid and not budging, though, and is going to require more force than you're mustering here. You place it on the floor, still in the plastic bag, but you're not sure how sturdy it is.

'I'm going to have to apply a lot more pressure,' you shout across to Catherine Smart.

'Be careful,' she cautions. You nod, and double your effort. Finally, you get somewhere. The lid starts to give as you apply a crucial bit of extra force to it.

'Stop!' screams a voice. 'Don't do it!'

That's not Catherine Smart's voice. She looks at you and knows instantly that it's not you talking either. Who the hell is it? And why do they want to stop you opening this?

Do you heed their warning and stop?
Put the brakes on by going to **158**.
No: you're doing this. You need **138**.

⇒ *18* ⇐

You need to do this properly. You're on the search for a murderer, and whatever you do has got to stand up in court. A crafty look at a confidential document might not do that.

You dial the Chief Inspector and she instantly picks up the phone. 'I need your advice,' you say, getting to the point. You explain the situation that you've found yourself in, and that you've been given these documents. You share the concern that you aren't sure they should be in your possession. You know oh-so-well that the Chief Inspector likes and demands that things are done by the book, and heaven help anyone who crosses her on this.

'You can't have them, and he shouldn't have given them to you,' the Chief Inspector says, alert to the danger. She's not cross with you, but she can see where this could go wrong.

'But Sara McLower's dead,' you protest.

'She is,' the Chief Inspector agrees, not controversially, 'but she still has the right to confidentiality. If you want to look at those documents, you need to get permission from whoever's deemed the personal representative, and that's almost certainly going to be Betty Grainger.'

'There could be a clue here,' you argue. 'Betty Grainger has a lot on her plate at the moment.'

'I agree. That's why we have to do this properly. Either get Betty Grainger's permission, or hand the documents back to Ralph Maddock and tell him in no uncertain terms not to do that again. He could be in serious trouble if he's not careful.'

You sigh. You know this is the right thing to do, but it's frustrating. This feels like a proper clue you've got here, but now that you've involved the Chief Inspector, you can't exactly go against her, can you?

Which is it to be?

Do you hand the documents back to Ralph Maddock?
You do that at **151**.
Or if you decide to ring Betty, try and get her at **166**.

→ *19* ←

You head back to the station, and finally get your head around the negative online comments being made about the Windy Dog. You feel that the problem with the complaints Causton police has received about the reviews is that there's always been a more important job to do. The complaints come in every month or two, and someone always says they're dealing with it, but a higher priority assignment has a habit of cropping up.

More in hope than anything else, you search when you're back at your desk for any kind of update. As it happens, there's been some progress, it's just that nobody had a moment to check. Someone – DS Lambie, you're presuming – had the bright idea to send the file over to the tech team at the heart of the county. They ran an analysis, and duly sent it back. The file looks like it has been sitting unopened. No wonder the Graingers were so annoyed about it.

You scan the findings, and because the central county team have more resources and posher computers, they've been able to run a pretty thorough analysis. There are terms in here you don't quite wrap your head around, such as 'IP address' and 'reverse DNS.' Phrases people involved with computers, you think, come up with to stop other people getting involved with computers.

That notwithstanding, the report in front of you is pretty conclusive. Every single review they've managed to do any kind of trace on originated in Causton. There's next to no doubt about it. But from where? Who in the village is writing them and, deliberately or not, trying to bring the pub down?

You head off for a drive as you mull this over, and then stop. You load up the copy of the findings that you've sent yourself as a thought hits you: you've missed the appendix of the report. You look again, and you're very glad you did, too. Because there it is, in front of you: the details of a user account on one of the online review sites, with a phone number attached to it. It must have taken some getting, but there it is. And it's waiting for you to dial it.

Are you going to make the call? Go to **115**.
Or do you go to the station and try something else? Go to **47**.

→ *20* ←

You check your surroundings and sit in your car, making sure to lock the doors. Something's making you feel uncomfortable here. Nervously, you take the sheet of paper out of the bag and peel the tape off. It's been relatively freshly applied. It's a simple message, in pencil, in the middle of the sheet. Presumably in pencil so that nobody could see through the paper and read what was written.

You kick yourself for not answering the door when you read the few words sprinkled on the paper. A very definite threat. 'Tell them nothing, or you know what'll happen.'

You inwardly gasp, and quickly report this to the station. It doesn't take long for a message to come back in return. Get back to Irene Whitley, it says. Backup is on its way.

You get back out of the car and walk back up the driveway, avoiding the obstacle course of gnomes. You realize you shut both the inner and outer doors fully behind you when you came out just now. Poor Irene is going to have to get up to answer. You knock on the door.

'Who the bloody hell is that?' she says, in a light tone.

'It's just me again. Sorry, something I forgot to ask you.'

You have to wait a minute or two while she struggles to the door, and eventually it swings open. She's out of breath, but smiling. 'I didn't need a drink that quickly,' she grins. 'But it's nice to see you again!'

She looks out. 'At least it's not raining. Do you like my gnomes?'

Once again, you can't help but smile. 'That one doesn't look like one of mine, though,' she says, pointing to a particularly fetching fellow right by the front gate.

You're impressed. She seems to mentally catalogue her gnomes. But what now?

You can talk gnomes with her if you really want to. Go to 77.
But still: you're here for serious business.
You need to talk to her about this letter. Go to 132.

⇢ *21* ⇠

Gasping for breath, you see in the car the little lever to pop open the boot. You flick the lever and hear the clunking click of the boot. DS Lambie's really struggling now, and you open up the other door for him as you run around as best you can to the rear of the car. At least if fresh air gets through, that's got to be something.

Still, you're practically wheezing as you get to the back of the vehicle, and it's as if the car breathes out too as you fully open the boot. A fresh blast of whatever's giving you and DS Lambie so much trouble hits you, and you have to take a step back. It's only because you're outside the car and in the fresh air that it doesn't entirely overpower you straight away, but it's had a very good go at that notwithstanding.

Water starts to form in your eyes. You focus as best you can.

You see a few boxes scattered across the boot. The car has seen better days, you observe. There's clearly been a leak here, as the boot is damp, and the cardboard boxes are damaged too. Someone must have dropped the car off in a hurry. Your chances of finding out exactly when are extremely slim, but that's not where your head is at the moment. Instead, you focus on the boxes themselves.

You recognize the smell, of course. It's car air fresheners. You've got one in your own car, but this time there are clearly lots of them. Strange, though. Your air freshener doesn't make you feel light headed, and doesn't leave you struggling to breathe. Are there more in there, you wonder? Is it worth trying to open the box? Or is this the point where you call in help?

If you want to try the box, go to **94**.
But if it's time to call in help, then you're better off going to **141**.

22

'One more thing before we go in, Mr Grainger,' you say, as the pair of you get ready to enter the building. 'Would you mind opening the boot of your car for me?'

If he looked pale before, he's positively ashen-faced now. He's trying to cooperate, but suddenly seems a little less keen. 'I'm happy to show you mine,' you smile, as you open up your door and click the release lever. The boot of your car pops open.

He knows he's cornered here. 'Okay,' he says. 'T–there's a button on this thing that opens the boot,' gesturing at his key fob. 'It doesn't always work.' He steps away from the driver's side of his car and moves to the back of it. You follow suit, putting on your politest, smarmiest smile. You think you're on to something here.

Hamilton keeps moving and, almost for fun you think, takes a look at the boot of your vehicle. You're a little embarrassed. As well as some car-care necessities, it's strewn with clothes, and a fair amount of rubbish you've not got around to cleaning out.

He pushes your boot shut, and then presses the button on his key fob. His boot clicks open, and you lift the lid, peering in. You let out an immediate gasp when you see what's there. Straight away, your eyes are drawn to two sizeable garden gnomes, sitting uncomfortably next to a collection of bricks. And several packets of air freshener.

Then – what's that? Oh no. You realize you left your keys in your car's ignition, and the telltale sign of this is when it suddenly bursts into life and jolts energetically back into the near-empty car park. You turn around and see Hamilton behind the wheel of your car – and he's still got the keys to his own vehicle. He bursts out of the car park before you can alert your colleagues for help.

But he's gone, and gone quickly.

It'll be days before your vehicle is recovered from Northfield Wood, well outside of Causton. By then, Hamilton will have made his escape. Also by then, the analysis of his car will determine that Hamilton is potentially far more than a person of interest. He might just be your prime suspect in the Sara McLower case.

Yet with him gone, and no obvious chance of a return, you resign yourself to this being a case you feel you got within touching distance of solving – but didn't quite manage it.

THE END

Go to p.313 to read your performance review.

⇒ *23* ⇐

It takes you a while to piece a few things together, and even then you're not entirely convinced that you've got the full story. Still, you *are* clear that Hamilton Grainger could have let you take the lid off that container and suffer the consequences, but when he realized what was happening, he intervened. Whatever his plans were seemed to have escalated beyond his control and intent, and he had little urge to add your life to his charge sheet.

Still, the charge sheet is complicated. The container was thoroughly examined, and opened up avenues of investigation. What it didn't do was directly tie Hamilton Grainger to a specific offence against Sara McLower or Archie Grainger. Although when Sara McLower's car was retrieved and properly searched, there was the feeling the air freshener in it had been contaminated.

The eventual death of Archie Grainger in hospital after the incident at the Windy Dog put Hamilton even more in the frame.

But in the end, his charges are to do with possessing the poisons. There's no direct proof that he personally used them, even though the circumstantial evidence looks strong. Certainly, under questioning, he's not giving anything away.

The phone? That might have helped. You remember seeing it in the bag when Caroline Smart pointed it out. Yet amid all the commotion, when they went back to retrieve the rest of the bag's contents a few things were missing. The phone was one, the masonry saw another. The picture remains incomplete. Who could have removed them?

Hamilton Grainger does plead guilty to a smattering of offences, and they're enough to put him at His Majesty's Pleasure for a short period of time.

Did you get the full picture? Well, no time to dwell on that, really. You need to get back to your desk and see what others crimes are fighting for your attention . . .

THE END

Go to p.314 to read your performance review.

⇒ *24* ⇐

You put the gnome down – the forensics team will need to take a look at that, although you'll assume the same pattern of brick trimming as the ones that stuffed Sara McLower's pumpkin – and beckon Irene Whitley back inside.

'Your front garden,' you ask her. 'I need to ask you about it.'

She takes a while, but sits herself down, looking expectantly at her empty coffee cup. You take the hint, pour more of the awful cappuccino powder into it over in the kitchen, and give her an approximation of a nice-looking drink.

'I can't do the garden myself,' she laughs. 'Can you see me racing around with a lawnmower?'

You can't. But you can see her telling someone else how to use a lawnmower properly.

'No, I get young Teddy to do some odd jobs for me. He's in charge of my garden.'

Teddy Jones? The grandson of Bob and Alison Jones? The young lad who does the deliveries for their shop?

'How often does he come around?'

'Not so much in the winter. I see him when he's dropping off my shopping, of course. But in the winter, he just tidies up the garden every few weeks. Hard worker, too.'

Perhaps you should go and have a word with him?
Head over to 25 for a chat.
Or have you heard enough? The clock continues to tick:
might this be Hamilton Grainger's work?
Head to your car and put out an alert. Go to 40.

⇢ *25* ⇠

You need to talk to Teddy Jones, you conclude. He was in the vicinity this morning, you think, and so might have an idea who put the note through Irene's door.

With his morning deliveries done, you find him back at Bob and Alison Jones's shop. As always, they're helpful and look pleased to see you when you walk in, even though Alison seems under the weather again. Whatever problems are going on in their lives, you'd never be able to tell by the way they smile and treat their customers. But it's Teddy you're here to see, and he reluctantly comes down from his room to answer a question or two for you.

It starts easy. He confirms that he was doing deliveries this morning, although he could hardly deny that, given that his grandparents were there and had sent him out on his bike to do his rounds. Just a couple today, though. Not many people booked a morning delivery slot with him when they were expecting to be out so late at the Windy Dog the night before.

It's when you turn the attention to the note that he goes a little sheepish. Teddy's not a good liar, and doesn't seem to be on very solid ground. He admits that he didn't write the note or know what was in it. He questions, genuinely, if it was something bad. There's an innocence to him, in spite of everything he's been through in life, that's hard to fake.

'I believe you didn't send it,' you tell him. 'But you need to tell me who did. Who gave it to you?'

The door clangs. It's Finn Grainger.

'Finn!' says Alison. 'How's Archie? Is he okay?'

'No,' snaps Finn. 'He's not. He died, this morning, and I think his dad has got something to do with it.'

He's pointing at Teddy.

'That'll be who gave him the note,' sighs Bob. 'There's your mystery.'

---

*You'd better go to **106** to see just what's going on here.*

⇢ *26* ⇠

You keep your expression neutral as you take in everything you've been told. But there's a loose end in your head. 'The Windy Dog,' you say.

'What about it?'

'Well, as we speak, Archie Grainger is lying in a hospital morgue because sabotaged Christmas lights exploded in his face. Are you saying that Betty sabotaged her own pub and tried to kill her own son? Isn't it just as likely that you did that, if you're the one who's been cut out of the will? You both have a motive.'

He doesn't like this line of questioning but, after a brief pause, gives you a considered answer. 'I'm not going to deny to you, Detective, that I feel part of that pub is mine. But also, Betty had decided she was going to be leaving anyway. You don't know my sister very well. If she's willing to kill her sister, she's willing to make sure that nobody else has the pub after her.'

'I thought the pub was important to her? A proper family business?'

'That's a question for her, not me,' he says, flatly. 'I thought it was important too.'

A formal notification of death for Archie Grainger pings through to your phone. That's two deaths now in the same family, in a matter of weeks. Could Betty Grainger really have killed her sister and now her own son?

---

*Head off to question Betty Grainger. She's over at **146**.*
*Confront Hamilton about the wills. Doesn't the evidence point a little more at him? Try that approach at **62**.*

If Betty Grainger isn't going to do anything about this, then you will. Good on you, Detective. You make your way behind the bar and towards the back room, the shrill light from your phone marking your path. You need to get this place lit up again, the faster the better.

'It's over here,' you hear a voice say. Finn, drawing you to a small corridor that runs to the left of the pub's back room. 'It's up here.'

You see the problem. The fuse box – a modern one, to your surprise – is quite a way up the wall, and is not instantly reachable. Not the best place to put it, you mentally note, but the time to challenge that isn't now.

You shine your light up at it, and a grateful Finn grabs stepladders from a small alcove set inside the opposite wall. He quickly erects the ladders and clambers to the top. He actually *did* need your help: if he had to do this without the benefit of your light, a few potentially valuable seconds would have been lost.

Finn lifts the cover of the fuse box and flicks what you assume to be the master switch. No joy: it trips the second it's activated.

'Try just the inside lights,' you suggest. He's ahead of you there.

He isolates the outside lights and leaves them off, then switches everything else on. He flicks the main switch again. Success! The darkness disappears, and you switch the light on your phone off. The problem's with the outside lights. Everything else has burst back to life without even a grumble.

You look at Finn, and see anger in his eyes as he comes down the stepladders. 'Someone's sabotaged this, and tried to ruin it for her,' he snarls, collapsing the steps and restoring them to their home in the alcove. 'And I won't let them get away with it.'

---

*Hang on: who does he think has sabotaged it? Why does he think this is sabotage? Go to **188** if you want to ask him. Or there's clearly a commotion going on outside – you can hear it now, and the calls for help are getting louder. Should you go and investigate that? Go to **214**.*

⇥ *28* ⇤

You check to see if there's anyone about, and pull back the door to the small storage cupboard. It's a bit dusty, and doesn't appear to be used too often. There's nothing really of note here that you can see, at least not without going in and having a good explore. The slight aroma of a car air freshener, perhaps – at least you think that's what it is. A few cleaning products on the shelves, and one of the biggest piles of own-brand toilet paper you can remember seeing in your life.

You chuckle to yourself at thought of how odd it'd be if someone found themselves submerged under it all, and died at the hands of loo roll. Still, if there's more here in this cupboard, it might be a job for the forensics team, who will already no doubt be working overnight and into the morning.

For now, there's not much more you can do. You head back to the front of the pub to rejoin the Chief Inspector. Go to **76**.

29

You look at DS Lambie, both of you losing the will a little by this stage.

But then, the simplest of hunches. The kind of hunch that justifies why they pay you the middling bucks.

'How far back does the footage go?' you ask. 'Does it go back a few days before?'

DS Lambie looks at you, puzzled. 'Would have thought so,' he nods, pointing at a folder icon on your screen. 'Take a look in there.'

With a few trusty clicks of your computer's mouse, you load up the footage from the day before, and it's more of the same. No wonder nobody in the thinly staffed office had gone through this before. You put it onto double-speed playback as you sip your bitter drink. After 20 minutes, you figure this still isn't going anywhere.

'The day before that,' you ask. DS Lambie nods. Surely somebody would have checked this, you resign yourself to thinking. But then the department is stretched. Two officers have left to go to the city over the last three months alone. Resources around here are not what they were.

There's a sense of going through the motions as you briefly scan the footage from 48 hours before the attack. Nothing. 72 hours. Nothing. Well, apart from Sara McLower popping in and out.

'Just one more day,' you ask. It's mid-afternoon already, and you need to be at the Windy Dog for 7pm, 7.30pm at a push.

'Stop!' Lambie suddenly says.

'What?' you jolt, nearly spitting out the mouthful of coffee you'd just taken.

DS Lambie urges you to rewind just a few seconds. It's fleeting, but it's definitely there. The back of what's almost certainly a male figure, seemingly placing something on the ground.

The penny drops. 'The pumpkin,' you realize. 'Whoever it is has gone there four days before the attack to put a pumpkin on the ground.'

'I think we can definitely conclude that this was pre-planned now,' DS Lambie wryly notes.

Now what? Leaving DS Lambie to circulate the image from the doorbell camera and inform the Chief Inspector, you figure you've got an hour before you need to make tracks.

It's already known that the murder pumpkin was filled with bricks and, in truth, the fruit itself isn't in a state to give it long in the evidence room. You can check the remains, though, if you want, at **104**.
Or do you want to take a quick look through the catalogue of other incidents reported on the same day the pumpkin was primed? Head to **98**.

⇒ *30* ⇐

You look at the phone and ease it out of its protective case. A chunky cover, too, that would keep the unit safe if it was dropped or left outside.

Straight away, two credit cards tucked into the cover fall out. These wouldn't have taken long for the forensics team to find, would they?

You examine them: both different banks, both in the name of

Mr H Grainger. 'Hamilton Grainger,' you say out loud, as you show the Chief Inspector.

'Why wouldn't he have cards under a fake name?' you add, a bit baffled.

This might be one of those moments where the simple explanation is the right one. 'Maybe credit-card fraud isn't one of his skills,' she replies. 'He couldn't even delete his internet history.'

Fair point.

She keeps musing. 'Maybe he just keeps a few different bank accounts, so that his more suspicious purchases all go through different routes. I don't know, really,' she says. 'But there are a few options.'

You start to ponder this as you go to replace the protective cover on the phone. Nothing else has struck you as unusual.

'Just be sure there's nothing else,' the Chief Inspector tells you. 'We might not be able to get our hands on this device for some time.'

You heed her words, and slip that protective case back off. You look at it extremely closely, but can't see anything. Then you switch your attention to the phone itself. It's not the most popular model, but still, it's familiar in feel, with one slight exception: it appears to have a changeable battery, and you slide the compartment open to confirm this.

A standard-looking battery drops to the desk, and you shine a light into the device. Again, nothing. You scratch at the surface, nothing again. You're getting a little frustrated here, and you can't help but feel you need a breakthrough. There must be *something*.

It's the Chief Inspector who spots it. 'The battery,' she says. 'It looks a slightly odd shape. I've got the same kind of phone.'

A good job she has, because holy heavens, she's right. It's a blink and you miss it difference, but the battery pack is a tiny bit thicker than it should be. A thin black film has been layered over it and you very slowly pull back at that.

It starts to peel back and you let out an audible gasp.

'What is it?' the Chief Inspector asks.

'This,' you tell her, as two tiny phone SIM cards drop onto the table in front of you.

He must take a SIM card out of the phone when he's not using it so it can't be traced. But why are there two SIM cards here: surely he'd only need one spare?

Is that the lead to follow, or should you be following up the credit cards?

No! This is all about those SIM cards now.
*Go to **73** and stop hanging around here!*
Hang on: follow the money. Always follow the money.
*Go to **167**.*

⟩ *31* ⟨

You elect to look for Finn, but it proves to be fruitless, at least for the moment. Wherever he's gone, he's presumably letting off a bit of a steam somewhere, and that might not be a bad thing.

Eventually, you temporarily admit defeat and decide to catch up with Catherine Smart over at the Windy Dog. You've known Catherine for a year or so now, and you're confident that if she's overseeing the forensics work there, it'll be done properly.

She greets you as you arrive, and quickly gives you a rundown on what's happened so far. But also: there's a useful discovery.

One of her team discovered a few items very well hidden away in a cupboard at the back exterior of the building. Some discarded food packaging: nothing to worry about there. But of far more interest is a small bag that had been hidden too.

The bag is where they discovered it, having been photographed and with key items put into plastic evidence bags. She walks you over to it: this might just be something.

There's some scattered tools – a saw, a hammer, a masonry saw, a few spanners, some screwdrivers – and some pencils and paper. Also, a pair of car air fresheners, a mobile phone, a flask-like container and some chocolate bars.

Your heart skips a beat – and not because you fancy some chocolate. This must have something to do with what's been going on.

It's the flask of liquid and the phone that take your eye, both nestled in their respective plastic evidence-bag covering. Which do you want to go for?

If you want to try switching the phone on, go to **81**.
If your priority is the container of liquid, then head to **165**.

⋗ *32* ⋖

You're asking for trouble if you stop to find out what the car is up to, you figure. You need to stick to the basics and not invite further trouble – and being on a secluded road with a strange car could definitely count as further trouble.

Instead, you make your way to Causton General Hospital. The news of Archie's death is shocking but, after the state he was in last night, not a huge surprise. The fact that Finn managed to keep Archie's pulse going until the paramedics turned up feels like a minor miracle.

They managed to stabilize him last night, but you all knew that the next 24 hours were going to be crucial.

So it proves.

It takes you a while to get to the hospital, though. All the way here, you were checking your rearview mirror. Whatever the other car driver's intentions were, they don't seem to be following you. You took the long route, just to make sure.

By the time you arrive, a familiar-looking vehicle, which you can't place but feel like you should, is exiting the car park. It's not the small vehicle that pulled up behind you earlier, but it was certainly by the Windy Dog last night.

You waste little time dwelling on it, and make your way through the corridors of the hospital, up to the intensive care ward. You're greeted by DC Isabel Blood, and her face gives away the news she's about to tell.

'It's been a very difficult morning,' she said. DC Blood was a uniformed officer up until the start of the year, so is already well used to difficult days at work. This, though, looks like one of the worst.

'Archie Grainger?'

'He passed away. Was on life support all night, but this morning they weren't getting any response from him at all.'

The ward nurse sees you and fills in the gaps. Archie had stopped breathing at the Windy Dog last night, and while they got his heart going, the damage to his body and brain was done. They were hoping for progress overnight, but this morning it became clear that his condition was not going to improve.

'Betty Grainger?' you ask.

'She had to make the decision,' the nurse explains. 'About an hour ago. She spent half an hour saying her goodbyes to him, and then agreed that the machine should be switched off.'

You realize that there have now been two deaths in her family, and neither of them were of natural causes.

'Where's Betty now?'

'That's where things got really difficult,' interjects DC Blood. 'She and Finn had a blazing row, and he's stormed out of the hospital.'

'Does anyone know where?'

'Just that he screamed, "He won't got away with this" as he smashed his way down the corridor.'

That must have been the car that you saw pulling out of the car park. That must have been Finn Grainger. But was Betty with him? In fact, where is Betty?

---

*Who do you try to track down? To go search for Finn, run off to **31**.*
*Or go and find Betty at **66**.*

You ponder your options, and figure that a quick conversation with Finn wouldn't do any harm. 'I'd like to chat to him, yes, please,' you say. Betty Grainger gives her usual smile, and lifts the bar counter for you to walk through to the back of the pub.

'Just in the back room,' she directs you. An honour: you've never been invited back here before. Few get to tread the crusty floor that leads to the Windy Dog's innards.

You make your way down a small corridor and through into the back room. When you enter, you find Finn nursing what looks like a whisky, playing with his mobile phone.

'They're bast—' he stops and corrects himself as he notices you.

His facial hair, as always, looks like a badly tended garden, but other than that he seems as alert as always. He's the one person in Causton who drinks more coffee than you.

'They're awful people, you know,' he says as he sees you. 'Have you seen what they've been posting?'

You confess you haven't and he hands over the phone. He's on the Windy Dog reviews page on a popular tourism website. After years of people leaving very positive feedback for the place, the last year has seen an influx of less positive responses. You'd think they were describing a puddle in the middle of a field, rather than a respected and much-loved local hostelry.

'What am I looking at?' you ask, knowing full well what you're looking at. But still, you want to find out just what Finn Grainger thinks of everything.

'You're looking at the online harassment that my mother keeps reporting to you,' he snarls. 'It's bad enough she has to run this pub by herself with no help from that disgrace of a brother of mine. But then she has to put up with someone trying to ruin her by doing this.'

'You think that somebody is doing it deliberately? You don't think these are real customers?'

You take it from his silent glare that he does not believe these people are real customers.

'Who do you think is doing it, then? If you think it's deliberate, then somebody's got to be behind it.'

'If I knew that, believe me, I'd be more inclined to give my brother their name and address than hand it over to Causton's useless police department.'

A little nod there to the incident that led Archie to prison; the Actual Bodily Harm conviction left unsaid.

Maybe Finn's not too happy with Causton's CID work. You're not a detective for nothing.

'What were you and your brother arguing about earlier today?' you ask, trying to shift the conversation.

'He's a leech,' Finn snaps. 'I'm working my backside off to fund my course, and haven't had a day off in three months. He's not had a day *on* in that time.'

'He was outside working on the lights when I arrived. He looked busy to me.'

'I bet he was. He gets off his backside at the last possible moment to make it look like he's actually doing something. I had to come back early yesterday to help Mum finish off the arrangements. Wasn't due back until next week, but the whole village is looking to her tonight, and she can't keep doing everything herself.'

'And you pointed this out to Archie?'

'And I pointed that out to Archie.'

That explains the argument. But still: the online reviews are a mystery. Someone seems to have Betty Grainger – or at least her pub – in their crosshairs. You'd imagine the reviews are hardly boosting passing trade.

You're going to have to keep pondering that. You ask a few more questions of Finn and he starts to thaw a little, thankfully. But now? It's time to head into the pub again, for the lights switch-on.

At the very least, the build-up to Christmas is about to be marked in a very Causton way.

Head to **162**.

⟩ 34 ⟨

'Have you ever had any trouble here?' you ask Irene, deciding not to tell her about the note. Why worry her, especially when she lives here by herself.

'I haven't. We keep ourselves to ourselves really, round here. We tend to get on.'

'You've never had trouble with anyone?'

'No. Well, unless they don't put enough chocolate in my cappuccino!'

She's laughing, but you know she's not being entirely truthful with you. Maybe that's how she gets by, though. If she doesn't think about it, it can't concern her. Or is she covering up? Is she protecting someone, or just plain scared?

You can't really tell. But you do sense that she doesn't want to do anything to puncture the life she's built here. She's happy, she doesn't want to feel threatened, and you decide to respect that. Still, probably worth asking someone at the station to keep an eye on the place. That can't hurt.

You leave her be. She's a lovely woman who deserves her happiness, even if you'd drive over seven counties to avoid her coffee.

You can take a stroll around the block if you want,
just before you head off. Amble over to 92.
Or you can go off to see how the forensics team is
getting on at the Windy Dog. Go to 79.

35

'Put the tinsel down,' you say, adopting your firmest tone. Somewhere deep inside, you know it's not the most assertive thing you've said in your life, but sometimes you have to make do with what you have.

The figure opposite you pauses, also assessing their options. A muffled voice responds: 'Just get out of my way.' Male, that much is certain. Is that a little bit of nervousness in their speech, too? They don't sound particularly confident, but they are very much standing their ground.

You take a second to glance at what they're holding. It looks like a Christmas gift bag from a store, around the size of a usual shop carrier bag. You can't make out the logo on the side of it, but it's not a big chain shop or a big brand. You can't make out at a cursory glance what's inside the bag either.

You quickly look back up. They're holding the tinsel in as menacing a manner as it's possible to hold tinsel, and there's no sign that they're putting it down. You repeat your request: 'Put the tinsel down.'

They don't blink. They don't move. They're waiting for you to make the next move, and an unusual stand-off has developed.

You assess the situation. You're alone, and you narrow your choices down to three options.

You should have gone in on the attack last time. You don't need asking twice! Lift your sign, and try and stop them. Go to **169**.
Let them go. At least that way you know you're going to get out of here safely. You think. Go to **109**.
Demand they hand over the bag, and then you'll let them go. Risky, but you never know. Go to **117**.

✦ 36 ✦

It takes you a little while to track the Chief Inspector down, given the fact she had a rather busy evening too. When you do get to her, she knows about the letter. She knew last night, when Betty had told her. She wanted it examined properly, away from the events at the Windy Dog.

'She knew she was dying,' are your first words to her this morning.

'She did. More to the point, she knew she was likely to die before Christmas too.'

'When was this posted?' you ask.

'End of October.'

'You think she knew she was going to be murdered on Halloween night?' you wonder out loud.

'We'll never know that. But look at everything else. She wasn't well, was she? And we know there were poisons in her body.'

'Do you think she did?' You seem to be asking all the questions this morning.

'I don't know. We knew for certain she wasn't well, but she wasn't the type to go to Dr Elliott to get herself checked out.'

You both realize who the 'him' in the letter is. That'd be Hamilton Grainger, of course. That Sara saw fit to mention him in it is a big clue that he's very much a person of interest in your case. But where are you going to find him? You suspect he's the kind of person who finds you.

'One more thing: it's pretty certain the lights were tampered with,' she tells you. 'Someone rigged at least some of them to blow up.'

'Archie Grainger?'

'He'll do well to survive.'

A grim 24 hours, then. But how are you going to fight back?

Something aroused Sara's suspicions enough to make her send a letter in the first place. Irene Whitley was her friend: would she know something about that? Track her down at **12**. Or maybe you're better off going to see how the forensics team is doing at the Windy Dog. Head to **79**.

37

The bark of a large-sounding dog booms back at you as you knock at the door of Ralph Maddock's house. He's a tall man, liked by pretty much everybody, but a stickler for things being done the right way. You remembered this, and rang ahead to ask for ten minutes of his time. Of course, as always, he genially agreed.

'Stop barking, Bonzo,' he says. 'It's only the Detective.'

The dog falls into line, and Ralph opens up the thick oak door. 'Come in,' he says, welcoming you into the warmth of his home. He's lived here alone since his much-loved wife Ethel passed away last year. Well, he has the company of Bonzo, of course, and his beloved cat Brenda. Yet there's no chance of Ralph ever striking up a relationship with anyone else. He and Ethel had been childhood sweethearts, and when she passed, he vowed that he wouldn't seek another relationship. Instead, he threw himself into work around the community instead.

'How's retirement?' you ask him, as he directs you towards his kitchen. There, he's set a couple of stools against a raised breakfast bar and – thankfully – two steaming cups of coffee are already set up.

'I'm busier now than I ever was,' he chuckles. 'The village council sees to that. We're already planning next summer's fete!'

You can't help but smile. It doesn't take seven months to organize a fete, you very well know. But it does give a lot of people something to work towards.

Ralph Maddock seems to read your mind. 'It's a lot more complex than being a solicitor ever was,' he says, laughing at his own aside. 'Honestly, just trying to get something in the local paper these days is a job and a half.'

'I've not seen the paper for a while,' you admit.

'You can have my copy,' he says. 'Not that there's much to read in it these days.'

'Oddly enough, it's a solicitor question I've got for you.'

He sits on his stool, and takes a gulp from his cup. 'Any way I can help,' he grins. 'But you know I've not actively practised since I retired. It's been five years now!'

'I'm aware of that,' you smile. 'But I want to talk to you about Sara McLower's will,' you say.

'Ah,' he replies.

'You acted for her?'

'I did. I still do the odd bit of legal work to help people around the village out. I've done a few wills now. That's a bit of law that doesn't seem to change.'

You smile, politely. But nobody is getting to the point really here. Ralph Maddock decides to take the initiative.

'What did you want to know?'

---

*Good question. If you want to know why she changed it so recently, then go to **102**.*
*Or – and this might be risky to ask him, if he values confidentiality – if you want to dig into what changed, follow that line of enquiry at **177**.*

38

You keep the door of your vehicle locked, but slowly wind down the window. 'Can I help you?' you ask, trying to hide the slight tremble in your voice.

'Hello, Detective,' smiles the man. 'How was Mr Maddock this morning? I hope he was helpful to your enquiries.'

Whoever this is, this encounter is no accident.

'He was very pleasant and helpful, yes,' you smile.

'Might I have a minute of your time?'

You nod. You weigh up whether to let him in the car, and decide to get out of yours instead. At least if things go wrong, you've got some chance of getting away. Not much, but it moves the odds a tiny bit in your direction.

You stand on the other side of the car, the pair of you weighing each other up. 'I'm Hamilton Grainger,' he says. 'You probably know I'm the brother of Betty and Sara. Not that the pair of them would ever utter my name.'

You put on your best poker face, and try to keep your expression steadfastly neutral, your tone measured.

'What brings you here? And what do you want with me?'

'I was trying to talk to you yesterday, but my sister – and her sons, especially the violent one – wouldn't particularly have welcomed me to their pub.'

'Why?'

'After our mother died, we didn't really deal with that very well. Betty had our mother wrapped around her finger, and got given the Windy Dog. Sara and I got some money, but it was Betty who got what we always thought we were going to split between the three of us.'

'Why are you telling me this?'

'You may or may not know that Betty's been having financial problems. I'm guessing if you've just been to see Ralph Maddock, you'll have got copies of the wills. And you'll see that Betty cut me out of hers. She told me she would.'

Wills? Why would he think you had two of them? Does he think you've got Betty and Sara's, rather than two copies of Sara's?

'And why would she do that?'

'Because I found out, Detective. I found out that she was trying to kill Sara.'

Your jaw drops. Betty Grainger? Kill her sister?

---

*Why would she want to do that? Ask him! Go to **171**.*
*Nonsense: tell him you don't believe a word he says, and that the Windy Dog was sabotage. Try that approach at **26**.*

✦ 39 ✦

'I'll get it,' you say to Irene Whitley, both of you absolutely sure that there's no way she's going to.

'Thank you,' she says warmly.

'Are you expecting anyone?'

'No. There's no post today, and I've not had a visitor for a while.'

You're wary, and very much on edge. Has someone seen you come here? Is it a coincidence that the doorbell rings when you're in the house? Or is this what the job does to you: makes you suspicious anytime somebody knocks a door? There's an inner and an outer door to the front of Irene's house, the inner door already open, as always.

You look through the peephole built into the front door and realize you needn't have worried. It's only Teddy Jones.

You open the door, and he looks surprised to see you. He's wearing a thick coat, and you wish you were too. There's a bite in the air.

You smile and say hello. 'E – er hello,' he says, eventually offering a small smile. 'Grandad asked me to check if Miss Whitley needed any extra deliveries this month. He's expecting a rush for Christmas.'

'Couldn't he have rung?' you laughed.

'I suppose so. He likes me to get out of the house, though.'

You know this to be true. 'He needs to get off his computer' is a common refrain from Bob.

You relay the message to Irene, who says she's okay, but can Teddy come and tidy up her garden this week if he's got time? He promises he will, hops on his bike and cycles on to the next street.

False alarm, then.

After a pleasant ten minutes or so more of chat with Irene, you get an alert. There's definitely been foul play with the lights at the Windy Dog, and the forensics team are on site now. You might want to go and take a look. Head to **79**.

➤ *40* ➤

Once again, you thank Irene Whitley for her time, and promise that an officer will come over shortly to have a good look at her front garden. 'Tell them they need to know where the kitchen is,' she smiles. 'You know where I am if you need anything!'

You do. But you sense she's in danger here. The note is one thing, but the bricks in the gnome? That suggests someone is planning something. Are they plotting to kill her, or is it in case they need to? Your mind is pointing towards Hamilton Grainger, someone Irene Whitley clearly has no favour for, and who has at least some motivation for Sara McLower's murder. Presumably, he stands to potentially financially benefit from it.

You take an extra 15 minutes – with her permission – just to look around her home to ensure there's no other obvious threat. Nothing you can spot. It's time to go, you figure.

You make sure to close both the inner and outer door of Irene Whitley's house, and get back to your car. You reach for your key, and depress the button on the key fob to unlock. It locks the car, and you curse yourself for leaving your car seemingly unlocked. You press the button and this time the doors unlock. You open the driver-side door and sit inside, slamming the door behind you.

It takes seconds before you're gasping.

If your mind hadn't been so concentrated on trying to work out what's been happening here, you'd have noticed the overpowering smell in your car from the outside. Inside, you've been hit with what feels like a concentrated blast of air freshener. You reach for the door handle, but realize whatever's in the car is robbing you of your strength, and at great speed. By the time you just about force the door handle, you're losing consciousness.

It's a good job you called in someone to come and talk to Irene Whitley a little more. Sure, it took them around 20 minutes to get here, but they discovered you while you still had some breath in your lungs, half slumped out of your car, but breathing in enough fresh air to keep you alive.

But still: the damage is done. When you come around a day later, you relay what's happened. Yet the note you had is gone, and the gnome has disappeared too. Unfortunately, so has any reasonable chance of catching the murderer. Hard lines, Detective.

THE END

Go to p.314 to read your performance review.

Go to p.314 to read your performance review.

→*41*←

There's a pleasing little ting from the bell above the door of the shop as you make you way in. You like the Jones's shop. It's tidy, full and – in spite of the relatively small space afforded to it – seems to pack a lot in. Alison Jones sits behind the counter, looking a little on the pale side. She offers a weak smile as she sees you, and you ask if she's doing okay.

'I've been better,' she admits. 'Can't seem to rid myself of this blasted bug. I'm going to the doctor in a little while.'

She abruptly changes the subject when Bob walks in behind her, offering his wife a drink. She turns it down, nursing instead the cup of something steaming that's she's keeping right next to her.

'Has Bob been helpful?' she smiles.

'Of course,' you reply.

You talk to them for a little while, as you try and get their take on what's been happening. The loss of Sara clearly hit them hard, and they're still shaken by what happened last night, too.

Teddy walks back in halfway through your chat, looking flushed from his latest delivery and brushing straight past his grandparents, heading upstairs. He grunts a response when they greet him. You let out a smile. You were a teenager once.

The fact that Alison's unwell is niggling you, though, and she reminds Bob that she's got an appointment. He's talking about shutting the shop to take her, but you offer to drive her to Dr Elliott instead. You'd get a chance to talk to her yourself in private, too. You wonder if there's any security footage around here. Just in case. That might be useful to see, and you might come back to that.

But then there's Teddy, already firmly ensconced upstairs, presumably playing video games. You might want to talk to him?

---

*You can talk to Teddy by going to **205**.*
Maybe you can take Alison to her appointment? She'd
*appreciate that at **215**.*
If you want to pursue the security footage now, though, do that
*at **116**.*

'Alison Jones and Robert Jones,' you say, as you read out their alleged offence. 'You do not have to say anything. But it may harm your defence if you do not mention when questioned something which you later rely on in court.'

'Our defence!' says Bob. 'Unbelievable.'

You leave the room for a minute and let them cool off. The Chief Inspector is waiting. 'Detective,' she says, 'do you have a shred of actual evidence that these two had anything to do with the murder of Sara McLower? Or is this some glorified fishing trip that I'm going to have clean up after?'

'I think they've got something to do with it, I really do,' you say.

You down a glass of cold water to try and refresh yourself, and head back in to question them. Yet you've got a growing feeling that you've made a very serious mistake here. You look at the pair in front of you: a woman whose health is in decline, and who's struggling. A man who would go out of his way to help anyone in the community. Now they're going to be tarred by suspicion. Once word gets out about this, their shop trade will never be the same.

That's exactly what happens. After hours of questioning, you accept that Alison and Bob don't appear to be hiding anything at all. Instead, they're caught up in the middle of something. But the way the gossips of Causton work, once they're released, some of their customers soon decide to go elsewhere. Gradually, more and more of them make the journey to the bigger out-of-town supermarket. They figure they've got less chance of being poisoned if they do that.

All you ended up doing here, the Chief Inspector admonishes you, is wasting time on a hunch with no substance behind it. You've made a rash arrest, on a charge that's dropped within days.

She takes you off the case immediately afterwards, too, her faith in you significantly damaged. Hopefully someone else can crack this, without feeling the need to arrest good, innocent citizens.

THE END

Go to p.314 to read your performance review.

↦ *43* ↤

As you dial the phone number of the Windy Dog, you're really not quite sure that Betty Grainger will be there. Won't she be at hospital with Archie? But it turns out this morning you get a little bit of luck, as she's popped back to the pub to pick some things up. She's understandably in a hurry, though. Nonetheless, she answers the phone, sounding a lot less shrill and on show than yesterday.

You quickly thank her for talking to you, and explain that you think there may have been a problem with the lights. But who, you want to know, would have had access to them? It's worth double checking at the very least.

'I keep them in a storage cupboard around the back of the pub most of the year,' she admits. 'The bolt on the door is one I always mean to get around to changing, but never did.'

'Did you test them before they were put up, though?'

'Yes, of course. We always do that. We got them out and tested then last week.'

That's promising: they were working a week or so ago.

'Who put the lights up?'

'My Archie did most of it. We were running quite late this year, though, so I gave young Teddy Jones a few pounds to help out as well. But I suppose once they were up, really anyone could have got to them. I'm sorry, Detective, I know that's not much help.'

She's right: it isn't much help. You thank her for her time, and wish Archie well. Fingers crossed that he manages to pull through, but you don't fancy his chances.

It's best you head off to the forensics team at the
Windy Dog now. They're at **79**.

44

You've nearly got this, you think. You skip through the options on the mysterious mobile phone and finish hooking it up to your own phone's data. Result: you've got a signal. You put your own phone down on the seat next to you and concentrate on the other device.

You scroll back to the internet browser and load up the history list again. You select a review website that appears to have been visited a few weeks ago. It's a little sluggish, but it soon enough loads up.

A page for the Windy Dog appears, and you gasp. The reviews here are *brutal*. Visitors are invited to score the place out of ten at this particular website, and while there are the positive reviews you'd expected as you scroll down the page, around half of the comments are downright hostile. No wonder trade was down: as early as last year, one vociferous commenter was complaining about getting food poisoning. Surely they weren't allowed to post things like that if they didn't have proof? That'd be a matter for the poli . . . ah, you sigh.

No wonder Betty Grainger and her family were so angry with the department. All of this would put you off visiting the Windy Dog in double-quick time, and you know the place and how good it is perfectly well.

The username on the reviews gives you no clues as to who wrote some of these, but for a minute or two you work your way through similar review sites you find in the phone's history. An identical pattern very, very quickly becomes clear. But who's doing this?

The answer isn't far away. In fact, the answer might be standing next to the window.

Turn to **137** *if you want to see who that is.*
Maybe you need to get something quickly from this phone,
though? Go to **163** *if you want to try taking a*
picture of what's on its screen.

45

You complete your circuit of the Windy Dog without spotting anything particularly suspicious. It gives you the opportunity to look a little closer at the lights that have been erected. What you hadn't appreciated before – and what you get from the little bit of extra thinking time you've given yourself – is that there are no lights whatsoever on the main pub sign set to the side of the road. These must have been ones that were swapped in next to the pub's main entrance door.

Which leads you to thinking: what if they'd exploded where they were originally placed? Then you'd be looking at a very different evening, with Archie Grainger still upright, and the pub at worst needing a new sign. The party would have had to stop, of course, with the fire risk, and the fact that the old pub sign is made of wood. Well, that would have caused quite a blaze. But would there have been a threat to human life? Probably not, you ponder.

Archie Grainger might just have been in the wrong place at the wrong time. As you amble back to the Chief Inspector, you figure you need to get to the station very first thing to pull information on Hamilton Grainger. At the moment, he's the closest you've got to an actual suspect . . .

Go to 76.

46

You drive to Trevor Davies' small house in the middle of town. He lives here, but you know he parks his delivery van at the edge of the village. For the minute, he's resting at home, and is genuinely delighted to see you.

'Is this about the ghost I reported?' he says, with some relief.

You struggle to remember. You know that there's a file on Trevor back at the office with some of the more spurious things that he's got in touch about. You and your colleague have always regarded him as harmless, even though he does have a habit of wanting you to follow up on outlandish matters.

You placate him a little, assuring him the ghost hunt is happening. He looks encouraged by this, and you steer the conversation as fast as you can to his delivery service. Alas, there's not much light he can shine on things for you here.

He confirms that he did indeed pick up the produce and drive it back to Causton when required. A fairly straight run, apart from the roadworks, and he saw no foul play. There's the possibility, you consider, that he might interfere with the goods in some way, but from talking to him, you gather that he continually feels he's being watched anyway. You're content to draw a line through his name.

You head back to the shop, for a minute wondering if you're being followed. But then you stop yourself, and think you might just have been spending too much time with Trevor Davies.

You've got the positive result from your testing still at the back of your mind, as you go via the station just to quickly check in, en route to seeing Bob and Alison Jones.

Go to **74**.

47

Back at the station, the latest lead appears to have gone cold, and the case seems no closer to getting solved. What on earth do you do next?

'Betty Grainger said that Sara sent her a letter,' the Chief Inspector offers. It's a loose clue, but it's something. 'She feared she didn't have long left.'

That's understandable, too. She may not have known *why* she was feeling so ill, but she knew full well things weren't improving. The Chief Inspector doesn't have the whole letter, but it does lead you to reconsider who Sara McLower's real friends were.

'In the light of everything, is it worth me going to see Irene Whitley?' you ask. Irene Whitley was a good friend to Sara, and always wants to help.

'Nothing to lose,' considers the Chief Inspector. 'It's a nice morning for a drive over to her house, at least.'

Head to **12**.

48

In truth, the majority of people attending the wake of Sara McLower are there out of politeness. In a village like Causton, it's best to be seen at gatherings such as this, else the gossips would wonder why you weren't there. And gossips are not in short supply.

You see a few familiar faces, greeting from afar the likes of Dr Elliott from the local surgery, and Bob Jones from Jones's Store. No sign of his wife, Alison, though. She must be minding the shop.

The Chief Inspector had requested that at least one member of the force showed their face, as was the custom. You'd pretended you didn't want to go, but you'd quickly concluded that a nice buffet and some polite conversation was better than sitting in the office listening to DS Brian Lambie talk about the latest old film he'd watched. Plus, it's a cold late-November morning, and the office heating never seems to work anyway.

The bracing chill of the outside gives way satisfyingly quickly to a blast of warmth as you step into the village hall. Standing awkwardly at the door is Reverend Martins, who looks a little out of place but greets you as if you were friends. You're pretty much strangers: that's the problem with him being an inexperienced late replacement.

Poor Reverend Harper was supposed to be here but, complaining of overwork, he'd booked a three-month sabbatical and had no desire to cut it short. Reverend Martins was just eight days into his stint as temporary cover, and this was already his third funeral, with a wedding to do next week as well. As you joked to him, though, the food was always good around here. He did not disagree.

After 15 minutes of doing the rounds and making sure you're seen, your stomach gets the better of you, and you head to the groaning buffet table. At last! A reward for your good deed of coming along this morning.

Of course, this is the opportune moment for a call to come in from the police station, and it duly does. For a moment, you consider prioritizing some of the delicious desserts over the dulcet tones of the boss, but the second shrill beep from your phone quickly refocuses you.

It's a good job, too, as it happens.

What you read on the small screen tells you there's a problem. You're wanted back at the station. The Chief Inspector has some fresh information you're going to need – the kind that can't be sent over the phone. Presumably about the detailed coroner's report that's come in – and, well, any hope of a munch from the traybake selection has gone. Maybe there'll be some at the winter lights switch-on tonight, although no doubt Betty Grainger at the Windy Dog will put her prices up for the occasion.

What do you do now, then? Here's where you need to start making the decisions! Do you:

Stay here! Half the village seems to have turned out, and you might have a chance to talk to one or two people. Go to 209.
Head to the station! That's where the report is. Maybe you can find out something important there? Run over to 128.
Hang on, here's a left-field choice: if everyone's here, then Sara McLower's house is empty . . . should you head over while you've got the chance? You need to jump to 78.

❖ 49 ❖

Deep breath, Detective. You get out of your car and head to your front door. You push against it, and it's still as you left it this morning: firmly locked, with no sign of having been opened. You take the key out of your pocket and put it in the lock.

Is that a noise behind you? You wait a second. No, no. You're alone here, you're pretty certain. You turn the key and open the door, quickly slipping inside and shutting the door behind you. You put the bolt on the door: it's not much protection, but it's something.

You hang your coat up on the hook to the side of the front door, and in doing so you know you've triggered one of the cameras. Hamilton Grainger will now know that you're in your house, assuming he's monitoring your phone.

Now it's a waiting game, and the problem here is that you don't have your phone. You realize you might be a bit isolated if there's a problem, with no easy way to raise the alarm.

It turns out to be a quiet night, though.

In fact, after an hour or two you allow yourself to relax a little. The occasional car seems to drive past, but nobody's stopping. You even put the television on for a bit, and start to unwind properly.

Well, until you see a blue flashing light pull up against your house. Then that familiar sinking feeling in your gut returns.

You look up, alarmed. Checking that it's a genuine police car, you unlock your front door and dash outside. 'Quick, get in,' says Sergeant Draper, driving the car. 'The Chief Inspector told me to get you: she couldn't get you on a phone.'

Of course she couldn't. You don't have a landline, and Hamilton Grainger has your phone.

'Where are we going?' you ask, dashing in to get your coat and then locking your front door behind you.

'The Windy Dog,' he says. 'There's been a murder.'

Quick! Jump in! Go to **129**.

→ *50* ←

Once he's finishing greeting people as they walk in, Reverend Martins makes an admirable and entirely understandable beeline for the hot drinks hatch. You sidle up next to him.

'Caffeinated or decaffeinated?' you ask.

'You're joking, aren't you?' he murmurs, a brief moment where his upbeat demeanour is allowed to slip. 'If I had bloody caffeinated coffee at every one of these things I have to do, I'd live on the ceiling of this place.'

'Busy week?'

He looks at you, and the lack of a verbal answer is all the answer you need. You know he's had a heavy schedule since he arrived, and no doubt he's got a meeting about another service before the end of the day. As it turns out, Reverend Martins has a second funeral to officiate today.

'Who's this afternoon?'

'Cyril from the bridge club. Ninety-one. About par innings.'

You vaguely remember Cyril. Always a bit of a grumpy man, but a firm fixture in the Causton chess team. Not that he ever won that many games.

Reverend Martins is in his late thirties, and in truth he's considering leaving the priesthood, but he hasn't told anyone that. For now, he's putting on his game face, drinking his decaffeinated coffee and making the requisite levels of small talk.

'Will you be at the lights switch-on later?' you enquire.

'Does anybody have a choice?' he smiles, before conceding that he's going to see how he feels after the next service. 'I think poor Betty would track anyone down who dares not to turn up,' he jokes. 'She seems to be a bit full on about it.'

You nod. Betty was always a one-woman publicity machine for her pub, but this year, she seemed to be in overdrive before she lost her sister. The planning started a month earlier than usual.

What is it about this evening's party that's so important? You file that, though, and continue to chat to Reverend Martins, but he's a man in demand. You say your farewells and, clutching his cup, he takes a deep breath, puts on his fake smile and continues to mingle. You, meanwhile, head outside into the crisp cold and get into your car.

The Chief Inspector awaits, and you're curious about the news she's got waiting for you . . .

Head to **128**.

You move towards the garage door itself, and there's definitely some kind of mechanism attached to it. There's no obvious manual way to open the door and, frustratingly, you can't find a switch or anything either. You clock that there's a receiver built into the door system: there must be a remote control here somewhere.

Given that all there is in this room is a big space where a car would go, and the aged shelving unit at the back, you decide to give the latter a thorough going-over. You chuckle at the array of ready-made screenwash bottles, though. You know country roads get dirty, but there must be 30 or 40 litres of the stuff here. A similar quantity of motor oil. You bend down to the bottom shelf to check the buckets out, and smile again, as you see what must be two dozen air fresheners.

Deep in thought, you wonder just how much Sara McLower put her car through if it needed this much maintenance. You keep rooting through the shelves as you ponder that, your search for the door control coming up short. Maybe there's a control on the other side, and you should try that instead, you think.

You should have stayed at the wake, you conclude. You'd have got a decent beverage there.

But you never did. Nor did you get to taste DS Lambie's famously treacly coffee. The creak of the shelf turned out to be the beginning of the end. Those rickety shelves? A little less rickety now, as they start to groan and then suddenly fall in your direction. Pelted by enormous bottles of screenwash, with an encore of motor oil, air fresheners and rusting metal shelves, the unit takes less than a second to suddenly lurch in your direction. You never stood a chance.

You made, the scene-of-crime officer would conclude later on, two mistakes.

Firstly, you got so consumed by whatever you were investigating, you must have lost a little of your sharpness.

More problematically, you left the door open, and didn't notice the figure creep into the room behind you. In fact, the figure was able to silently slip out too, and the assumption was the shelves had simply collapsed, with no human help whatsoever.

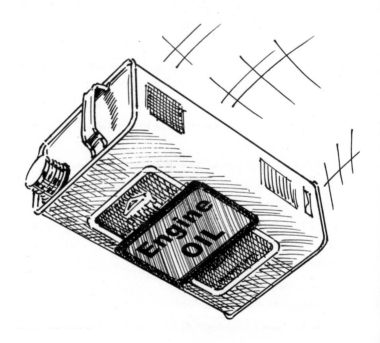

Out of a kindness to your family, the cause of death on your certificate wasn't recorded as 'pummelled by roughly 80 litres of assorted car-care products landing on head.' But everyone at the station knew, as the rickety shelves were abruptly pulled down collapsing on you, that's what'd happened.

Your journey ends here, Detective.

Flowers will be sent on behalf of the department to your funeral, as usual. Maybe Reverend Martins will be able to fit your service in before Christmas.

THE END

Go to p.314 to read your performance review.

➤ *52* ➤

You caution DS Lambie that his days auditioning for *Fast & Furious* movies may be over, as your face shows every sign of someone happier to be outside the car than in it.

You retrieve the bag, as the figure – around six foot tall, you both guess – heads off into the distance. They're avoiding the roads and going over fields. Best you don't let DS Lambie loose on them.

The bag that they were carrying, though: well, it's a bit of a mix. The two of you examine it, but there's nothing really of note that strikes you. A few car-care products, mainly. An air freshener or two, there's a breathing mask, a bit of screenwash in sachets cosily nestling at the bottom. A few bags of sweets as well. DS Lambie takes the bag and pops it in the boot of his car. Neither of you even takes a sweet.

'I'd best drop you back at your car,' correctly assumes DS Lambie.

He duly does so, and motors off ahead, keen to get to the biscuits back at the office first. You call the Chief Inspector on your own drive back to the station. She does give you a bit of a ticking off, but only a little one. You decide not to answer back, knowing that, once she's had her say, she'll move on.

She hangs up, and you put some music on for the rest of the drive, vowing to forget all the words of the cheesy pop songs you've been listening to before you walk through the doors of the station. Otherwise you'd go crazy, crazy, crazy.

Head over to **128**.

53

You opt for caution and let Finn Grainger fumble with the fuses. He'll know what he's doing, you're sure.

That, in turn, leads to a few potentially valuable minutes that you can spend in the main bar of the Windy Dog, still cloaked in darkness. You hear some banging from the back, which you assume is Finn trying to get the electricity back on – was that the clatter of a stepladder? – and, after what feels like a minor eternity, success.

Well, for the inside lights anyway. The electricity is back on at least, and the inside of the Windy Dog is illuminated. The outside is still looking distinctly lacking where festive sparkle is concerned, with just the dimly shining streetlights visible through the strong, thick windows.

A cheer goes up in the pub as the place flickers back to life, though. Smiles are back on all faces but one, and that's the woman standing behind the bar: Betty Grainger. Just as several people take the opportunity of renewed light to head to the bar for a refreshing shandy or two, Betty promptly turns around and heads to the back room. It's unsettling, the almost-broken way she exits, and she gives you cause for concern there. She's never one to turn away a customer. Something's wrong.

At the same time, the noise of a further commotion makes its way to your ears. All the kerfuffle inside has drowned out the noise that's been going on outside. It now becomes clear that something has gone very, very wrong.

'It's Archie,' goes a scream. 'He needs help!' You hear this. The patrons in the pub hear this. Finn, from the back room, hears this.

Which, though, deserves your attention the most? Is Archie in trouble? And where exactly has Betty gone on what's supposed to be one of her biggest nights of the year?

Try and get to Betty Grainger now! You've not seen her like this before, and she might just talk. Go to **192**.
Get outside and find out what all the fuss is about. Go to **214**.

Glumly, you weigh up that you've lost the car, and if there was a lead, it appears to have gone now. You decide to cut your losses and do an about turn on the narrow country road. It takes around 20 minutes to get back to the car park of the Windy Dog. As you pull back in, an ambulance is leaving, its blue lights piercing the dark, frosty night. Uniformed officers are on site too, taking details from people at the pub, before letting them start to filter off home.

You pull up in the car park, and head back to the bar. Betty is struggling to keep things together when you see her, and that's not really a surprise. What's more of a surprise is who she's sitting next to. Your stomach sinks as you realize it's the Chief Inspector. She's come down personally to see what's been going on. As you'll learn, she was particularly surprised to find her officer had left the scene.

You have little choice but to approach her and Betty. 'Good evening, ma'am,' you meekly say.

She turns and looks at you. 'Good of you to come back, Detective,' she responds, ice dripping from her words. 'When I've finished talking to Mrs Grainger, we shall be having a nice, long conversation. I trust you didn't manage to catch anyone or find anything useful out?'

'No, ma'am,' you whisper in response. 'I followed a car that I felt was acting suspiciously, but I couldn't catch it.'

You at least wrote down most of the number plate. However, you got a letter or two wrong, you assume, as the subsequent search won't reveal anything useful.

'So you, the senior detective at the time, left the scene on what, a hunch? Did you not think the safety of everyone here might just have been a little more important than going off on some kind of car chase?'

You start to protest, but you know in your heart of hearts that you've broken one of her cardinal rules. You could have perhaps got away with this had you made an arrest or captured someone. The hard truth here, though, is that you didn't, and you left the remaining members of the public potentially at significant risk.

You've not seen her like this before. If it's any consolation, you're not going to have to see her too many times again. Once the weekend is over, and this incident is properly filed, she informs you that she'll be starting the process of transferring you over to uniform. And not in the Causton area.

This has not been your finest hour, Detective. You might want to start putting together your CV . . .

THE END

Go to p.315 to read your performance review.

The Chief Inspector shows you the message, and seconds later the phone rings again. You don't get time to investigate as she answers, and hands the device to you.

You decide to introduce yourself. You figure he knows who you are anyway.

'Hamilton Grainger,' he says. He figures you know who he is too.

'I think we should meet, don't you?' he says. 'Just you and me.' You don't like the idea of this at all. Nor does the Chief Inspector. However, you've been dancing around making progress with this investigation, and this is a chance to get it all out in the open, to have a full conversation, and try and get some proper answers.

'I won't offer again,' he says. 'I will send you the details of the time and place. But it's got to be you. Alone. That's the condition. Nobody else can know when or where.'

You tense up, and look at the Chief Inspector. She knows she can't ask you to do this. But you're very tempted to put yourself forward. It's that, or ignoring Hamilton Grainger and examining the phone.

Take your pick . . .

Pursue the examination of the phone? Go to **30**.
Or do you take up the offer of the meeting? Go to **134**.

⇒ 56 ⇐

After saying your farewells to Irene Whitley and checking she's settled – at the cost of another of her awful coffees – you head outside and decide just to knock on the door next door. Maybe they heard a car, or saw someone put the note through Irene's door?

She has two immediate neighbours. You knock at the first door, but the chance of getting Ann Williams out of bed on a Saturday morning are not high. You figure she's not answering: she's either in bed, or out. Either way, she's not going to have seen much this morning.

On the other side you have a bit more luck. That's where Pamela Peters lives and, having brought up a couple of children, there's no chance of her ever getting used to the idea of a lie-in again.

She greets you warmly and offers you a drink. Haunted by the thought of whatever was in Irene Whitley's cup, you decline, but get to the point. You bite your lip a bit as you tell her that there's nothing to worry about, just that there was a knock at Irene Whitley's door, and you wondered if she knew who it was?

'She's always too late to open the door,' smiles Pamela, 'But I didn't see anyone, I'm afraid.'

You feared as much. You could ask some of the other neighbours, but the further away from Irene's house you go, the less chance you have of their having spotted someone.

'I'll have a quick look on the doorbell camera if you want, to see if that picked anything up?'

No, you're wasting your time, you figure. It's not too late to take
*a stroll around the block. Go to **92**.*
It might take a bit of time, but it pays to be thorough.
*Go to **185**.*

57

Whoever it is that's next to you, they've given you a slight advantage, even if it doesn't feel like it. You might be seated and they standing, but their arm is through your window, and they're not entirely in control of the situation. That doesn't stop them trying: a second arm comes crashing through the remains of your window, reaching for the phone.

Now you're on the back foot, but still, it's clear that your attacker is more interested in the mobile phones than they are in you.

You strike their arm, although without much backlift it's far from any kind of decisive blow. In fact, if anything, it just irritates them, and they switch their attention from the phone to you instead. They've clearly gone for a change in strategy: if you're out of the way, that'll make getting what they want a whole lot easier.

Their arms move towards your neck, and as they switch focus, you seize your chance. You put all of your weight into your move, and slam down on one of the arms. Your attacker roars with pain as their left arm smashes into the remains of your driver-side window. This gives you a temporary advantage: the glass in the window isn't jagged enough to do significant damage, but it's certainly enough to cause pain.

You look in horror, though, at what the attacker's other hand is doing. They're reaching for your car keys, and if they manage to grab them, you have absolutely no getaway here. If you're going to move, you need some kind of distraction, or else the keys will be theirs. Or you can opt to stay here and fight this to the end.

You have a split second to decide what to do with the opportunity you've bought yourself. You've worked out that you're outpowered physically: but do you want to take your chances and continue the fight? Or, here's an idea: throw a phone out of the window to distract your attacker, and then you can try and get away.

---

*Throw the phone! Hurl it over to **82**.*
*Battle on, and see if you can land a blow at **199**.*

The inside of the pub is all but pitch black, the lights and electricity clearly off, with just a few mobile phone screens trying to light the room up.

You figure you're best located where you can actually see something. There must be a bit more illumination from the streetlights outside, you believe, and head straight for the exit and into the car park.

Had all gone to plan, this is just where the choir would have been found; you were expecting to see them huddled together for the moment when the bulbs finally spring to life. But they're not huddled, at least not where you were expecting. Instead, there appears to have been some incident around the Christmas tree that was next to the Windy Dog's main door.

You look at the tree itself and instantly see that something's gone very wrong here. You thought you'd heard something amid the bustle of the pub itself, but those thick double doors are very good at muffling sound when there's nobody around. Among a crowd of people, especially so.

The tree's once-handsome branches now look like they've been on the wrong side of an argument with a box of matches. They're singed and steaming, but that hasn't stopped a bunch of people from being hunched down by the tree itself.

You then spot the feet. There's someone on the ground there and, given the concerned faces on the people around here, they might just be in serious trouble.

'Who is it? What's happened?' you ask, urgently.

'It's Archie Grainger,' gasps Alison Jones. 'The lights . . . They just, they just . . . *exploded*.'

'Exploded?'

'We all saw it,' adds Irene Whitley, looking shaken. 'He was stood right by the tree, smoking a cigarette. I—it just seemed to blow up, right by him.'

They describe how Archie hit the floor fast, a flash just by his face. Urgent care is needed, and you call for an ambulance. Someone, it turns out, has already called one, and help is on its way. You hope it doesn't take too long to get here.

You take a second to look around. This doesn't look right. Christmas lights don't explode or blow up as a rule, and even if they do, not with enough force to knock someone clean to the ground. What on earth has happened?

'Did anyone see anything else?' you ask, loudly, as care is given to Archie on the ground.

'No,' Alison replies. Then there's a shriek from the ground. 'I—I don't think he's breathing.'

By now, word has spread and people are exiting the building to see what's going on, some here to help, others here because it sounds a lot more interesting than standing in a pitch-black pub.

Finn Grainger rockets out of the door, and gasps as he sees what's happened. He jumps into action. 'Step back,' he screams at the choir, as he puts his medical training to use and starts emergency care on his brother. This is clearly very, very serious and, to your eye, Archie Grainger will do well to get through this.

You step back as you wait for the ambulance. But what do you do now?

---

*If you want to help Finn, then stay right here. Go to **145**.*
Who's with Archie's mother? You need to get to Betty Grainger,
*and fast. Go to **172**.*

⇒ *59* ⇐

The two of you stare at the phone for a moment that feels like a whole lot longer. 'I'll see who's available to get you some backup,' she says. 'There's no way you're going back to your house by yourself. You have no idea what you'll be walking into.'

If it's anything like usual, a small house that needs tidying with a couple of microwave meals in the fridge.

But you stop for a second. 'Chief Inspector,' you ask. 'Why does he need the phone back?'

She looks at you for a moment, and the silence gives you the encouragement to continue.

'By now he'll know that we have it, and surely he'll assume that we've found some way into it. So why is he so keen to get it back, and why would he risk going to my house – and potentially getting caught – to get it back?'

She looks at you. 'If he knows anything about the way we operate,' you go on, 'he'll know that we have to use it through one of these evidence bags. Perhaps we should be taking a closer look at it?'

'It's a risk,' the Chief Inspector admits. 'Even if we use gloves, we risk contaminating what's currently our best piece of evidence.'

'What's the alternative?' you ask. 'Even if we fast-track sending this to the lab, we're not going to have anything concrete to work with until next week. They'll be long gone by now. And it's not as if we're getting particularly close to an arrest.'

You can see the Chief Inspector wrestling with this. Early in her career she had a couple of major prosecutions fall through due to process not being followed, and she knows the pitfalls of taking shortcuts.

'Open the bag,' she says, quietly. You look at her, checking for affirmation.

The Chief Inspector's phone starts to ring again, with your name appearing on the screen. 'It's him again,' she says.

'Buy us five minutes,' you ask, as you slowly open the evidence bag.

A message flashes up on the screen. 'Put the Detective on the phone, or things are about to get a whole lot worse.'

Gulp. Examine the phone properly, by going to **30**.
Speak to him: take a breath and go to **55**.

❖ *60* ❖

Time is running short on the investigation, you fear, and that's why you've had to take the drastic step of bringing two of Causton's most popular residents in for questioning. Back at their shop, a steady stream of customers are puzzled as to why it's shut: that's not like Alison and Bob. Right here, though, you figure you need to take a risk to try and break the case.

You lay out the facts as you see them. 'I have evidence that Sara McLower was poisoned,' you tell the pair. 'That before she was murdered on 31 October, she was already dying. And I believe that the poisoned items were purchased from your shop.'

'W–what?' splutters Bob. 'What are you saying? Why are we here? Are you saying we poisoned her?'

'I'm ruling nothing out at this stage.'

He can't believe the words that he's hearing. Alison, meanwhile, is silent, but scowling.

You lay out what you know, which in truth doesn't take very long. You explain that, in your view, only a small number of people had access to the items Sara ordered. That you're contacting the original supplier, but you're expecting tests there to come back clean. You believe the items were contaminated in Causton, and on their premises.

'And how were we supposed to have done that?' Alison fires back. 'I'm ill, he can't even use a computer or file a piece of paper. We're just doing the best we can with what we've got.'

'I appreciate that,' you say, truthfully. 'But something doesn't add up.'

The back and forth goes on for some time. 'Detective, we're getting nowhere,' Alison Jones eventually says. 'If you believe that we're something to do with this, then charge us. But otherwise, we're going home.'

---

*Your call, Detective. Do you want to charge them? This is a huge step if you do. Go to **42**.*
*Or quietly apologize, thank them for their time, and take them back to their shop. Do that at **202**.*

→ *61* ←

You feel like you're overpowered here, and that if you're going to get to safety, this is your very brief moment to be able to do so.

You reach for the ignition key and go to turn it. Get away from here, you think, and then you can send a copy of the picture you just took.

To your dismay, your move has been anticipated. The assailant's arm is not short of strength, and you've done nothing to discourage them from continuing their attack. To your continued horror, they don't try and go for your arm, though, or initially aim their ire at you. Instead, they've grabbed the keys to your car, their move taking you by surprise. The engine to your vehicle dies, and they throw the key far into the wooded area behind them.

For the sake of decency, you decide to go with the words, 'Oh dear.'

This leaves you in terrible danger, because now that the car keys are gone, you've got no obvious means of escape. You can hardly make a run for it, as it'd take you a valuable couple of seconds to even get out of the car. You have little choice but to stop fighting, you decide, and to accept your fate. You don't want to anger your attacker any more.

But while you're pondering this, it's very clear that the damage has already been done.

'Hand everything over now,' they snarl. The tone of their voice is beyond hostile, and it immediately sends the chills down you. There's nothing in the car you can use to fight back. There'd be no point anyway. You hand over the two phones in your possession, and watch with horror as the hand to the side of you curls into a fist.

The punch to the side of your head is swift, firm and brutal.

You don't remember anything about it, other than it knocks you firmly out.

When you awake the following morning, it's with a pounding headache. It's also without the evidence that could have got you to the bottom of this particular case. The moment to solve just what happened passes, and the deaths of Sara McLower and Archie Grainger will go on the very small list of unsolved suspicious fatalities at the station.

All you have to show for your work is no arrest, a princely wound on your head, a few days off work and the need for a new set of car keys. This has not been a very successful investigation, Detective.

THE END

Go to p.315 to read your performance review.

You absorb the news about Archie Grainger, and Hamilton – still to the side of you – recognizes that you've been told something important. For the moment, you don't tell him. Instead, you're focused on the two different wills. 'Are you aware that Sara McLower changed her will?' you ask him.

He clearly wasn't, as the question takes him aback a little.

'Ch–changed it? When?'

'You didn't know?'

He remains silent. He's on the back foot. 'She originally was leaving everything to both of you. It was only a little while back that she cut you out of it. Now why would she do that?'

He mumbles that you'd have to ask her that. You retort, stating the obvious, that that's rather difficult for you to do.

He's absorbing this when you hit him with the news about Archie Grainger. The colour drains from his face.

'I didn't think you were a fan of Archie Grainger?'

'I'm not,' he mumbles. 'But he didn't deserve that.'

You wait a second. 'This isn't stacking up for me, Mr Grainger. I've heard your accusations, and I've heard what you have to say. But it strikes me that the evidence is not in your favour. I've now got two dead bodies, both relatives of yours. I have to conclude that you're a person of interest to my enquiry.'

He tries to regain the upper ground here. 'You need to be talking to Betty,' he says.

'Maybe I do. But I think you ought to come with me to the station. I'm sure you wouldn't want to be seen not helping our enquiries, when a young man has just died.'

He thinks about fighting this, you think, but decides against it. Instead, he drives to the station with you, and parks his car next to yours. It's a surprisingly empty car park today: you'd imagine the station is down to bare bones, with people still over at the Windy Dog, gathering evidence.

The pair of you get out of your vehicles, side by side.

What now, though? Do you go in for questioning? Go to **113**.
You could ask him to open up his car? Try that at **22**.

$\Rightarrow 63 \Leftarrow$

Every other day in the eight years that he's had Charlie, Derek James has completed the morning walk with little drama. A few occasions when Charlie would chase a rogue squirrel or sniff where he shouldn't, but he's always trusted him from an early age. Charlie, of course, loves running around with his lead off.

Today's happenings have obviously shaken him, though, and Charlie isn't his usual bouncy, enthusiastic self. He looks at you with sad eyes, panting.

Charlie, not Derek.

Derek, wrapped up in a thick coat to ward off the rain and chill in the air, is making a fuss of the dog when you start to quiz him. He tells the story again of his extensive search to find his pet, and how, when he did find him, he was halfway into the bush over there. When Charlie realized Derek was near, he started barking.

'Did you look at the car, open it?'

'Nooooo,' says Derek. 'I just looked through the window when I saw it to check, you know . . .'

'That there wasn't a body in it?' you say, cutting to the chase.

Derek James nods. 'And then I called you lot, and got told to wait.'

'Did you notice anything else? Any people around?'

'No. I mean, look at it. I'm no detective, but it doesn't look like it's been parked there in the last hour, does it?'

He does have a point there. You thank him for his time, get his contact details and check that he's taking Charlie to the vets.

Derek James is a man who just wants a quiet life, and all of this has clearly spooked him.

They start to make their way back down towards the car park, Charlie whining just a little again and chewing on what looks like a packet from a car air freshener. Must have blown out of the car, you guess.

Your phone bursts to life again, alerting you to the arrival of an ambulance for DS Lambie. In all, it takes around 45 minutes to get him back to the car park, and the ambulance whisks him away.

Now? You've not got too long left before you're due at the Windy Dog for the lights switch-on. Off you go to **201**.

⇒ *64* ⇐

'You're not making sense,' you say urgently. You want answers, and Finn Grainger isn't giving you anything specific to work with. 'Tell me: who sabotaged the lights? And why do you think they were sabotaged in the first place?'

Finn takes a second, sighs heavily, and starts giving it both barrels.

'I bet that good-for-nothing brother of mine had something to do with it, for a start,' he retorts angrily. His brow is furrowed and his ears look like steam might pop out of them at any minute. This is not a happy man.

'What's your brother got to do with it? Why would he sabotage anything?'

Finn scoffs. 'You know where he's been, don't you, for most of the last couple of years? Residing at His Majesty's Pleasure? That man is capable of anything.'

'Really?' you push back. You know Archie Grainger has made mistakes, but he clearly loves his mother. Why would he sabotage her big night?

Finn isn't in the mood for counter-arguments, though. 'Mummy's favourite, isn't he? Her golden boy. The boy who wrongly – ha! – went to prison.'

'You think he's the preferred son?'

'Well, what do you think? He brings shame on us all. He'd have got out of prison quicker if he'd behaved himself in there. Then he arrives back on her doorstep as if nothing's gone wrong. He feeds her a sob story and she falls for it. Every single time.'

'You're not answering my question, though: why would he sabotage her lights, if she's the one who looked out for him?'

Finn pauses for a minute. The red mist is falling away from his eyes just a little, but he's still clearly upset.

'I don't know,' he says, resigned. 'I don't know. But he reappeared out of the blue earlier in the year. We weren't expecting he'd get out. And then Aunt Sara started getting ill, all those horrible comments about the pub appeared . . .' This time he trails off, cooling down.

'And you don't think all of this is coincidental?'

Finn looks at you dead in the eyes, and not in a friendly way. 'No, Detective. I do not believe it's coincidental. Do you?'

Good question. But before you can answer it, a voice from the bar calls, suggesting – no, urging – that Finn goes outside. He can ignore the call no longer.

Go to **214**.

The door is a little stiff, but with a bit of pressure you're able to open it, and see the short staircase leading down. Nothing too taxing, just a couple of steps, with a support beam alongside them.

A breath of cold air hits you as you make your way down, and you realize that you're heading to the garage, and not a well-heated one either. The little door to it is unlocked, and gives you no quarrel as you open it. You step through, leaving it ajar as you begin to explore.

Not that there's much to work with here. There's no vehicle, for a start.

There's nothing unusual about the fact that there's not a car in the garage. After all, you think of the little garage next to your own home, which spends its life storing lots of boxes you never seem to have the time to unpack.

Still, Sara McLower's car wasn't on the drive either. Had she got rid of it? If not, where could it be? The forensics team would have flagged it if they thought it'd been moved around the time of Sara's murder, but to your knowledge, it got a cursory mention at best.

Looking around, you appreciate that Sara McLower was a woman who clearly liked to be well stocked and prepared. There's some very rickety-looking metal shelving, gasping under the weight of multiple ready-made screenwash bottles. Bags of grit underneath, too, although what use they'd be when Sara McLower's drive and front path are gravel-based you're not quite sure.

A waste bin has the discarded packaging of car air fresheners and a few chocolate-bar wrappers. Several discarded plum stones, and some bottles of drinking water, too. Sara must have spent chunks of time in here, but there's no sign of any recent activity.

It strikes you that there's everything here *but* a car. There must, surely, have been one in here at some point, else why would Sara need all the car-care materials?

You wonder if there might be some tyre tracks or clues the other side of this door, to at least offer an idea as to whether there's been a car in this garage recently? Might be worth quickly checking out.

But what do you want to do?

You could search for a control for the garage door,
and try and open it from this side? Go to **51**.
Or you could head out around the front of the house again, to
see if there are any clues there? You need to run over to **196**.

≫ *66* ≪

It takes you a little while, but you eventually find Betty Grainger in a quiet side room, mourning her loss. Her latest loss, as it happens.

'He hates me,' she whispers when she sees you. 'Finn hates me. I had to turn the machine off. I couldn't watch Archie suffer.' She cries, uncontrollably, and who can blame her? Betty Grainger's awful year has just got even worse.

You ask about the row. She tells you, through her muffled tears, that Finn didn't want the machine switched off. That he's angry with her.

You know it's difficult for her, but you also know you need details. Where did he go? What did he say? Finn Grainger is not usually an angry man. If he's snapped . . . well, you need to intercept him.

She's light on details. Is she protecting him, or does she not know? She's insistent that he just went to let off steam, but did he? He never strikes you as a loose cannon, but surely everyone has their breaking point – and he's just lost the brother he tried to save.

After spending a little more time with Betty, you're relieved by Reverend Martins, who's heard the news and come to be with her.

You, in turn, check back in at the station and tell them the latest on Finn Grainger. They've not heard anything there, so you head back to your car.

You decide you're best going off looking for Finn Grainger. But where do you start?

---

*Try over at **2**.*

You manage to get a few hours of very precious sleep before waking up with a start just before 7am.

Through bleary eyes, you instantly check your messages. An update from the hospital: Archie Grainger is critical, but stable. He's far from out of the woods, but it looks like he's got through the night, just.

But as you get yourself dressed and fix yourself a coffee, you realize that you've got a couple of leads you need to get on top of quickly. Today is going to be critical, you're well aware, if you want to crack this particular case.

You can't get Sara McLower's will out of your head. Why was that changed so late in the day? And just what changed? But also, you wonder if any clues have sprung up overnight at the Windy Dog. There must be a lead there somewhere, surely?

You scan your phone: an early-morning update from the Chief Inspector is waiting for you. Does she ever sleep? Confirmation from the forensics team that there was something wrong with the lights at the pub. They were tampered with. And it looks like this was not as accidental as it first seemed.

Do you pay Ralph Maddock a visit, and see what he can tell you about Sara McLower's will? Go to **37**.
Or head to the station and gather what you can from the forensics report. That's at **155**.

⇢ *68* ⇠

With Finn valiantly applying what – hopefully – is lifesaving support to his brother, you move towards the very sorry Christmas tree just to the side. It's now been blown over, and you swiftly identify the shards of glass around it. Betty Grainger must have been using the same old glass lights on this tree for years. Heaven knows how many times the bulbs must have been changed over that time, and it didn't appear to be an option to anyone to simply replace them. Too late now.

With no sign of any electrical current running to them – the whole of the outside is reliant on streetlamps, which aren't wired to the circuits of the Windy Dog – you take a couple of the damaged lights in your hand, still attached to their electrical cable. Nothing catches your eye at first, certainly in the first few lights that you examine.

But by the time you get to the fourth, there's something not quite right there. You look at it as closely as you can with your very tired naked eye. Is that a bit of powder? Just a few grains, and it may only be a little bit of debris. But you were trained to look for things out of place, and, well, this is something out of place.

As you ponder this, you become aware of the flashing blue light approaching. It's the ambulance, which thunders onto the car park.

In double-quick time, paramedics have taken over the treatment of Archie Grainger, and they're soon getting him into the back of the vehicle to rush over to Causton General Hospital. It's only ten minutes away, given that the roads are pretty much empty thanks to so many people being here. That must be how the ambulance managed to get to the pub so quickly.

As it roars off into the night, Finn heads back inside, looking shellshocked. You go back to the lights, clip them and slip a few into an evidence bag.

Nobody's going to be at the station on a Friday night to examine them properly. Once statements have been taken here – and you see that uniformed officers have now arrived – it might be worth calling it a night, and starting again first thing tomorrow.

---

*By now, Betty Grainger's been told what's going on, of course, but she isn't keen to come out. Do you want to get a quick word with her? If so, go to **168**.*
Other than that, you're all but done here for the night.
*Head to the station on Saturday morning to get the lights checked: you can do that over at **97**.*

≈ *69* ≈

The air in the car suddenly feels frosty as you quickly try to work out where the voice came from. You assume that it's come from your back seat, and as you draw the car to a stop on the secluded, hedge-lined lane, your assumption proves to be correct.

From under a blanket on the back seat emerges a figure. You curse yourself. You dashed to the car at such speed, you didn't do the basic checks. You're in trouble.

'Hamilton Grainger,' you gasp out loud.

He reveals himself, wearing a protective face mask.

You look around for anything that could help you, but come

up short. He's holding the cards here. You decide to tough this out: you figure it's your only chance.

'We know,' you say.

'Know what?' he replies. 'Just what do you know, Detective?'

'We know about Teddy Jones.'

He stops for a minute. You get the sense that's a surprise to him.

'You leave him out of this,' he sneers. His emotions are bubbling up now. How far can you safely push him?

'He's knee-deep in it. It's not just me that knows it, too. Even as we speak, the Chief Inspector is sending officers out. It's over,' you say.

'You don't know what you're talking about,' he blasts back, but he sounds a little nervous now. A car, you notice at the last minute, zips past. You pray for it to stop. It doesn't.

'Sara McLower. Your attempt to put the Windy Dog out of business. It's just a matter of time before we get the evidence that links you to Archie Grainger's death.'

'Archie Grainger was never supposed to die,' he snaps back.

You gasp. You've got him. He's slipped up. The problem? He knows it too. He lunges for you with his hands, and you move a split second in time. You unbuckle your seat belt, but you know you're going to struggle to get out of the car. That'll give him the extra second or two he needs.

Instead, you reach for your phone, but he's anticipated the move. He gets to it first and throws it into the footwell on the passenger's side of the car. But: you've linked the phone to your car, too, and you hit the screen on the dashboard to urgently dial someone. Anyone.

This throws him for a second, and you try to make your exit. Bad luck, though: he recovers in time, and his hands snake around your seat and slither up to your neck. They close your windpipe, and you start to struggle, gasping for air.

Which is when a rather large fist goes straight through the nice tinted window next to where Hamilton Grainger is sitting, and connects at some velocity with the side of his somewhat unpleasant face. His grip around you instantly loosens, and you turn around: you've never been happier to see DS Lambie in your life.

'What kept you?' you gasp.

He smiles. 'Need some help?'

---

*A groaning Hamilton Grainger falls back on the seat,
and you move swiftly to arrest him. It's with some relief
that you get him back to Causton police station, and begin
to fully put together just what's been happening . . .
Head to* **85**.

❖ *70* ❖

A familiar-looking car is exiting the car park of Causton General Hospital as you pull in. You ascertain quickly where Archie Grainger is being treated, and head up the flight of stairs to the right of the reception desk.

You've arrived at a heartbreaking moment. You ask to go in and see Archie, but the nurse advises you that his mother is with him, saying goodbye.

'Goodbye?'

'She made the decision to turn his life support off. She had no choice, really.'

Despite the best efforts of Finn Grainger, and of the paramedics, the treatment that Archie got at the Windy Dog last night simply wasn't enough. It was established very quickly this morning that the only thing keeping him alive was the machine, and Betty was faced with the kind of decision that nobody should have to make.

You pass the news back to the station as you wait, and ask where Finn Grainger might be.

'He left. He wanted the machine kept on,' the nurse says.

Betty had seen Sara suffer, though. You understand why she wouldn't want Archie to go through something similar. But what a way to go: an exploding Christmas light.

You wait to try and catch a word with Betty, and pass on your condolences. She's getting a little too used to them these days, and could live without more. She accepts them quietly, and sits down, muttering, 'He'll pay for this.' She's not willing to expand on that, though. Even if you tried, you're not likely to get more out of her.

You call Reverend Martins, who agrees to come to the hospital and be with her. The nurses assure you they'll take care of her too. You decide that you need to go and find out where Finn may have gone – not that you've got much chance of catching him.

Go to **31**.

⇒ *71* ⇐

You look puzzled. 'Your dad?' you say, turning to Teddy.

'Teddy, don't . . .' says Alison, softly. 'You've been through enough.'

He certainly has, but he also brought this up. You didn't even know Teddy's dad was still around. You ask Teddy again.

'I think my dad is the one who was breaking in here. I saw him once, and he told me not to say anything.'

He doesn't sound entirely certain of his story, but you let him continue.

'I–I thought he was just stealing some food or something. That he just needed a few things. I–I didn't think he was . . .'

He didn't think that his dad was tampering with the produce, you assume, as Teddy melts into tears. The three of them have no shortage of water in their eyes. Any more, and you might have to put out a local flood warning.

'Who is your dad?' you ask. It feels like the elephant-in-the-room question.

'It's Hamilton,' says Alison Jones, softly. 'Hamilton Grainger.'

The car outside the window speeds off. Teddy presses a button on the phone he's holding, you notice.

'Hamilton Grainger is your dad?'

Now there's a secret you never saw coming – not that you learned it in time. He suddenly becomes the key person of interest in your case, but it's as if he knew about the conversation that was taking place in the shop. You put out an alert, and the message goes out to neighbouring police forces, too. But Hamilton Grainger, you eventually surmise after several days of searching, is gone. You don't know this now, but he'll never return.

It's too late for Betty Grainger and her pub. She has no choice but to carry through with her plan to leave. What's more, because you can't directly interview Hamilton Grainger, you can't be sure just how involved he's been in what's happened around Causton and, indeed, if he's responsible at all. You'll never quite know. But you do observe that things seem to have got a lot calmer following his disappearance . . .

THE END

Go to p.315 to read your performance review.

❧ 72 ❧

You're not quite sure what's making you and DS Lambie feel like you do, but you know you're not hanging around to find out. You quickly scoop up what you can from the footwell of the car, and then focus your attention entirely on the job of getting DS Lambie to safety. It's not easy, but your determination and a seam of strength you didn't know you had drag him out of the vehicle.

It takes some time to get him away from the car, and you also make sure Derek James and his dog are at a safe distance, too. Only then do you turn your attention to what you grabbed from the car. You put in the call for support – DS Lambie will need to go to hospital to be checked at the very least – and then study the collection of litter.

You lay it on the ground in front of you. Sara McLower was a neat person: would she really be the one to throw the packet of a triple-decker all-day-breakfast sandwich down on the floor of her car? Come to think of it, was she an all-day-breakfast woman at all?

There's an air-freshener packet, a few other items of little note and a piece of paper that gives you hope: a receipt from the filling station just five minutes from these woods. Is there a date on it, you wonder? You're out of luck, Detective. If there was, the dampness of the car has smudged whatever was printed on the piece of paper.

Judging by the logo on the sandwich packet, you'd imagine that it was purchased at the same time, but without that receipt, you've got no way of . . .

'The best-before date,' says DS Lambie, catching his breath.

He's right. You go back to the all-day-breakfast sandwich. The best-before date is marked as 1 November: the day after Sara's murder.

When, then, did the car disappear? Did Sara even notice it'd gone?

'You buy these sandwiches a lot,' you say to DS Lambie. 'If the best-before was 1 November, when would they have bought it?'

'A day or two before,' he says. 'Less if they put it on offer at the end of a day.'

Whoever took this car – and you can't imagine it was Sara McLower – must have got it out of the way either on the day of the murder, or a day or two before.

---

*You're still waiting for help here. Do you want to call the filling station, where the receipt is from? A long shot, but you've got a small amount of time to kill. Go to **218**.*
*Or is that all you can glean from here? Once everyone is settled and help is on site, it's time to get ready for the Windy Dog and the lights switch-on. Head there by going to **201**.*

→ *73* ←

'I need to try them,' you say out loud, gesturing to the twin SIM cards. You root through the drawers to get a needle or pin so you can release the catch on the side of the phone. You put the phone back together first, with the battery back in place.

After a little bit of rootling, you find a safety pin and slip the sharp part into the minuscule hole on the edge of the device. The tray for the SIM card pops out. You pick the first of the two cards on the table in front of you, slipping it into place and closing the tray again. You switch the phone back on and watch it light up.

A quick glance at the menus and there's no clue to any identity here. Any history that may have been stored on the SIM card itself has been cleansed. But one thing can't be: you navigate to the system information option, and write down the code number for the SIM card itself.

You head back to the main screen, and note down the name of the mobile phone operator, then repeat the process with the second card. The SIMs themselves look quite old, and show signs of wear. At the very least, they've been taken in and out of the phones a fair amount.

Both have also been sold by the same phone network, and you write all the information down on a well-worn pad of paper next to you. The Chief Inspector snatches paper and gets one of her team to trace the names on the accounts. The preliminary request for information should be done in a matter of minutes. You can sit tight for that amount of time, so you take a rare opportunity over the last day or two to simply breathe out. The Chief Inspector's phone has stopped ringing, too. A brief sprinkling of peace.

And you know what? You're not wrong. It ends up taking about ten minutes, but a breathless officer comes back into the room, and they have information. Both of the SIM cards are tied to individual contracts, both are funded by the same credit card. You look down at the table and reckon you can hazard a guess as to which card that is.

'Do you have a name?' the Chief Inspector asks.

'I have two. The first card is registered to Mr H Grainger,' they tell you.

'Hamilton Grainger,' mutters the Chief Inspector.

'And the other?' you ask.

'Well, that was the reason for the delay really. I wanted to double-check. It's Teddy Jones.'

Wait: Teddy Jones? The grandson of Bob and Alison Jones? The young lad who does all the deliveries around the village? Why is his name on one of these cards? You need to get to him – and quickly.

You need **89.**

→ *74* ←

The positive result is only a crude indicator that there's a problem, you understand, but it does confirm a nagging suspicion that you've had for some time: that the poisoning of Sara McLower had to have a local source somewhere.

Thing is, you didn't expect it to be Jones's Store. You can't imagine that Bob and Alison knew that the plums they sold were contaminated, and it's going to take a few days and a more in-depth examination of their produce to work out just what's inside them. But they need to be informed about what's been going on, and you have to be certain that they've had no part to play.

It's Alison behind the counter when you walk back in, although she's sitting down again, feeling a little fatigued.

'Hello again, Detective. Forgotten something?' she asks.

'Is there somewhere we can talk?' you reply, adopting a more formal tone than usual. Alison reads the situation quickly and looks a little perturbed.

'Er, okay,' she says, pressing a little bell by the side of the till. A minute or so later, a sweaty Bob stumbles through the front door.

'You rang?' he smiles, before noticing you.

'Have you been getting sweaty in your shed again, Bob?' you ask.

'Well, Detective, those vegetables don't move themselves.'

'Do you need to talk to both of us?' Alison asks. 'I've got a doctor's appointment in half an hour.'

Bob looks a little confused, but realizes there's a reason for your return.

'It's best if we have a minute of privacy,' you reply. Bob takes the hint and drops the lock on the shop door, putting up a little sign that says 'Back in 5 Minutes.'

'I need a full list of everything Sara McLower had ordered in specially from you,' you say. 'And I need to know who else would have had access to her order.'

They don't ask questions. The pair have always been law-abiding, and always helped the police with their enquiries. 'I've got the last few invoices in the other room,' says Bob, and trots off to find them. From what you've gleaned of his filing system, it may yet take him a little while.

Alison deals with the other question. 'All our stock is stored in the facility next door.' The one with the lock that may as well not be there, you think. 'And then Sara had her order delivered. Bob would make it up and pack it, Teddy would deliver it.'

---

*Do you want to examine Sara's orders? Do that at **96**.*
Maybe you want to find out more about the doctor's
*appointment? You could offer to go along. You need **215**.*

---

75 ∻

You elect to follow Finn Grainger, assuming he's heading back to his mother, but curious to know if he's going directly there. You try to keep a fair way back from him, in the hope that he won't spot your small, reliable car. The tinted windows on it help a little, but you're still not entirely hopeful you'll remain hidden from him.

Your hunch was correct, though. He's *not* going straight back to see his mother. He's taking a detour, and after a short while you realize just where he's taking you. He winds his car down the country lanes, and eventually arrives at the small shop run by Bob and Alison Jones. They're a friendly pair, who have tended their store for years, but what on earth is Finn doing there?

You watch as he pulls up, gets out of his car and heads inside.

Do you want to follow him in? Or is this his business? He might have just gone for a drink or something. You might be better off at the station.

---

*Go into the shop at **8**.*
*Or it's back to the station at **47**.*

⇒ *76* ⇐

The Chief Inspector takes Betty Grainger off to Causton General, and you hang around for another half an hour or so, before handing over to the uniformed officers and the forensics team. When you get home, even though you fall asleep quickly, it's a restless night.

It's still dark when you decide to stop fighting it and get out of bed. A quick shower, a warm drink and an oddly shaped banana later, you decide to make an early start and arrive at the station just before 8am. The word overnight on Archie Grainger is that he's stable, but in a critical condition.

You head to your computer and search for everything in the files you can find for Hamilton Grainger. There's nothing that comes up. No crimes on record, no incidents logged. No sign of any criminal activity at all. You've been doing this job long enough to understand that the most vital information often isn't held on a computer. It's in the heads of people who've been working in the area for some time.

Sergeant Alan Draper is the longest-serving member of the Causton police force, and he happens to be on duty this morning, sitting at the reception desk to the station.

You prepare a warm drink and take it over to where he's sitting.

'You must want something,' he says, gruffly. Rumbled.

'Hamilton Grainger,' you say, handing over the drink.

'There's a name I haven't heard for a while,' he admits, reaching for a Hobnob to dunk into his cup, oblivious to the coating of crumbs his mini-quest leaves.

'His name came up last night, to do with the incident at the Windy Dog. Nothing on the computer about him.'

'There wouldn't be,' Sergeant Draper. 'Clever little sod, and a pain in the neck. I can't say I cared for him at all, but he was never a criminal.'

'You remember him, though?'

'Oh yes. He was horrible to those sisters of his when their mother died. Kicked up a right stink over the will. Proper entitled little whatsit he was. Really upset Betty and Sara.'

'He may have been in the area yesterday,' you confide. 'I'm trying to work out if he had something to do with the explosion at the pub.'

'Who thinks he did?'

'Betty.'

'Well, she'd know better than us,' he mutters, cursing as his biscuit prematurely crumbles into his cup.

'Is he capable of something like that?'

Sergeant Draper pauses for a second.

'I've been working here for 30 years now, Detective,' he responds. 'I've seen things in Causton I never believed I'd ever see as a working police officer. After some of the things I've had to deal with, I've come to the point where I believe that anyone is capable of anything. The cheese, for crying out loud . . .'

'But what does your gut say about Hamilton Grainger?'

'My gut says two things. One, it wants better biscuits than whatever I've just dropped in my drink. Two, that I always thought Hamilton Grainger was a nasty piece of work, indulged by a lovely mother who couldn't see the bad in him at all.'

'Where do you think I might find him?'

'Can't help you there. Slippery fella at the best of times,' he says, as he peels back a banana.

'Would it surprise you that he's a suspect?'

Sergeant Draper ponders that for a second, doesn't give you an instant reply, but then admits: 'It wouldn't surprise me really, no.'

He puts the banana in his mouth, and you thank him for his time. Now what?

---

*You could try and find out a bit more about the finances of the Windy Dog? Try that, over at **125**.*
*Or how about seeing what the forensics team came up with overnight, if anything? Check in with them at **155**.*

✦ 77 ✦

'How long did it take to collect all of these?' you ask, going along with the gnome conversation.

'Oh, years,' she says, enjoying being asked about them. 'I'm no bother to buy things for at Christmas. Sara always used to buy me a new gnome, for one. That, or she had a thing for singing Santa toys.'

She continues to look out over her front lawn, awash with plastic men in hats. 'That really isn't one of mine, you know,' she insists, again pointing to the gnome by the front gate. You indulge her, and go over to take a look.

'This one?'

'No.'

'This one?'

'No.'

'This one?'

'No.'

'This one?'

'No.'

'This one?'

'Yes, that one. Can you pick it up and bring it here?'

That's when you hit the problem. You can't easily pick it up, and you should be able to. It's plastic, like all the others. But even though the others are weighed down with water inside them, this

one is a lot heavier. You have a sinking feeling as you lift the gnome and realize the poor man has been opened up from underneath and resealed.

This gnome is full of finely cut bricks. And you know where you've seen that before.

What does she know about this? Has she seen anyone in her garden? You can ask her by going to 24.
In your head, there's now a clear threat to Irene Whitley, though. Why? You might have to ask her about that. Head to 34.

→ *78* ←

It takes a few minutes to bid your farewells at the wake, but you eventually quietly exit and make your way to your car. You bristle at the cold air, but thankfully your trusty vehicle's heater has you covered.

Sitting at the outskirts of Causton, Sara McLower's home sits isolated from the others in the area. In fact, there's not another house for a few hundred metres down the windy road. The whole village is a lot quieter this morning. It's hardly bustling with traffic on a Friday morning anyway, but with the funeral going on, a lot of people remain at the wake.

You're not completely alone. There's the occasional passing car, yet there's an air of quiet as you pull onto the long, gravelly drive. The police tape was taken away just last week. It'll be down to Betty Grainger, you assume, to ultimately sort all of this out, and you'd expect a For Sale sign to be up before Christmas.

Sara's car isn't on the drive, but that's no surprise. She'd been going out less and less, and you assume it's locked up in her garage. The house itself has been pretty much left alone since the ambulance left nearly a month ago, and then since the forensic teams have completed their work.

You take a minute to pause, and just look at the building itself. It's an old house, but it's been modernized, albeit by the previous owner rather than Sara herself. You clock that the doorbell is one of those new-fangled video devices. You vaguely remember that someone had gone through the limited footage from the day of her murder and come up with nothing.

The front door to the house is locked, as expected, but you take a look around the perimeter of the property and note with some surprise a window that's very slightly ajar. That's either new, or an oversight from the forensic team. You didn't even spot it yourself at first, and it took a double glance for it to grab your attention.

Still, presumably nobody's been back to secure the property: it's not a massive surprise that the window might not have been checked, given how hidden it is. You walk up to it, set behind a tree and well-trimmed bush, and poke your head through it. You can still make out the Halloween treats and decorations that Sara had prepared. Going back around the outside, you count a few of the remaining pumpkins she'd laid, but they've seen better days. The fatal pumpkin was taken away, of course, and the others are decomposing of natural causes.

There's no obvious reason to explore the house further, you figure. After all, it was combed over after the incident, and nothing of note was flagged. But if everyone else is over on the other side of the village at the wake, you might be able to have a cursory look around the place.

Your call, Detective. Do you:

Open up the window and squeeze into the house?
It's risky, but you might find a clue. And it doesn't
look like there's an alarm . . . go to **130**.
Whoa! Play safe! That doorbell is likely to have some
video footage somewhere you can access. Perhaps this is where
you go back to the station to find out more? Go to **128**.

go to **130**.
Go to **128**.

→ *79* ←

It's a very different scene to when you first arrived here yesterday. Replacing the throng of locals is a lot of police tape, a couple of vans and police vehicles, and a smattering of people working to gather evidence. The remnants of the lights near the entrance are scattered, the once-handsome Christmas tree looking the worse for a heavy night on the town.

As you arrive, you get a message through, and your heart sinks as you read it: Archie Grainger has just had his life-support machine switched off. It's official: someone died here last night.

You get out of the car and Catherine Smart approaches you. Her surname does not sell her short. She's clever, has a habit of spotting details others don't, and you're instantly comforted that she's here.

She efficiently takes you through what you'd gleaned from the earlier report, but also informs you that one of her team went around the perimeter of the pub in broad daylight this morning, and was alerted to a storage cupboard tucked around the far side of the building.

This wasn't the main cellar – although the exterior doors to that had been left unlocked, unusually. But a little further on the edge of the building, next to the kitchen. The kind of door that looked like it hadn't been opened for years.

It's the contents of it that Catherine flagged. The door to it was very slightly open. A discarded drinks carton and all-day-breakfast sandwich packet were the first things that looked a little off to her. But then there was a small bag tucked inside, too.

'A bag?'

'This way,' she directs you, and leads you to where it was discovered, stepping under the police tape that's cordoned off the small cupboard area. The bag has been opened, but left where it was found. They've photographed it, of course, and you don a pair of gloves and examine its contents, which are now lying next to it in evidence bags.

There's a mixed collection of things here. A few bottles of drink, a bottle of a mysterious liquid in a tightly sealed container, some chocolate bars, two car air fresheners, and – oh hello – a mobile phone. A few tools as well. You don't know if they were part of the collection or belonged to the Windy Dog, but you see some screwdrivers, spanners, hammer, pencils, paper and a masonry saw.

You look up at Catherine Smart. She reads your mind. 'The phone, right?'

'Right.'

Someone has been squirrelling things away here, and that feels like at the very least a small breakthrough.

Do you focus on the phone? Doesn't that have to be key to this?
You might want to try switching it on, at **81**.
The bottle of liquid, though: prioritize that instead?
You need **165**.

→ *80* ←

Your hand is shaking as you reach over and take the Chief Inspector's phone. You flick it to speaker mode, so that you can both hear what's being said. It's a male voice at the other end, and you have little doubt that it's the man who put his arm through your car window.

The Chief Inspector clearly recognizes the voice: Hamilton Grainger. You offer a quiet hello, and your blood freezes as he reads out your full name, and your home address.

'It's amazing what you can find on someone's phone,' he muses, a sinister edge to his tone. 'Their friends. Their family. Their taste in music. The kind of websites they visit.'

'It's interesting what's on this phone, too,' you retort, opting to try and land a blow or two yourself. 'A lot of interesting internet reviews here: you really don't like the food at the Windy Dog, do you?'

'No, I do not,' he snarls. That remark clearly got to him. 'And if I was you, I'd stop looking through that phone right now. You shouldn't mess with things that don't belong to you.'

You point out that he's calling from your own device, but he doesn't bite.

Instead, you tell him in no uncertain terms that him going through your phone is a crime, and he has to return it.

'Are you sure it's a crime, Detective?' he challenges you. 'In fact, this is a phone you chose to dispose of by throwing it out of your car window.'

'How's your arm?' you ask, trying to score a quick point back.

'Nothing that won't heal in time,' he coldly retorts. A pause, and then he's got a suggestion.

'How about I meet you at your house, Detective? How about you get yourself there in half an hour, and you give me back what's mine?

None of your colleagues. Just you. And I'll check my phone when you get there: if you use it at all between now and then, I'll know. And it won't be you I come to find. You know very well that the names and addresses of people very dear to you are on here . . .'

The line cuts dead, and you exchange a panicked glance with the Chief Inspector. Between the two of you, you need to make a very fast decision – and it might just be life or death. Not just for you, but for the people closest to you. A very real threat.

A niggle, though: why does he need the phone back? He'd know that you'd got information off it. Is there more hiding there somewhere?

This feels like the endgame. Head to your house alone.
Go to **90**.
But shouldn't you discuss with the Chief Inspector the matter of why this person needs the phone at all? You need **59**.

⇒ *81* ⇐

You lift the mobile phone out of the evidence bag and examine it. Catherine Smart tells you that they simply found it as it was. Nobody has tried to switch it on, and she's no idea if it's charged.

It's not a new phone, you note. If anything, you'd place it at around five to six years old at least. Whoever owns it doesn't seem to have an interest in getting the latest and greatest. Instead, it strikes you as an ordinary phone that's just not used very often.

'Can I try switching it on?'

'Be my guest,' says Catherine Smart. 'But can you do it through the bag? There may be prints on it.'

That's no problem. You find the power button for the device, and to your surprise it takes relatively little time to light up. About a quarter of the battery life remains.

The buttons don't look particularly well-worn to your eyes, even though the phone itself is reasonably old. You wait a few seconds for the main screen to appear. Whoever owns this device has put the bare minimum of effort into customizing it. The background screen is the standard one from the manufacturer. There's no photo of anyone, or anything that might identify it.

You're hoping that there's a list of numbers here, some kind of call history, something that would give you a clue to the phone's owner. Your hopes are dashed when a message appears on the screen. 'Insert SIM card.'

'There wasn't a card or anything for this, was there?' you ask Catherine Smart. She replies in the negative. Great, you think to yourself. You finally find something that actually might be of use, and what you appear to be left with is a phone that's not connected to any network, and that doesn't have any personal information on it.

But then, a hunch. Just because the phone doesn't have a SIM card in it, it doesn't mean that it can't have connected to someone's wireless internet network. That way they'd still be able to send a few emails, wouldn't they? Or visit some websites?

Websites, you ponder. Websites. You load up the internet web browser on the phone, and – as you were expecting – it tells you that there's no connection. As such, you can't load anything up, and Betty Grainger never thought to add wireless network facilities to the Windy Dog. 'Can't people just sit and talk to each other?' she'd grump. You still recall her two-word response when one of the regulars asked her to put televisions in so they could watch the football. 'Yes' was not one of the two words.

Yet just because you can't load up a website, that doesn't mean you can't check the internet history here. You press a few buttons, and select the option to do so.

You've got something, at last. It seems that the owner of this phone has been going to a lot of review websites, and leaving feedback about – wouldn't you know it? – the Windy Dog.

If you can connect this to the internet, you might at least get a username of the person who'd been doing it. Mind you, you're also tampering with valuable evidence here. Maybe you should leave this to some technical experts to do a proper search?

*You need **176** if you're going to try the internet idea.*
*Or if you want the experts to take a look, you need **147**.*

→ *82* ←

As much as you wish this was an even fight, and in spite of the damage you've just done to your assailant's arm, your feeling here is that the longer things go on, the more they will have the advantage. Ultimately, you're stuck in the seat of your car. If you try to get out, that gives them valuable time. If you stay put, you're an easier target.

Their arm is nearly at the keys to your car now, which you know will trap you here. In a moment of very quick thinking, you grab the mobile phone next to you and throw it out of the window. This temporarily stops them as they realize what you've done. Your gamble is that it's the phone they were after, and this time you've called it right: they decide to cut their losses and run to retrieve it.

That, in turn, opens up the window of opportunity that you've been looking for. You turn the key in the ignition. Your car may not be the flashiest in the CID car park, but you know you can rely on it. The engine fires into life and your foot hits the accelerator hard. The car jolts off, leaving whoever was attacking you behind.

It's come at a cost, though. You realize you may have lost the most valuable piece of evidence from the Windy Dog last night: what looked to be an incriminating mobile phone.

You decide your best bet here is to go straight to the station and try to regroup. If your attacker decides to follow you, they're very unlikely to pursue you into a police station.

During the journey to the station your eyes are all but fixed to the rearview mirror. You half expect to see your assailant appear, but they don't. They've got what they needed, and presumably your chances of apprehending them have gone with the phone they retrieved.

You park your car. Only then do you allow yourself to stop and breathe out. It's been a hell of a day or two, and it doesn't look like a crime is going to be solved here.

You turn to the left and rummage under the passenger seat to see where your phone has disappeared to. Your heart skips a beat when your hand seems to find it.

But that's when you realize the problem: this phone is in an evidence bag. That means the one that you tossed out of the window . . . oh no.

You left it unlocked. It has all your personal emails and contact details on it. They'll know where you live, what you like . . . all the information that's drilled into you at work to keep private. It's just landed in the hands of someone who smashes their arm through your car window to get their own device. They presumably still want their own phone: but how far are they willing to go to get it?

You dread to think. What do you want to do?

Work with the evidence you have: go into the station and get when you can off the phone, fast. Move – at speed – to 108. Run home, and take someone with you: you need to get some stuff and get out of there, fast. You need 189.

⇀ *83* ⇀

It's been a genial gathering here up until around ten minutes ago, and most of the faces are both familiar and friendly. Even though things have gone wrong, there's still no animosity. Concern, certainly. Fright? Sure.

Right at the start of the day, the Chief Inspector had asked you to come here, thinking Sara McLower's murderer might be around.

But are they? None of the people here are instantly making you suspicious, and your senses are usually pretty good. Not for murderers, maybe, but at least for people who stick out a tiny bit.

Still, you know that you're making quick, snap judgements in a very pressurized moment. You head back into the bar and scan the faces there. Again, nobody strikes you as particularly out of the ordinary here.

Yet the lights, as you know, could and likely would have been sabotaged in advance, if that's indeed what had happened. There'd be no reason for the person who did it to be here, unless they wanted to see if their plan had been realized. Again, you're making assumptions that all of this is planned. There's too much you don't know.

Returning to the car park, you look around again one last time: nothing really. It must have been someone setting something up beforehand, you conclude. Look at the facts: it's a fair bet that the light switch was going to be flicked at a certain time. It's not as if a place like the Windy Dog is calling out for lots of security, either: no CCTV that you can see, and it's a very easy site to access. Anyone could have snuck on here without anybody batting an eyelid.

Then you spot something, and just in time. A car you absolutely don't recognize. That in itself isn't the problem: it's the fact that it's exiting the car park in a way you think is desperately not trying to attract attention. It's trickling around the outside, not making the most obvious path to the exit. It's going just a smidge too slow to your eyes, too.

It may be something, it may be nothing. But you don't recognize the car. You don't recognize the man behind the wheel. Just at a point where everything and everyone is looking like they belong, it's the one thing that might not.

What do you want to do?

Get in your car and follow them! Rev yourself up to **173**.
Hmmm. Best not leave the site until the ambulance is sorted.
Go back to the front of the pub, which you'll find at **15**.

⟩ *84* ⟨

Teddy Jones has had a tough life. You know it, everyone in the village knows it. He never met his dad, who was long gone before he was born. Then, when he was just ten, his mum – Alison and Bob's only daughter – got ill.

Aneta Jones had fought valiantly but – as per her own request – she went to the seaside just months after her diagnosis, watched the tide come in for the last time, and then quietly slipped away overnight. Teddy wasn't there, and he's always struggled – understandably so – to come to terms with it.

He's now been living with his grandparents, Alison and Bob, for the last few years. It's hard to tell just who needs who the most. Teddy's regularly in trouble at school, but fundamentally he's a good person. It was Bob's idea to give him the job delivering groceries, and he's done that for the last 18 months or so. It doesn't give him a lot of free time, but it does earn him money, which he then invests in video games, from what Bob and Alison can tell.

'Where can I find Teddy?' you ask.

'Where do you think?' smiles Bob. 'If he's not out on his bike working for us, he's in that room of his shooting some aliens!'

Bob really doesn't understand video games.

You head into the shop, and ask Alison if you can pop upstairs to see him. She nods, and directs you to **205**.

✦ *85* ✦

With Hamilton Grainger safely in a police cell, Teddy Jones is brought in to help with your enquiries, and the full picture as to what's been going on becomes clear. Thanks to the evidence from the phone, it's apparent that Hamilton has been behind the savage online reviews for the Windy Dog pub, enlisting Teddy Jones to help him. Presumably, he paid him well for that, too.

Teddy is a picture of regret as he reveals his involvement. He, after all, also delivered the groceries that Hamilton had poisoned to the door of Sara McLower. Sure, he didn't do the poisoning himself, but he alerted Hamilton every time a new delivery was due. After the death of Sara, though, Hamilton presumably took the SIM card he provided back from Teddy so they couldn't be linked. That didn't work out too well.

The judge will take Teddy's difficult background and young age into account, and not give him a custodial sentence. But the boy has a lot of rebuilding to do.

No such leniency will be afforded to Hamilton Grainger. So desperate was he for the money from the pub, that he first wanted to see if Sara McLower's demise could be put down to some natural causes. Hence the light, long-term poisoning. But when he learned that Betty was adamant she wasn't leaving her pub and was going ahead with the festive lights again, even though she was clearly broke, he had to accelerate his plan. Hence, Sara's murder.

Then he had to sabotage things so the lucrative lights switch-on at the Windy Dog couldn't dig Betty out of the financial hole she was in. The problem? The old lights, which meant what was supposed to be sabotage became something a lot more. Bulbs that were supposed to be by the road sign ended up by the front door. Poor Archie. The judge did not go light.

As for Betty, she lost so much, but at least kept her pub. When news spread about what had happened – and let's face it, in Causton it doesn't take long for news to spread – the villagers rallied round. It may be an emptier one, but Causton remains Betty's home.

Then there's you, Detective. The pride of Causton CID, cracking a very difficult case, and just in time for the festive season. In fact, so impressed was Sergeant Draper that he let you have one of his home-made mince pies. Better than any commendation, that.

Well done, Detective. An excellent job.

THE END

Go to p.315 to read your performance review.

⇾ *86* ⇽

You try to keep your composure as a vehicle that you're sure you saw in the car park of the Windy Dog yesterday comes to a stop. Your eyes don't leave your rearview mirror as you tuck the pieces of paper back in the envelope and hide them under your seat.

A tall male figure steps out of the car and walks towards yours. You don't instantly recognize him, and you certainly can't remember seeing him either at the wake yesterday, or at the pub. But still: it's you he's heading towards.

He walks towards the driver-side window as another car brushes past, heading into the village. He taps lightly against the glass, and you turn to look at him. You still can't place him, but you suspect that, in a struggle, you're not going to finish in first place.

If you want to make a getaway, this is probably your last chance, you figure.

*Do you wind the window down and talk to the stranger?
Give that a go at **38**.
Not a chance! You've got to get away – and, for once, at as
much speed as your trusty car can muster. Put your foot
down and head off to the hospital instead: that's at **32**.*

87

'W–what are you doing here?' Bob exclaims. He's directing his question at Hamilton Grainger, who's standing with some discomfort, limping just slightly over to a chair to lean on. He remains silent.

'Teddy?'

'He just turned up here and started threatening me,' Bob's grandson retorts. 'He said I was to pass a warning onto you two not to talk.'

'You're lying . . .' Hamilton interjects.

That's enough for an already enraged Bob, who's not been in the best of moods courtesy of his trip to Causton police station. He lunges forward to try and strike Hamilton Grainger, and you instantly move to restrain him.

'Stop it,' you order him. 'What's going on here?'

'His grandson is a liar,' sneers Hamilton. 'A flat-out liar.'

The colour of Bob's face is changing, and it's not getting lighter.

'You're the liar,' screams Teddy. 'You're the one threatening them.'

'Typical Teddy Jones, always the victim,' Hamilton fires back.

'I told you,' splutters Bob, 'never to come here again.'

Wait: what?

'He's your man,' says Teddy, in a softer voice.

There's something you don't know here. Something nobody's

telling you. You look around. The fridge door is slightly open. There are papers scattered about. And then . . .

You head to where the video system is set up, as the three of them stare each other out. You can't believe it: there's a tape in, and it's recording. Bob, for once, has put a tape in. You stop the recording and eject the tape, walking back into the middle of the room.

'I think you should all calm down. This should explain a few things.'

Hamilton Grainger's eyes narrow, and he makes a sudden lunge for you. Unfortunately for him, Teddy Jones is much younger, faster and more powerful. One swift kick to the leg, and Hamilton Grainger is on the ground and your handcuffs are out.

You take him, and the tape, back to the station. Go to **119**.

88

You decide to head to your home, figuring – and fearing – that this is where everything will come to a head.

A quick decision, though: he's got your phone. You have a security system that will alert him if you go through the front door. Is that what you want? Or do you want to break in to your own home, so he doesn't know for certain that you're there?

Choose quickly: he's very likely on his way.

Break in! That's exciting. Go to **212**.
Stride in through the front door. It's your house, after all.
Go to **49**.

→ *89* ←

Both you and the Chief Inspector rise in unison: 'Go,' she tells you. 'Get him here, get him safe.'

'Are you sending backup?' you ask.

'He's only 15,' she replies.

'It's not him I'm worried about.'

'I'll see if DS Lambie is free.'

As she goes off to get more details on what's just been discovered, you race through the station and get moving. You need to get to Teddy Jones, and you need to get to him quickly. You know not to go too fast around the windy lanes here – a car goes off these roads at least once a month – but you also appreciate the need for haste. It's not just that you've discovered a fresh lead, it's that you have to work two steps ahead: if you've found this out, you have to assume that your discovery will have been anticipated.

If Hamilton Grainger thinks you know, he might just try to get to Teddy first. Teddy Jones has now become your best lead, you consider, as you head along the country roads, a scattering of houses occasionally breaking up the greenery to the side.

You're completely in the zone, concentrating and considering the case.

'I think that's far enough, Detective,' says a voice. 'I think you should pull over here.'

What on earth is going on?

---

*Do you pull over, as the voice suggests? Go to **69**.*
*Or do you race towards the Jones's shop, to try and get to Teddy Jones? Go to **210**.*

≫ 90 ≪

You retreat to your desk for a few minutes, knowing what you're going to do. The Chief Inspector always recommends caution and safety, but you can't miss this opportunity. You feel you need to talk to Hamilton Grainger, and your best chance is in an environment you know better than him. You do wish you could ask for some backup, though. However, you're doing this behind the back of the Chief Inspector, so this is clearly how it's got to be.

After helping yourself to a biscuit from the CID tin – needs must – you grab your coat and head to your car. You look around before you get in, though, just in case Hamilton Grainger has risked coming to the police station. He's not that daft, though, is he? So you drive back to your small house outside the village. You couldn't afford a property in the middle of Causton, which is why you're residing ten minutes away on the outskirts.

It's a ground-floor flat in a small street, with a tiny driveway. As you pull up, you keep checking behind you to see if you've been followed. Then you remember: he wouldn't need to follow you. He's got your home address. For all you know, he's accessed the feed on the . . .

Oh no. You remember for a second. You've got the little security cameras that your last place gave you as a leaving gift. You go to load up your phone to see if there's been any movement in the house, and then remember: Hamilton has your phone. And Hamilton will get an alert once you step inside the property, too. As soon as you walk through your own front door, he'll know exactly where you are.

*That does come with an advantage, though. You could walk
straight in – at least it speeds things along. Go to* **49**.
*Or you could try and break into your own home, through your
own back window. At least that way, it won't set off an alert.
Give that a go at* **212**.

❖ *91* ❖

You and DS Lambie may have your moments, but he's been the one
who's most had your back since you joined Causton CID, and the pair
of you always agreed that you'd look out for one another if you were in
trouble. This is very much one of those moments, and with everyone
now at a safe distance, you turn your attention to him.

He's struggling at first, but you eventually get everyone far enough
away from the car.

'I'm not feeling great,' he admits. 'T–the air refreshener,' he
splutters. You were already ahead of him. There was something that
felt a little overpowering about the aroma around the car, and it's as if
the air freshener was, well, could it have been covering something up?
There was no evidence of anything else, though; a thorough search of
the car will take place, but neither of you is expecting human remains
or anything dramatic.

'I'm going to have to give tonight a miss,' says DS Lambie. You
knew he'd find a way out of it anyway but, you tease him, he didn't have
to go this far. Still, he's going to head off to Causton General Hospital
just to be checked over, and you know it's the sensible thing to do. It
takes a little while for help to arrive, along with some local officers to
take things from here.

DS Lambie is taken off to hospital, although he'll be back at work
tomorrow, he promises. Derek James, meanwhile, will take his trusty

hound Charlie to the vet. And you? Well, you've got to be at the Windy Dog this evening. You'd better get a move on . . .

Go to **201**.

92

You decide it's worth just taking a quick look around the street, and the one next to it, on the off-chance. It pays to be thorough, although you're reaching a little if you're hoping there's a killer clue just around the corner.

There isn't. It's just a quiet Saturday here, and the only thing that strikes you is a car you can't quite place, but feel that you should, in the distance. Other than that, you might just have come up with a blank here.

You're probably better off with the forensics team at the Windy Dog, in truth.

They're waiting at **79**.

93

'At the moment, I don't have much to work with,' you admit. 'But from examining the lights that exploded, there appears to be a powder of some sort that was in the casing of the lights themselves. It clearly wasn't there last year, as the lights would have exploded then. Between the time they were packed away and the flicking of the switch this evening, somebody has been at them.'

Finn Grainger can immediately recognize how hopeless that seems. The lights were packed away in January as usual, and then were unpacked again earlier in November. He tells you this, and you sigh.

'We're looking for someone who had access to all the lights during a ten-month period?' You confirm this, as you stare down at what looks like a dead end.

'No,' says Betty Grainger, slowly looking up. 'When Archie unpacked them for me, the first thing we did was switch them all on and test them. And they were working fine.'

That's helpful: she's just narrowed down your investigation a lot there.

'And when did you test them?'

'That would have been the start of last week,' she tells you.

'Did you buy any new lights, or was it all the same as last year?'

'I can't afford new lights,' she softly confesses. 'I wish I could. I've not been able to afford new lights for years.'

That narrows it further. In the last week and a half, somebody has been meddling with the lights.

Do you want to bring up Archie, since he unpacked the lights?
Go to **103**.
Thank them for their time. You need to get to the station in the morning to test the lights. Go to **97**.

➤ *94* ➤

Doing your best to ignore the fact that your head is starting to feel light and a bit woozy, you edge towards the boot of the car properly and reach for the cardboard box. As you open it, the soggy cardboard falls away in your hand, and you see inside: there's nothing immediately suspicious that catches your eye.

It's a temporary reprieve, as it turns out.

The first big clue that things are going wrong for you lies with your eyes. They're watering, just a light sprinkle at first, like a few drops from a rusty watering can. Then the water keeps coming. Then more of it. It's getting harder and harder to see.

You do your best to focus, then you notice that inside the box are around a dozen or so air fresheners, but the packets of all of them seem to have been opened and badly resealed. It's odd, too, it strikes you. Surely the scent from the air fresheners wouldn't be so strong if the packets had been opened? Either the car had been left here in the last couple of days – weeks after Sara McLower was murdered – or there's something strange about the air fresheners themselves.

You turn back to look towards DS Lambie as you ponder this, and that's when your eyes start to give way, and your vision leaves you. The sense of faintness, a weird light-headedness. S–something isn't right, you realize. Problem is, you've realized it very, very late. Almost too late.

Thankfully, help was able to arrive in time, but when you wake up in hospital and finally feel like your head is coming back together, days have passed. The winter lights switch-on is over. Your chance to solve this particular crime has gone.

At least you live to fight another day, Detective. But whoever it was that killed Sara McLower, it looks like they've got away with it . . .

THE END

Go to p.316 to read your performance review.

→ 95 ←

'I know it's been a few weeks now,' you say to Bob, 'but I don't suppose you have any of the items Sara McLower used to order in hanging around, do you?'

Bob stops and thinks about this for a minute. 'Well,' he ponders, his hand by habit stroking the end of his bristly chin. 'She did like a particular type of instant coffee. I'm sure we have a jar of that somewhere. There may be a little bit of leftover fruit and veg in the corner of the fridge, but we're very thorough about making sure produce doesn't hang around too long.'

You take a look at the disorganized appearance of Bob Jones and don't believe that for a second. If Alison was in charge of the stockroom, then you'd be convinced. But she isn't, and you're not.

Bob leads you back to the storage area, with its hardly convincing security precautions. He quickly locates two jars of local coffee – 'They don't grow the beans, of course,' Bob chuckles – and then heads to the fridge where Sara's orders were presumably kept.

He digs around for a moment, and extracts half a punnet of plums, a few carrots, some apples and a jar of damson jam. 'This is all we have left. We always used to order double the number of plums, though – Alison was quite partial to them,' he chuckles.

You ask if you can take the items away. He bags them up for you, and you thank him. Your immediate priority now is to get these back to the station and get them examined. Before you do, you ask Bob for details of the supplier, jot those down in your notebook, and get moving.

*You need to get these tested. Don't you have a basic kit back at
the station? Head there! It's at **126**.
Or wait until you're clear of the shop, and give that supplier a
ring. See what you can find out there. Call them on **105**.*

96

You accept the small folder from Bob Jones and open it up, as a
customer comes through the front door of the shop. It's Jack Linus,
you recognize, presumably coming in to buy that newspaper he likes,
which always puts him in a bad mood. You acknowledge him, he
acknowledges you, and you quickly look through the orders.

They roughly tally with what you were expecting. Over the
months, presumably as she was getting more and more ill, Sara upped
the amount of fruit in particular that she was ordering in. In fact, what
you can glean from these documents is that Sara bought her milk from
Alison and Bob, but the fruit, vegetables, coffee, cheese . . . that was
all shipped across from the place near where she used to live.

Still, all this has done is validate some of your suspicions. If the
food was indeed poisoning her, then it's no surprise that the more
she had of it, the quicker her health declined. But also: you don't feel
any closer to working out why someone would do this. And, indeed,
who would do this.

*It's a long shot, but do you think you need to formally
question Bob and Alison? If you want to take them
down to the station, then head to **179**.
Or come clean with them. Tell them what's been going on,
and see what they think. Go to **204**.*

97

After a pretty restless sleep – you assess that you've barely managed three hours, and even then it was interrupted by jolting awake all too regularly – you grab the evidence bag with the lights from the tree and make your way to the station. There are a lot of people milling around this morning, even though you've got here early. While it's going to take some time for the full forensic work to be done, you can get some preliminary ideas.

You take the evidence bag to the most experienced officer at the station, Sergeant Alan Draper. Now in his early sixties and happily still in uniform, there's little he hasn't seen across his career, and he's a useful person to go to.

'I heard about this,' he mutters, as you give a brief overview of what happened last night. He wasn't at the Windy Dog, but he treats social occasions with the same disdain he's treated the last few years on the job. At least once a week, you can rely on Sergeant Draper to confirm that things aren't like they were in the old days.

He's instantly interested in the lights, though, and the little speckles of powder. 'Can I take it out of the bag?' he asks.

'Best not. Not yet,' you reply. 'I'm just looking for a pointer in the right direction at the moment.'

'Well, Detective,' he ponders. 'I might be wrong, but this looks like, well, some kind of gunpowder. Something like that, anyway.'

'Would that have made the lights explode?' you check.

'Well, even at worst, it would have given them one hell of a helping hand. I'd get this to forensics. They'll be able to tell you for certain. But there's no way that powder should have been in those lights.'

You mull over this for a minute. 'Who would sabotage them? Who would do it?'

Sergeant Draper munches on his banana. 'That's your job to sort out,' he muses. 'Always been a troubled place, that pub. The three of them have never quite agreed on it.'

The three of them? He explains that it was left to Betty Grainger, with a share too to her siblings, Sara McLower and Hamilton Grainger. Hamilton has long wanted them to sell it to cash in: but that doesn't mean that he'd sabotage the place.

---

*Who, then, had access to the lights? You know Betty might be struggling today, but is it worth asking her? If you want to do that, try and get in touch with her at **43**.*
*Since it's clearly sabotage, you could go to the forensics team at the Windy Dog, to see what they've turned up overnight? Go to **79**.*

98

Draining the remains of your now-tepid coffee, you start examining what other incidents and messages were logged on 27 October.

Jack Linus was in touch, as usual. This time he was complaining about his neighbour – Ralph Maddock – making too much noise after 9pm. Oh, and that Ralph's cat is a menace. No surprise there. Jack and Ralph are frosty at the best of times. Nobody really knows why they hate each other so much but, well, they do. The cat is a bit of a pest as well, considering her litter box an optional extra rather than a day-to-day necessity.

Betty Grainger from the Windy Dog wanted to know if anyone had looked into those internet reviews for the pub that she'd been told about. You curse yourself for not getting back to her, but also, you'd imagine she's had other things on her mind since.

The department's stretched enough without having to police the internet as well.

From the local shop, Alison Jones said the theft she'd reported the day before was actually a false alarm. Her husband, Bob, had found the missing delivery baskets after all. You're not surprised at this: Alison and Bob have been running the shop for 30 years now and Bob's memory isn't what it was. It's a good job their grandson, Teddy, does all their deliveries for them now.

What else? Well, Trevor Davies reckons he's been seeing ghosts. Not the first time, either. A small file is kept on him, but his reputation for making things up stops you taking him seriously.

Peter Page reckons the cider they bought at the summer fayre a few months prior tastes a bit funny. Martine Moffett meanwhile wants to know if anyone wants raffle tickets to try and win the big wheel of cheese.

Oh, and your colleague at Little Worthy has confirmed that the model village should have reopened in time for Christmas, if anyone fancied popping over.

You sigh. This log is for reporting incidents, and it's just a local free-for-all now.

Nothing strikes you as particularly out of the norm, though. Certainly nothing that would give an instant clue to the identity of the mystery figure at Sara McLower's door. Not that you get much thinking time here: just as you sit back to relax, in walks DS Lambie. 'They've found Sara McLower's car,' he hurriedly informs you. 'I think we need to go.'

He's probably right, too. Head to 7 to scoot over to where Sara McLower's car has been discovered.

No, DS Lambie can handle this by himself. You've had another hunch: you can check in with the Chief Inspector instead, and see what she makes of all you've discovered. She's at 182.

⇢ *99* ⇠

You turn back to Betty Grainger as the ambulance pulls away. Finn has gone with Archie, and you fear things are touch and go.

'I know this is a difficult moment for you,' you say to Betty, as she tries to deal with the fact that her son is on his way to hospital, his life in very real danger. Her haunted eyes offer no protest at the prospect of your questions.

You offer to get Betty a drink. She declines, but softly. After some supportive small talk, you follow up on something she said just before that's niggled you.

'You said just then that you'd give someone the pub if Archie was okay. Has someone been trying to take it off you?'

'Ever since Mum left it to us,' she quietly tells you. 'She wanted the three of us to have it. She always thought it would give us an income, no matter what life throws at us. Who was expecting that we'd have to deal with something like this?'

You assure her that Archie is in the best possible hands at the moment. The conversation soon swerves back, at your behest, to the ownership of the Windy Dog.

'Who did she leave it to, exactly?'

'Her three children. Me, Sara and Hamilton.'

'Hamilton?'

'My brother. I don't suppose you've met him, have you? I can't say you're missing out. He's not a very nice person,' she tells you.

She fills in the story for you, through tears and silences of varying lengths. The pub had always been at the heart of their mother's life, and when she passed she split it equally three ways, thinking that Betty would take over the running of it. Hamilton, though, had no plans to hang around. Instead, he wanted to sell the pub and split the money: but Sara and Betty held firm. They knew how much keeping it going meant to their mum.

'And you think he's the one trying to get you out? How's he doing that?'

'I wouldn't be surprised if he had something to do with those awful reviews, too.'

You know the ones. The reviews that the pub had been getting online had been reported to the police, but nobody at the station had really looked into them.

---

*If you want to know more about the online reviews, then ask her: head to **216**.*
*Maybe you should go outside now, and scope out the outside of the pub? Go to **195**.*

→ *100* ←

'Are you sure about this?' you say to DS Lambie as your fingers dig deep into his musky upholstery. DS Lambie is a good driver, he just sometimes dreams of hotter pursuits than his current position allows.

Both you and your suspect leave whatever they've dropped behind, as they zigzag across the road, and wisely decide to go where even DS Lambie's driving skills can't take you. They duck behind a detached house some way up from Sara McLower's, and head across its back garden.

'Don't say it,' mutters DS Lambie, knowing full well he's been outwitted just minutes into the chase. Both you and he know that by the time you knock on the front door of the house here, your suspect will be gone. In fact, you know they've got options here anyway: the wooded area at the back is a good place to lose yourself, and from there, there are umpteen places where they can rejoin the road. You and DS Lambie – even with both of you in cars – would struggle to catch them now.

Just to make matters worse for you, when you head back to where you think the bag they dropped should have been – appreciating it takes you a little while to do so – neither of you can spot it. Sigh.

DS Lambie meekly accepts that his stunt-driving days may be behind him as he drops you back at your car. You head back to the station, calling the Chief Inspector to get a talking to on the way. Now that's out of the way, when you get there, you can see what information she has that she wasn't revealing over the phone.

Pop off to **128**.

➢ *101* ➢

You're pulling into the car park of Causton General Hospital just as a car you can't quite place appears to be leaving at haste. As you stop, though, you get confirmation of news you'd been dreading: Archie Grainger's life support has been turned off. Betty Grainger gave consent for the plug to be pulled. It's awful news.

You decide to head up to pay your respects and briefly pass on your condolences to Betty Grainger. She's a shadow of the woman you saw yesterday. One day after burying her sister, she's now lost her son. What's more, her other son isn't here. She's alone, and broken.

You talk for a few minutes. She turns down your offer of a hot drink, and just asks that she's left for some quiet time. She's struggling, and you're relieved when you see the face of Reverend Martins coming to take over. He'd been ringing to check on the news too, and when he heard, he got here fast. You thank him, and your thoughts turn to Finn Grainger. Where has he gone, and what is he doing?

Chatting to the nurse on the way out, she tells you that Finn and Betty had a tremendous row about switching the machine off. You're not surprised and, thinking about it, you assume it was him speeding off as you arrived.

You head back to the car with a choice to make, though.
Are you going to try and find out where Finn may have gone?
If so, you need to go to **2**.
Or is this where you head back to the station
and try to regroup? That's at **47**.

→ *102* ←

'I gather Sara wanted to change her will very recently,' you say, deciding that it's time to get to the point. 'Do you know *why* she wanted to change it?'

'I asked her that myself when she came to me in the first place,' Ralph Maddock admits. You're not asking specifics, so he's comfortable answering this.

'She seemed in a real hurry to do it. She rang me in the morning, and asked me to pop round in the afternoon. She wouldn't take no for an answer. I had to cancel my game of bowls.'

'What did she say to you? Did she explain why it had to be done that day?'

'It was a bit odd, really,' he admits. 'She made a joke of it, but she was saying things like she needed to get her affairs in order. She was telling me she was planning an enormous Christmas this year; even when I was there a couple of boxes of gifts arrived. That, and her shopping delivery from Alison and Bob's shop.'

'So you went to her house?'

'Well, as you know, her health was declining this year. In truth, I offered to drive round. She said it'd been a month or two since she'd even been able to think about getting in her car.'

'What about the delivery from Alison and Bob? Was that just some groceries?'

'Yes. Same reason, too. Her health had been getting worse. She couldn't come to me. But still: the urgency of the will change did alarm me a little. I could have easily sorted it the end of that week, but that wasn't good enough.'

'You told her that?'

'I did. And, well, she got quite emotional really. To be fair to her, too, she's never been the kind of person to ask someone to drop everything.'

'She always wanted to be liked, didn't she?'

'She did, very much so. It was so sad. Her funeral, lots of people who were acquainted with her, who'd taken gifts off her. But very few who actually knew her.'

You feel your phone start to buzz in your pocket. It's not just you who's starting early today, but you're trying to concentrate on the matter in hand.

'When was the last time she'd done a will?' you ask, as you reach for your phone.

'Just after her mother died. Betty did hers around then, too.'

'And did you sort their mother's estate?'

'Yes, I did. But that's a whole different story,' Ralph sighs.

You glance at your phone. A reminder about the forensics work that's waiting at your desk. Is it time to switch attention to that?

You can continue questioning Ralph and try to find out what Sara wanted changing at 177.
Or head off to find out about the forensics at 155.

→ *103* ←

You know that Archie Grainger's life is very much in the balance at the moment, just as he was getting himself back together. He may have served his time, but he's got a track record of trouble. Without his mother taking him back, he'd likely have spent a lot more time in prison. As it stands, he's in hospital, and your gut feeling is that the signs don't look good.

You utter his name. The two of them look at you in unison.

'What about him?' growls Betty, activating her protective mother shield.

'I have to ask. I'm sorry, I have to ask. But could Archie have been involved in some way?'

'My Archie,' she says, her face a mixture of rage and sadness, 'is a good boy. A good boy. Just because he made a few mistakes, it doesn't mean he has to be linked with every single thing that goes wrong.'

Finn tries to calm his mother down. He's not his brother's biggest fan, yet you don't get the sense that he's blaming him for this either.

'No,' she snaps at him. 'I won't have it. I see how people look at him. I see how people look at me. Just because something's gone wrong, that doesn't mean it's down to Archie.'

'But did he say anything? Had he spotted anything? He's one of very few people who's been involved with checking the lights.'

'No,' says Finn. 'He didn't say anything, but he wouldn't. He'd just get it fixed. The only thing he mentioned was switching one stretch of lights for another. But you already knew that.'

You did already know that. Also, part of you thinks that Archie's too obvious a suspect, given his criminal background.

Much to ponder: but your next priority is getting to the station in the morning to follow up on the broken lights. Go to **97**.

⇥ *104* ⇤

If you're double-checking lines of enquiry and investigation that have already been covered – especially now you have new evidence – then you may as well go back to the murder weapon. Not that it's in much of a state.

'I've come to look at the pumpkin,' you say formally, as you head to the evidence room at the station. You know it's been photographed and videoed, and you've examined the images on your computer. Furthermore, the samples from it have confirmed that it was indeed used to smash Sara McLower in the face.

Still, you'd like to examine the fruit yourself. At the very least it might remind you you're a bit peckish.

Thing is, it's been stored here now for just over four weeks. Even though the evidence-room fridge wasn't the usual lowest priced piece of equipment that the department's become famed for, it's still only capable of so much. A tired Emma Jameson – the guardian of the evidence room – sees you coming, and knows what you're after. She heads to the fridge, retrieves the pumpkin and places the exhibits on a table for you.

She's been cataloguing evidence here for years, yet has to admit that fruit and veg aren't her speciality.

You're expecting to see a smashed pumpkin that's slightly gone off, and as it turns out you're looking at a smashed pumpkin that's very much gone off. Emma returns and places separately on the table the heavy bricks that were inside. They were tested, but no prints came up. On the day of the murder, though, the killer handled the pumpkin itself, not its contents. And, well, just look at the state of the pumpkin.

You conclude that this might just be a dead end. There are splatters of blood and a few hair follicles mixed in, but everything tested has come back as Sara's.

'Anything unusual about the bricks?' you ask, more out of hope than anything else.

'They're bricks, Detective,' Emma deadpans.

'Slightly odd shape, though?'

'Have you ever tried to get a normal-sized brick in a pumpkin?'

Fair point. But somebody has had to cut these to size. Work has gone in here.

'It's a clean cut,' you say.

'I noticed that,' Emma replies. 'I looked it up. A standard saw wouldn't do it. That's the cut of a masonry saw. The cut's too clean for anything else.'

Interesting. It's not a massive lead, but it's something, although you'd imagine that even masonry saws wouldn't be particularly rare around here.

'And they wouldn't have bought the brick ready sized?' you check, readying yourself for the inevitably delivered answer.

'You can't really walk into a shop and ask for a brick that you can hide in a pumpkin, Detective. Tends to arouse suspicion.'

Suitably chastised, you thank Emma Jameson for her time. She files the exhibits away, and gets back to whatever she was doing before you arrived.

You head out of the room and back in the direction of your desk. Which is when the call comes in: Sara McLower's car has been found by a dog walker, and you need to get over there fast . . .

Go to 7.

⇒ *105* ⇐

You step into the car with the number of the supplier in question, and quickly get through to a small family business many miles away. The man you speak to couldn't be more helpful as you give him an overview of the situation. He seems genuinely shocked – as you'd hope and expect – when you tell him that his produce may have been poisoning one of his favourite customers.

He tells you how Sara McLower had been coming to them for years before she left to return to Causton, and that she had mixed feelings about her move. She wanted to be closer to her sister, but never really felt at home in the village. Still, she felt that Betty needed her, and decided to up sticks for what she said was going to be the final time.

They got the call from her a while back that she was missing some of her favourites from their store, and Betty put them in touch with Bob and Alison Jones. The man takes you through the process, how they packed things up ready to be sent by special delivery for arrival every other Monday.

He admits he's baffled as to where any suspected contamination could have crept in, and is keen to help. He's never had an issue like this before, and your instinct here is he's on the level. He offers as much information as he has on Sara and her orders, which you thank him for, but there's nothing out of the norm in what he sends across. Your growing assumption is that the poisoning – if that's what it was – took place closer to Causton rather than in the vicinity of his business.

You need some certainty here, you reckon. You need to go and get this produce tested. Go to **126**.

→ *106* ←

Teddy Jones looks nervous. Alison and Bob Jones look worried. Finn Grainger looks angry. You're absolutely baffled.

'Will someone tell me what's going on here?' you ask.

It's Finn who gives you the piece of information you don't know, but everyone else in this room does: Teddy Jones's father. It's Hamilton Grainger. A father who abandoned him before he was born, a secret known only to a few. A father who came back into Teddy's life sporadically after his mother died, the father Teddy longs for, but never really had.

'And you know where he is?' you ask, incredulously. 'You know how I can contact him?'

Teddy has a tear in his eye. He knows the last 24 hours haven't gone well. He nods, slowly.

'Ring him,' you ask. 'And put it on speaker.'

'You don't have to do anything you don't want to,' says Bob, trying to reassure his grandson.

'My brother is dead,' says Finn Grainger, flatly.

Teddy looks up, shocked. He reaches for his phone and starts dialling.

It takes two rings before Hamilton Grainger answers the phone. 'Teddy, I can't talk now,' he says, clearly in a car, and clearly on the move. 'What do you want?'

*Do you let Teddy talk? Go to **152**.*
*Or are you going to do the talking? Go to **208**.*

⇒ *107* ⇐

You creep out of the room and along the narrow landing. This suddenly doesn't feel like a very good idea, and you're very aware that the soft sound of your feet against the bushy carpet isn't entirely inaudible. If there's someone else in the house, they certainly know you're here now, you figure.

Was that another sound? The house may have been modernized over time, but its foundations are still old. Is there wind rattling around the loft making a noise? Or is there someone else hiding in the house with you?

Alert, your eyes fix magnetically to the door at the end of the landing. A door that you thought was closed, but now seems to be just a tiny bit open. Was it like that before?

Time is short here. The first thing you have to do is make yourself safer. You quickly look around for anything you can defend yourself with, fumbling through the pile of boxes just inside the room you came from.

You find something that feels bulky, and inwardly sigh when you realize what it is. You allow yourself a quick look to confirm it: a 'Santa Stop Here' sign, about the size of a newspaper. You're improvising, but it'll have to do. You do question whether Sara McLower would really have a sign like this outside her home, but you have a more pressing priority now.

That's because the door that was just slightly open at the end of the landing appears to have opened a tiny bit more. You are not alone, surely.

You try and get on the front foot. Clutching the sign, trying to keep on top of your nerves, you call out. 'I know you're in there. I'm from Causton CID. Come out now and there won't be any trouble.'

Quite whether you're in a position to say that is open for debate. But the door ahead of you creaks open. Any doubt is removed as you see a figure, dressed all in black, their face covered. They appear to be holding several strings of tinsel, and they're clutching a bag, too.

The two of you quickly fixate on each other, neither looking like you desire a fight. But is it a fight you want? There are a couple of options, which you quickly weigh up.

---

*Ask the intruder to stop, and try and engage them in conversation. Surely that's got to be worth a try? Go to **35**. No time to waste! Lift your Santa Stop Here sign, and go in for the attack! Head to **169**.*

⇢ *108* ⇠

You're in a lot of danger and you have to get moving quickly. You lock your car and get into the station building as fast as you can, checking behind you as you do so. The coast appears clear, but you fill in Sergeant Draper on the desk about what's happened, and advise him that someone may be tracking you. Sergeant Draper may be grouchy, he may be half way through a cheese and pickle sandwich and counting down the days until he can get his pension, but he's just the kind of person you want on your side in a moment like this.

He urges you to get the phone examined, and fast. This may now be a race against time to see who can find who the quickest.

You immediately bring the Chief Inspector in, and the pair of you reconnect the phone to the internet, using the installed-by-the-lowest-bidder office wireless network.

You briskly go through the phone's internet history again, taking snapshots of the assorted online reviews as you go. But is there something here that can give you a clue as to whose phone it is?

There are a few other websites listed, but nothing of note. You tap the email option on the main menu screen, and here you do get a name to work with, but it's clearly fake. No surprise there. There are only a couple of dozen messages in the in box, though, and once again, you're coming up short.

'Try the sent messages,' the Chief Inspector suggests. 'People are very good at keeping their inbox clean, but – and this happens time and time again – less diligent when it comes to sent messages.'

'I've got something,' you quickly exclaim. 'Right here!'

It's not a message that's been sent: instead, it's a message that's been composed, but is sitting in a folder marked 'drafts'. One with an image attached: the picture is unmistakably that of Archie Grainger. Another review makes up the body of the mail: 'I ate at the Windy Dog last week, and I saw this man: not only was the food bad, but this is a pub that attracts dangerous criminals.'

For some reason, the phone's owner either had second thoughts about this particular review or the message just failed to send.

Next to you, the Chief Inspector's phone bursts into life. She answers it, fast.

'Who is it?' you ask her.

She looks you dead in the eye. 'It's you,' she replies.

Take her phone: pick it up at **80**.

⇒ *109* ⇐

Safety first, you think. You can hardly solve a crime if you're not alive, can you? Even though you think there's a possibility you might have been able to apprehend the intruder, it's not worth the gamble. There's no useful description you can get of the figure opposite you either, short of their fairly six -foot-ish height and mid-build stature. Male, too.

You slowly put your Santa Stop Here sign down on the floor, and step out of the way.

The intruder needs no second invitation, and breezily scoots past you, taking the bag with them. You try and catch a quick look as they go past, but they move so quickly that you were never going to find anything that way. They're gone before you know it.

They seem to exit the same way you came into the house, and once you're sure they're gone you head to the room they'd come from.

After several minutes of searching, you realize it's just a mix of fairly anodyne Christmas presents: selection boxes, biscuits, wine sets. As if Sara McLower kept a stock of gifts for every occasion.

What you can't deduce is what, if anything, the intruder may have taken. You know you're not supposed to be here, and figure that since this isn't the first time you've done this, your time at Causton may be over if you tell them at the station what you've done. In need of a job, and with a mystery to resolve, you decide to keep quiet, leave the house, and head back to the station.

Go to **128**.

110

Betty buttons up her coat and wraps a warm, woolly scarf around her neck as you carry on talking. Along with the Chief Inspector, you walk alongside her into the car park.

'I need to know more about Hamilton,' you press. The Chief Inspector takes a step back and lets you pursue this. You're coming to him cold, and might be able to mine some useful information.

'You said things tend to go wrong? You think he had something to do with what happened tonight?'

Betty nods. 'I'm afraid I do. I've not seen him in person for months. He didn't even come to Sara's funeral. But on the same day we bury her, his car is skulking around as everything goes wrong here. And as for poor Archie . . .'

She breaks down again. She's got a point, though. That he'd be here now, hiding in the corner of a car park, but not seen earlier today? That's odd.

'Why?' you ask. 'What does he stand to gain from things going wrong here?'

Betty Grainger looks at you, her eyes absolutely locked on yours, but her hand gesturing to the building itself. 'This, Detective. He wants this. He always wanted this.'

'The pub?'

'Oh, he doesn't care about the pub. He just cares about the money. I know it. Sara knew it. When Mum died, he thought all of this should be his. He just wanted to get his hands on it and sell it. To take the money that other people had earned, as usual.'

It starts to fit together. If the pub wasn't running anymore, it'd have to be sold. That'd be a fair payday for Betty and Hamilton. It would have been a lucrative one for Sara, too, who you understand stretched her finances to buy her house a few years ago. For all of them, a far richer return than trying to run the pub and live off its profits.

The Chief Inspector opens the car door for Betty to get in. You know she needs to get to the hospital, and it's not as if she's likely to disappear from the area in the next day or two.

'One more thing before you go,' you say, as the Chief Inspector starts her car. 'You said Sara knew it? Was it something you talked about?'

'No, Detective,' says Betty Grainger. 'She sent me a letter.'

Betty roots through her handbag and pulls out an envelope with a handwritten address on it. With that, the Chief Inspector pulls away, warning you to run that by the station before you open it, and they start their journey to the hospital.

You look down at what she's given you. The postmark is stamped 31 October. The handwriting seems to be Sara McLower's. This was sent on the day that she died.

---

*Go to **207**, and find out what's in the letter.*

⟫*111*⟪

'Who could that be?' you ask, looking at Irene.

'Oh, could be anyone. It's non-stop here,' she chortles. You're unsure if she's joking, but you know she's popular. They don't knock again, so they're hardly insistent. 'If they really wanted to see me, they'd ring twice,' she grinned.

They're not ringing twice. Instead, Irene continues to tell you about Sara, and you can't help but feel sad. A friendship that ended too soon. She's not got too much more she can tell you, but you wait for her to finish her gruesome cappuccino, and go and wash her cup for her.

You bid her farewell. 'Stay there,' you say, as she starts to struggle to get up.

You're about to open the door when you notice the letterbox is half open. In it, there's a folded sheet of paper. You instinctively get your gloves on, grab an evidence bag and take the sheet. It's not in an envelope, it just looks like a folded note, sealed with a tiny bit of tape.

You look up and down the street. It's been a good five minutes since the door was knocked, and you don't see anyone. Strange: you didn't hear the sound of a car. It's been a very quiet morning here.

You decide to take the note to your car, and bid Irene Whitley farewell. She tells you to come again anytime you like, and to feel free to make her a drink whenever the urge takes you. You can't help but smile.

But now: you've got this note. What are you going to do, Detective?

Do you want to open the note? Go to **20**.
Or should you do this properly, and take it into the station for examination? Go to **11**.

→ *112* ←

You head towards Alison and Bob's shop, letting Alison make her own way back. You're a little unsure, but she's insistent, and you cede to her wishes.

With just Bob at the helm of it, things are inevitably more chaotic than usual. You decide it's best not to sneak around, and go straight into the shop, greeting Bob as he stands behind the counter, trying to deal with a growing queue of increasingly impatient customers.

'Bad moment?' you ask, looking at the queue, then kicking yourself internally for your lack of tact, given the news that his wife has just received.

He nods. 'You could say that. Where's Alison?' he adds, a look of concern draping his face.

'She wanted to walk back.'

'That'll take her at least an hour! Why didn't you bring her back in the car?'

'I think she needed the hour,' you reply, calming Bob a little, as he moves on to the next customer. 'She said she'd ring if there was a problem, and I could go and get her.'

You wait for a few minutes while he clears the queue and then approach him, as he weakly smiles. It's all been a bit too much for Bob.

'Do you know what could have made her ill?' you ask him.

'Nothing. I've been wracking my brain as best I can to think what it could be, but I just don't understand it.'

'Do you eat the same meals?'

'Every night. We've made a habit of it right throughout our marriage, and we're not stopping now. We've always done things the same way.'

'What about when you're working here? Do you have the same sandwich or something?'

'Usually, yes. Sometimes we don't get time for lunch if we get a rush on. Most of the time we end up eating some fruit from the shop or something. And we've always got this trusty thing' – he's pointing at the kettle behind him – 'when we need warming up.'

'Do you drink the same drinks?'

He's getting a bit frustrated by the questions, but he understands the need to ask them. He nods, as a customer slips into the shop.

'And eat the same fruit?'

'I'm more of a chocolate-bar man, really,' he admits. 'Alison doesn't approve, but I've always had a sweet tooth. She sometimes went for the fruit when it came in, though.'

'And Teddy?'

'Well, h—he doesn't talk to us that much these days,' says Bob, sadly.

'Why did you tell him that?' bellows a voice from behind. Teddy Jones. He's been listening to every word, and he's not happy.

Bob looks surprised. 'I—I thought you were playing your game?'

Teddy gives him a look of disgust, and races out of the shop.

But what do you do here? Do you follow Teddy? Or do you stay with Bob? Your call, Detective.

To stay with Bob, go to **174**.
To follow Teddy, head to **203**.

→ *113* ←

You lead Hamilton Grainger, voluntarily on his part, into the station and settle him into an interview room. You explain to Sergeant Draper, who is enjoying some peanut-butter brittle, that he's not being charged with anything, and can leave at any time. He knows the drill, and brings you in two coffees.

Hamilton is clearly upset, and close to breaking point, you think. But you don't have anything specific you can pin on him, and after an hour of questioning that fills in some background details, he starts to realize this. His answers get vaguer, and he moves into self-protection mode. Every now and then, you mention Archie, a name that seems to upset him a lot more than Sara. But then he's processing the news, you suspect.

You end up interviewing Hamilton for most of the day, and he answers your questions calmly, occasionally getting upset. Yet you don't seem to be able to land anything close to a knockout blow here. The longer the questioning goes on, the more time you end up wasting, and the more impatient the Chief Inspector gets.

She's the one who, in the end, puts you out of your misery. She calls the interviewing to an end, and tells you that you're simply going to have to let him go. That you've run out of time and, without any evidence, you have to thank him for his cooperation and bid him farewell.

Which is what you do, through gritted teeth. You're not entirely sure if Hamilton Grainger was responsible for what's been happening around Causton these past few weeks, and possibly longer. But you do feel he knows something, at least. Your suspicions are cemented by the fact that you ask him to leave a contact number, and when you try it the following day, the signal at the end of the line is dead.

Hamilton, you realize, has gone. And with him, perhaps your best chance of ever solving the case.

THE END

Go to p.316 to read your performance review.

→*114*←

You decide to get in the car and head towards Jones's Store on the other side of the village. You mull over the news that Archie Grainger hasn't survived his injuries. His confirmed death this morning casts an even bigger shadow over your investigation. You can't help thinking that this has to be treated as a murder.

It takes around 15 minutes to drive across and park up in the small area to the side of the shop. It's a standalone building with a storage garage set to the side. The shop is doing a brisk trade, as you'd expect from a Saturday morning. You see Teddy Jones loading up his bike with bags, ready to make another delivery. You greet him, and he briefly returns your greeting.

'Busy day?' you smile.

'Busy week,' he sighs. 'If it's not school, it's helping with the lights, or doing all these deliveries. My grandad keeps saying he'll find someone to help me with this, but he never does.'

He fastens his helmet and sets off. The storage garage has a firm door on it, but the lock looks like it's seen better days. As you're taking a look at it, out comes Bob Jones, checking his grandson is on schedule.

'Good morning, Detective,' he says. 'I keep meaning to change that lock.'

'Teddy says you keep meaning to get him some help, too,' you say, lightly.

'That's what I tell him,' Bob chuckles. 'Keeps him out of trouble, and he makes a few pounds. Alison keeps saying we should hire someone else, too, but it's helped him a lot. Brought him out of his shell.'

'Any news about the Grainger boy? Last night was quite a shock.'

The look on your face gives him the answer. It's not been a happy few hours.

Still, you're here to investigate. What do you want to do?

You take another look at the garage door. Do you want to look inside? You could ask Bob and see what he says. Try that at 157.
Or, while he's here, why not find out where he gets his fresh fruit and veg from? Worth asking, right? Do that by going to 198.

⇾ *115* ⇽

You dial the number. Initially, you try from the police landline, and you're not surprised when there's no answer. People aren't too inclined to answer the phone to a private number. You try a second time. It rings out again. If they don't answer on the third, then you're going to have to call from a mobile, and you're trying to avoid that.

But on the third attempt, curiosity gets the better of whoever's on the other end of the line.

'We need to talk,' you say. You're going to assume that whoever's on the other end of this line will have an idea who you are.

'Ah, Detective,' they respond. 'I won't ask how you got this number.'

'I won't tell you.'

'I think it's time we met and sorted some things out, don't you?'

You agree. That's what you were hoping for, too. But you're a little alarmed at the logistics. You have to go alone. He'll tell you where and when to meet. The slightest sign of anyone else, and the meeting is off. Agree, and he'll meet you. Disagree, and you'll never see him again. What choice do you have?

Go to **134**.

→*116*←

'Mr Jones,' you ask. 'Do you have any security cameras anywhere?'

'You'll have to talk to Alison about that,' he says, a little nervously. 'That's a bit more her department.'

You note that it's a very, very organized shop, and you're guessing that is more down to Alison than Bob. Considering the fact that the building itself is on the small-ish side, you've always been impressed at just how much they manage to get into it. And, as always, smiling at the checkout is Alison, where she's been for the past 30 or so years. She has to sit more than she stands now, though. She's been a little under the weather.

Still, she smiles as she cheerily serves another customer. There's only one till here, and it's always got a human behind it. Alison almost reads your mind. 'None of that "unexpected item in the bagging area" nonsense here,' she remarks. 'You can't beat the human touch!'

You can understand why Alison Jones and Betty Grainger have always been such firm friends. They're very much cut from the same cloth.

'Are you okay?' you check, remembering how shaken she was by last night's events.

'I think so. Didn't help that I was a bit under the weather still. Also didn't help that I might have had a drink or two. Poor Archie. Poor Betty.'

The news of Archie's death hasn't stayed secret for long. Typical village life.

You turn to the matter in hand.

'Bob said you're the person to talk to about any security footage,' you politely ask.

'He would! You want someone to put up a shelf? Call Bob,' she continues. 'You want someone to operate the VHS player? Run a mile!'

'VHS player?' you reply.

'Oh yes. They were all the rage when we bought it. It's served us so well.'

'Are you saying your security system works off a VHS tape?'

'Well, when Bob remembers to change the tape over! Oh, we've had people coming to try and sell us new-fangled devices, and we keep getting catalogues through the post. But this is Causton, Detective. We barely need what we have!'

She promises that she'll get Bob to put a fresh tape in.

It already feels like a lost cause, but you can pursue the VHS tapes at **10**.
Maybe it's worth just seeing if there's anything Sara ordered left in stock? If you want to ask that, go to **95**.

⇒ *117* ⇐

'I'll do you a deal,' you offer, hoping the trembling nervousness you're feeling inside isn't obvious in your voice. 'You leave that bag behind, and I'll let you go.'

The slight pause leads you to believe the offer is being considered.

After a few seconds that feel like an eternity, the figure opposite you slowly nods.

They ever so slowly lower the bag to the floor, clinging to the tinsel for protection.

You honour your side of the bargain, stepping to the side and allowing them to suddenly sprint past you. When you properly appreciate their size – around six feet tall, you figure – you'd have been struggling had it gone to a fight. Instead, you make no effort to stop them, save for a slight twitch of your Santa Stop Here sign.

As you hear them exit, you wait a few more seconds just to be sure.

You turn your attention to the bag, assuming it's going to be full of Christmas gifts, or something of that ilk. Only it isn't. Instead, what you're looking at is just a few bags of sweets, some disposable breathing masks and a couple of car-care products: some screenwash sachets, a couple of car air fresheners. It's as if a few things have been scooped together and bundled together in a hurry: did Sara do that, or did the intruder?

It's an odd collection of things, and there's nothing particularly striking about them: why would someone come into the house to try and get those? Did they just stumble into a random room and start helping themselves? Do they own a car with a bit of an odour to it?

You shrug your shoulders, make a mental note of the contents of the bag, and put it back in the room where presumably it came from. After all, you can hardly walk into the station and say you entered the property unauthorized. Not without a solid piece of evidence, and what you've just discovered isn't anything close to a smoking bullet. You feel like you're no further along than you started – but at least you've got your life, and the investigation goes on.

You cut your losses here and decide to head over to the station, keeping what you learned to yourself.

Head over to **128**.

⇘ *118* ⇙

You can't win this. In a one-on-one fight with Hamilton Grainger, you have to assume that he's very much got the upper hand. You have no idea what weapon he may have in his coat. He seemed to want to meet you to say his piece. He's said his piece. Now, he's going.

'Don't leave here for five minutes after I've gone,' he demands, walking away.

You'll leave it three, you think. But you're hoping that the plan you've put in place pays off. It all depends on DS Lambie. Well, DS Lambie, and a little hunch the pair of you had: that it might be worth getting hold of some very particular air fresheners. You really hope this is going to work.

Hamilton Grainger cuts through the chilly night with some haste. He's devastated about the death of Archie. That was never supposed to happen. There's a tear in his eye as he locates his car. It'll take DS Lambie a few minutes to find it, having correctly guessed the best places to hide a vehicle once you'd told him the location of the meet.

Neither of you wanted to tackle Hamilton Grainger in a one-on-one fight. Instead, you came up with something else. Hamilton only realizes what it is when he sits in his car, and DS Lambie makes his move. He doesn't attack Hamilton: he just jams himself as hard as he can against his car door.

Inside the vehicle, Hamilton Grainger realizes what's happening. The odour from the air fresheners has hit him, and on the back seat it becomes clear that DS Lambie has really delivered. A box of them, belching out whatever Hamilton had inflicted on Sara McLower. Just in a far more concentrated dose. Hamilton Grainger loses consciousness in less than a minute, his strength in half that. You instantly call for backup and, once content that Hamilton is out for the count, open the car doors and step back, letting the odours dissipate in the night air.

Hamilton Grainger comes around early in the morning, in the medical facility at Causton's police station. He has questions to answer, and a long life behind bars to prepare for.

All thanks to you, Detective.

THE END

Go to p.316 to read your performance review.

$\rightarrow$ *119* $\Leftarrow$

Sergeant Draper is licking the lid of his creamy yoghurt as you walk to the front desk with Hamilton Grainger in tow. You ask the Sergeant to book him in, as you root through the office cupboard to see if the old VHS player is still around.

The Chief Inspector's heard about your arrest, and lends you a hand. Within minutes, you've set up the player and wheeled in a television to attach it to. You insert the cassette into the machine, and press play. What plays out makes both of your jaws drop.

The footage is shaky, but the sound isn't bad. You ascertain that Teddy was in the stock garage, and Hamilton got past the rudimentary lock to confront him. The conversation between them starts quiet, but quickly gets intense.

Later that day, you read the notes that you took from it. About how Teddy was upset that his grandparents had been taken to the police station. Hamilton says he saw them go, and wanted to talk to Teddy, knowing he'd be alone here. The two of them know each other, you and the Chief Inspector quickly realize.

It's about five minutes into the recording when the bombshells start to hit. Teddy screaming at Hamilton that he did this, that it's his fault. How he wanted no part of it. Hamilton screaming back that he thought Teddy hated his grandparents, and just wanted to save the money to get away from them.

But it's when Teddy's voice softens and he says that he didn't know people were going to die that the penny drops. Just when you think the revelations are over, the line that sits in your head every time you think of the case: Teddy, saying quietly to Hamilton, one single sentence.

'You're supposed to be my father.'

When confronted with the tape under questioning, Hamilton's defences fell apart. He had no choice to confess. About how he wanted his money from the pub, and that Sara and Betty wouldn't let him have it. How he knew Sara was unhappy, and that he'd been breaking into the shop's storage garage when Teddy alerted him to a new order being readied, and applied poison to Sara's plums. He hadn't expected Alison to munch on a few of them, though.

When he learned that Betty was not going to give the pub up, despite all the reviews that Teddy had helped him with, he knew he had to accelerate his plan. He was nearly out of money.

The murder of Sara was thus a necessity. The sabotaging of the pub was supposed to make Betty change her mind. What he hadn't anticipated was the last-minute switching of the lights from the road sign to replace broken bulbs over the door to the Windy Dog. The death of Archie Grainger was never intended.

But it still happened. In the end, Hamilton Grainger would be charged with both deaths, and would plead guilty. The locals would rally around Betty, so she could keep her pub.

And Teddy? This young man, who's had a difficult life, still faced charges. You and the Chief Inspector decided to go as easy as you could. He just, in the end, wanted his dad. Hamilton Grainger might have been his father, but he had no interest in being a dad. Teddy escaped a custodial sentence, but had a lot of making up to do with his grandparents.

As for you, Detective? Well, you're the toast of Causton. You've solved the murder. The Windy Dog lives another day. And you can relax for a while in the idyllic surroundings of Causton, ready for your next case . . . Well done. An outstanding job.

THE END

Go to p.317 to read your performance review.

→ *120* ←

'I need you to explain what you just said,' you say to an enraged Finn Grainger. 'Are you trying to tell me that someone has attempted to interfere with the lights this evening? That this is deliberate?'

'That's what I just said, isn't it?' Finn snaps back. Not the most patient man at the best of times, and this is clearly not the best of times.

'Who would want to do that to your mother?'

'You're the detective,' he retorts. 'You can start by talking to that brother of mine. Maybe he's got something to do with it. Or some of his prison friends. Mommy's blue-eyed boy.'

'Do you really think Archie would do this, though?'

'What I can tell you, Detective, is that with those horrible reviews and now this, somebody's had it in for the Windy Dog. And yes, to be clear, I do think this was deliberate.'

The calls from outside are getting louder now: something's gone on, and the pair of you need to go.

Get to **214.**

⇀ *121* ↼

The three of you walk across the car park towards the Chief Inspector's car, and you decide to quickly change the line of enquiry. 'Is there anything we don't know that we should?' you tenderly ask. You want to hear what Betty has to say here.

It takes her a minute to compose herself, and then she takes in the sight of the building behind her. 'I'm leaving,' she murmurs. 'This is my last month here. My last lights switch-on.'

She continues, admitting that things aren't good, and things haven't been good for some time.

'There's only so long I can keep the show going on. And . . . well, it's not the most important thing at the moment, obviously,' she says quietly. 'But without the money from tonight, I can't go on.'

'Finances? How important was tonight?'

She looks around, back at the pub. 'The income from this always got me through January and February. And, well, March and April. Without it?'

Tears start to form again in her eyes.

'Why are you giving it up? Is it because of money?'

'I'm not giving it up. I'm being forced to stop,' she states, firmly. 'I never wanted to give the place up. I–I just can't afford to keep it going now.'

'But this place is always busy,' you reason.

'It used to be, yes. But since those reviews starting going up on that internet . . . Sara told me there are so many of them now. It just puts people off, doesn't it? People have been saying the most horrible things on those internet pages. I don't know why. I don't know why they turned on me.'

'What sort of things?' you ask.

'Oh, you know. Just talking the pub talk, criticizing the food and drink, telling people to avoid the place. That sort of thing.'

'Could you do anything about it? They're just reviews. Won't people make their own mind up?'

'What do I know about computers and all that stuff?' she argues. 'Sara was better at that stuff than me, but even she couldn't stop it. How am I supposed to?'

You have no answer for her.

'Where will you go?'

'Sara's old house, I think,' she says. 'She left it to me in her will. Lucky she updated it, really.'

'When did she update it?' you ask.

'Three weeks ago. Ralph Maddock helped her. He's such a good soul.'

You and the Chief Inspector exchange a glance. You look at your watch. It's nearly midnight now. Tomorrow, you sense, is going to be a long day. You'd best try and get yourself some rest, because tomorrow morning you've got some big choices to make . . .

Go to 67.

You drive your car away from Ralph Maddock's house and park in a secluded spot just outside Causton. Checking that there's nobody around, you slide the two pieces of paper out of the envelope and set them side by side.

They're virtually identical, you note. One dated three years previously, presumably once the estate of Sara McLower and Betty Grainger's mother was settled. The other dated at the start of October, just a few weeks ago. You scan the text, and you quickly spot the difference here.

You're wary that one or two cars are driving past you, so you pretend to be on the phone. But you know you need some peace and quiet to take this in. Once the second car is comfortably ahead of you, you concentrate again on the documents.

Sara McLower kept it simple. She'd decided not to split her estate, and simply left everything – her home, its belongings, her assets – in one lump. The earlier document determined that it was all to be left to her surviving siblings, Hamilton Grainger and Betty Grainger. The later document said that it was to be left solely to her sister, Betty Grainger.

Sara had cut her brother out of her will, and had made the decision recently. A brother who hadn't been seen around the area for some time.

Cars continue to creep past. Your head goes into overdrive, though. What could have led to Sara changing her will? And was it a coincidence that it was changed so late in the day? There's only one person who's likely to have any answers here, and that's Betty herself.

She's just made her way to the hospital, though. And the alert you've had on your phone tells you her day has not improved. Archie, says the message, has had his life-support machine switched off.

While you're pondering that, you heart jumps a beat as you check your rearview mirror. There's a car behind you, and it's just pulling up.

What do you do?

---

*Is this the moment to get to the hospital, see Betty and find out just what's happened? Go to **32**.*
*Or that car: should you give it your priority? Wait and see what it's doing by staying put at **86**.*

⇾ *123* ⇽

You've come this far, you tell yourself. You decided to follow the car, and you have to follow through to see where it ends up.

You slow your car down slightly as the vehicle coming in your direction appears to be picking up pace. As it gets closer, a lump in your throat forms: it's definitely the car you were following. Whoever it was seems to know that you were behind them, and they're closing the gap between you. Gulp.

You look around, fast. No other cars, and just a field or two either side. The road is narrow, and two cars could just about pass each other without having to trade any paint. However, when you look up, you see the other car is less interested in staying in its lane, and more interested in coming your way: fast.

Are they actually trying to hit your car, though? Or are they just trying to escape the other way? Maybe they're nothing to do with all of this and they just got spooked. These are the thoughts that run through your head, as you come to decision time.

Swerve into the field! Yank the wheel and go to **206**.
Gulp: keep going! That's at **140**.

⇒ *124* ⇐

'Hang on,' you splutter, trying to catch up with what Finn's telling you. 'Your mother is leaving? When is she leaving? What's happening?'

'Like she has any choice!' Finn fires back. 'They've forced her out, haven't they! Someone never wanted her to have this pub, and someone has been doing their damnedest to make sure she can't afford it anymore.'

'But I thought the pub was doing well?' you respond earnestly.

'It *was* doing well!' Finn spits. 'It was doing really, really well. Right up until the passing trade started to dry up. You see them driving through the village every day now, and they get on their little phones, they read what people have been saying, and they just keep on driving. It's been getting worse all year.'

'Is this the online reviews you reported?'

'Yes. The online reviews that you and the rest of your precious colleagues couldn't be bothered to investigate. The reviews that have helped drive her out of business. Decades, Detective. Decades this pub has been in our family.'

'And now she's got to leave?'

'She can't afford it anymore. What do you think we are? Rich? Granny's inheritance was this! She didn't leave money, she left the pub. Mum's entire livelihood is tied to it.'

He continues to simmer. 'Some detective you are. Are you even listening to what I'm saying? She put her notice in last month. The place is about to go up for sale.'

'Who knows she's going?'

'I know. That brother of mine knows. And her sister knew.'

'Sara?'

'Sara. She must have told her a while back. Probably told her first, knowing Mum. They were talking about it more and more on the phone, even as Sara was finding it harder and harder to get out of the house.'

'When is she planning to go?'

'She wants to get to Christmas. And then she'll be gone for New Year.'

'That soon?'

'She can't get out of here quickly enough. And I don't blame her. You'd want out if you'd had the year she's had.'

You hear a voice from the bar shouting to you. 'Finn, I think you need to get outside. Now.'

Looking at Finn Grainger, you see a man shaken, angry and clearly not in the mood to continue this conversation. He gets up and heads outside: as do you.

Get to **214**.

One of the first things you remember being told when you started as a detective was a simple phrase: follow the money. A lot of the time, behind a crime there's a financial motive. You're curious to see just how much trouble the Windy Dog is actually in.

It's not too hard to get financial records for the pub off your computer system, and the predicament for Betty Grainger becomes very clear. The last three years have been trading quite steadily, but even then the pub was struggling to make much money. At best, it broke even. You can't get the information for this year, but you can't imagine it'll paint a very healthy picture at all.

You then ask for Betty Grainger's personal financial details, and these take a little longer to obtain. Once you offer assurances that they form a legitimate part of your enquiry, you get the information you were after. This time, the numbers are far more up to date. If anything, they make things worse. Betty Grainger is broke: up to her overdraft limit, and absolutely can't afford to prop up a struggling business, too.

The pressure on her must have been intense. Trying to keep her mother's legacy going, while also covering her own bills. You scroll through the history of her accounts: the legal fees she had to pay to try and keep her son, Archie, out of prison, really didn't help.

She's clearly desperate for money: but what benefit would there be in her own lights switch-on ceremony going wrong?

You go back to Sergeant Draper at the front desk, and quietly talk this through with him, as he nibbles at a bap.

'Interesting,' he says. 'I play bridge on Monday nights at the Windy Dog. Got talking to Ralph Maddock a month or two back. Said he was back doing wills if I wanted to get mine updated, the cheeky . . .'

'What's this got to do with this case?'

'Well, Ralph is very upstanding and proper. Always was, when he was the local solicitor. Even in retirement, he tends to keep tight-lipped. But after some of the homebrew at the Windy Dog, he can get a bit loose-lipped. Mentioned one or two people who'd been in to change their wills: and I'm sure he mentioned Sara McLower.'

Hang on: what if she changed her will to benefit Betty, and then . . .? Betty surely wouldn't . . . would she?

Go and see Ralph Maddock. Find out about the wills, but
tread carefully with him. He'll be sober at this time of day.
Go to 37.
Or – gulp – might you have a new theory to talk
through with the Chief Inspector? Go to 131.

❖ *126* ❖

You waste no time taking the produce to the station to get it examined: you can hopefully get some indicative results, at the very least.

There isn't a lot of expertise in the small Causton police department, so you know for a thorough examination you're going to have to send everything away. But you keep a small stock of testing equipment around here somewhere: you've had a few instances of food-related contamination, and the Chief Inspector reluctantly approved the budget for a few test kits to help get quicker information. Finally, they might come in useful.

You ask Sergeant Draper to give you a hand, and he'll take on any old job to get away from staffing the front desk for an hour. He even puts down the nuts that he's been nibbling on. You figure, too, that as the most experienced officer at the station, he's also the one who's hardest to surprise.

You explain the situation and he looks at you with caution. Mind you, he always looks at you with caution. He's got two years to retirement, and very much wants a quiet life. Every night he can get home by 6pm is a bonus.

But when it comes to the work, Sergeant Draper can absolutely be counted on. The pair of you go off into a side room, and you get the tray of testing equipment.

'What are we looking for?' he asks, as you both put on protective gloves.

'I'm not quite sure. I just know that Sara McLower—'

'This is the McLower case? I thought that was a straightforward murder.'

'We all did. I just know now that not only had she been unwell for some time, but she was also ordering special produce to be shipped in to Bob and Alison's shop. Paying a bit extra for the privilege, too.'

Neither of you have used one of these kits before, and you carefully slice off a tiny part of one of Sara McLower's plums. You put it in the tiny mixing container, and add the solution. You seal the lid of the container and shake it, while Sergeant Draper gets a little dropper from out of the packet.

'Ready?' he asks.

'Ready,' you say. You put the container back on the table and let it settle for half a minute. Then you gradually peel the lid back off, and Sergeant Draper sucks up some of the liquid using the dropper.

You place the testing card next to the container, and he releases a couple of drops onto it.

'What are we looking for?'

'This one's a simple indicative test,' you explain, reading the instructions roughly five seconds ahead of telling Sergeant Draper what's going on. 'If the card goes red, we're in trouble . . .'

'Like that?' he says, pointing the card.

You look down at it. It has indeed gone red, and quickly. You're not quite sure what was in Sara McLower's plums, but you're reasonably certain it shouldn't have been there.

Now what?

You need to get back to Bob and Alison's shop, to trace the source of their plums. Rush over to 74.
Switch focus to the supplier. Isn't that where the problem lies?
Go to 150.

127

Now that Pamela has managed to get access to the footage on her phone from the camera, you may as well just see who else was about.

'How far back does it go?'

'Not that far,' she laughs. 'This wasn't the expensive model!'

She's not kidding, either. It goes back about an hour, from what you can tell. 'You have to pay them money if you want to keep more footage than that,' she explains. 'I only got the basic package.'

It feels pretty hopeless, though, and Pamela is clearly keen to get back to her sewing. But there is one small thing that her doorbell camera has picked up: the same car going past twice. Slowing down as it passes her house and, in turn, Irene Whitley's house. The picture isn't clear enough to identify the vehicle, but you do get the impression that someone was very aware of where you were.

It's probably time to get moving. You thank Pamela for her time, and head back towards your car.

*What do you want to do, though? Do you want to go and talk
to Teddy? Go to* **8**.
*Or head off to see the forensics team at the Windy Dog if you're
done here. Go to* **79**.

→ 128 ←

As you head to your desk at the station, Sergeant Draper – the duty
officer on the front desk – informs you without a single pleasantry the
Chief Inspector wants to see you now.

'Now?'

'Right away.'

Best not roll your eyes. You'd best not argue either, and you traipse
your way around to her room.

'Close the door,' she says, as you walk into her studiously tidy
office.

She turns her attention to Sara McLower. Unusually, she
apologizes to you too, but only for messaging you when you were at
the wake. Still, she explains, she'd got some fresh information that she
needed to share, and she didn't want to put it on a phone screen where
someone might catch glimpse of it.

'This is just between a few of us for now,' she says, her eyes
indicating there's no hint of compromise on this.

'It's Sara McLower,' she confirms. 'It was definitely murder.'

Why is she telling you this? You worked that out from the brick-
filled pumpkin being used as an attack weapon.

'With all due respect ma'am,' you say, trying not to let on you think
she's stating the obvious, 'but we knew that already, unless I missed
something.'

'We all did,' the Chief Inspector acknowledges. 'But it turns out there's a bit more to it than we originally thought. In fact, it was a lot more premeditated than we suspected.'

'What makes you say that?'

'This,' she says, as she pushes a buff-coloured folder across the desk. Now you understand the secrecy.

You open the folder and take in the information on the three sheets of A4 paper that were snugly tucked inside. The Chief Inspector wasn't kidding. It seems that the attempt to kill Sara McLower wasn't just restricted to Halloween: it had been going on for some time. The pumpkin/face interaction you knew about. Heck, everybody knew about that. But the two other factors you didn't.

The report details a slow poison that was in Sara McLower's system. Almost undetectable, and it's only because such a detailed post-mortem was required that it'd been picked up at all. It'd taken a while to get the results back because the traces were difficult to register. The working theory is that it was something she was eating, but for the minute, that's all you have to go on.

Well, that and another crucial piece of information.

For there was a second poison at work too. Something that she had probably inhaled or been in contact with. The cumulative effect of both? Independently, they could each have killed her over a period of time. Both had been eating away at her in tandem.

'She was being poisoned? Twice?'

The Chief Inspector nods. 'Only you, me and DS Lambie know. And the coroner, of course. Keep this as quiet as possible. This wasn't an opportunistic murder. Someone wanted Sara McLower dead, and had been slowly trying to kill her for some time. I'd also suggest – although this is of course only a theory – that they ran out of patience, hence the incident at Halloween.'

It's a lot to take in.

'Are you absolutely sure it's murder?' you say. You know the answer, but you know you need to be thorough, and establish the basics.

The Chief Inspector nods.

'Any idea who?'

'That's part of what you're going to have to find out,' the Chief Inspector tells you. 'I don't need to tell you that the next month is a busy time in Causton. I don't want you causing alarm. But I do want you at the Windy Dog tonight. Virtually everyone will be there, and work on the assumption that the murderer might be as well.'

The last sentence drops the temperature of your bones. What have you found yourself in the middle of?

'If you get a moment, you might want to double-check the computer, too. Go back over the footage from Sara McLower's door camera.'

A knock at the door. DS Lambie walks in, and offers a nervous smile. 'You're up to date?' he asks.

You nod.

'What next, then?'

Well, you came here intending to check the footage from the door camera. Is that still worth doing?
Head to 135 if you think it is.
Perhaps, though, you could find out a bit more about these poisons. Is it worth a quick chat with the coroner?
Got to 213 to give them a call.

→ *129* ←

You've got a sinking feeling about this. For the second night running, the Windy Dog car park is awash with activity, with uniformed officers milling around, and the forensic team who thought they might have the night off are back on the ground.

The Chief Inspector intercepts you. 'You went home, didn't you?' she says sternly. 'You know you shouldn't have gone home like that.'

A bit unfair, you think. She can hardly stop you going home, even though you acknowledge that she had warned you not to. But when you learn just what's happened here, you understand why she's not happy.

Hamilton Grainger, she's assuming, *did* monitor your phone. When he realized that the detective on his case was relaxing at home – courtesy of alerts from your phone pinging through – he figured the coast was clear. If you were at home, you weren't at the Windy Dog. And the only person who was likely to be there? Betty Grainger.

Hamilton headed straight there, thinking the coast was clear. But you see a body on the ground, covered by a white sheet. As she tells you the story, you have a sinking feeling. 'Chief Inspector,' you ask. 'Who's under the sheet?'

She walks over with you, ducking under the police line. She nods at the officer standing alongside and they pull back the sheet. The face of Finn Grainger stares back up at you, his eyes lifeless.

'W–what happened?' you ask.

Hamilton Grainger: that's what happened. He came here, just as Finn Grainger was returning after going off to look for him. The pair of them arrived in the car park at the same time – and when Finn saw Hamilton, the red mist descended. He leapt out of his car and started running straight for Hamilton.

Thing is, whereas Archie Grainger knew how to handle himself and would have been a tricky opponent for Hamilton, the same couldn't be said for Finn. As it turns out, Hamilton Grainger had your mobile in his hand, and as his fist connected with Finn, it was your second-hand smartphone that hit Finn's Adam's apple.

It was a fluke hit: just enough force, just enough precision to induce fast swelling in his throat.

As a final-year medical student, he knew what was happening, but was powerless to stop it. The swelling quickly blocked his throat, and as Hamilton leapt into his car and left Causton for the last time, Finn Grainger was spending the last few minutes gasping for air, knowing that he'd been killed by a phone. And not even a new one.

You know what the Chief Inspector is going to do tomorrow when she hauls you into her office. You know that however you explain this, it's not going to look good in her eyes. You know that it might be best, when you do get to the station tomorrow, to take a box along with you. You're likely to be clearing your desk . . .

THE END

Go to p.317 to read your performance review.

❧ *130* ❧

Deep breath, Detective. You open up the window, and – thanking yourself for not having eaten anything off the buffet table this morning – squeeze into the property through the gap. The chill hits you again quickly: this must be the only house in Causton where it's probably warmer to stand outside, and that's saying something today.

Your hunch about there being no intruder alarm or much in the way of security precautions is correct. The window leads to a side passage, which in turn gives way to the main downstairs layout. In less than a minute you find yourself in the middle of Sara McLower's kitchen, with baked treats that likely would have been delicious a month ago, now standing looking really quite sorry for themselves. A few have been taken away for testing, you presume, the rest left there to rot.

There are the remnants of a grocery delivery from the local shop as well. That would have come from Jones's Store. It's not too far down the road, but the shop does a roaring trade with deliveries to people who struggle to get out and about themselves.

You open the fridge and take a look, and soon wish you hadn't. Even though the electricity hasn't been cut off, you'd have thought that one of the forensics lot would have thrown the milk and punnet of plums away. You shut the door rather than let the smell of any more curdled milk make its way to your nostrils. Still, the many valiant air fresheners should help settle it, too.

Clues are not in abundance here, and you're struck by just how neat and tidy everything is. Sara wasn't known as a big socializer, and never had anyone round to her home. Yet the place looks as if it's about to welcome in royalty. Maybe she was expecting a visitor this time? You're not convinced she was, but you can't rule it out.

You've not got much time here. Two possible avenues of exploration catch your eye.

The big staircase, leading – uncontroversially – upstairs. Is it worth having a quick snoop up there? That, or there's a door off to the side of the hall that looks slightly different to the rest. You reckon you've got time to try one of these, as you check your watch and figure the wake will be coming to a close soon.

*If you want to try the stairs, climb your way over to **133**.*
*But what about that other door? You'll need **65***
if that's where you want to go.

⇥ *131* ⇤

'Ma'am, can I have a word?' you ask, as you catch the Chief Inspector. The two of you bring each other up to date with what you know. That a person of interest has come to light: Hamilton Grainger, Betty and Sara's brother. Meanwhile, Archie Grainger is at best clinging to life, courtesy of the lights explosion.

And then there's the little bombshell you're about to throw into the mix.

'I was always told don't overlook an obvious motive,' you say to the Chief Inspector, a little apprehensive, as you know full well which way this is going.

She looks puzzled.

'Betty Grainger needs money.'

She's silent. You continue.

'The Windy Dog isn't making a profit, and hasn't been for years. The downturn in its trade this year is bound to have made things worse there. And then there's Betty herself: she's not got a pot to . . . well, have a wee in.'

The Chief Inspector does not appreciate the analogy, but lets you continue. You tell her what Sergeant Draper said about Sara McLower changing her will.

'I spent time with Betty Grainger last night, Detective,' she says. 'I'm afraid I just don't buy it. We talked a lot, and she bared her soul a bit. And also, what's the benefit in blowing up her own lights ceremony?'

She thinks again. 'Bear it in mind,' she says. 'It doesn't stack up for me, though. And also, we did financial checks on relatives after Sara was murdered, and did some quiet snooping around. It's not her.'

Well, that put you in your place, at least for the minute. Still suspicious? Keep it in your back pocket if you are. You might as well go and see how the forensics team is doing at the pub.

Go to **155.**

→ *132* ←

You ask if you can step back inside, and Irene Whitley opens the door. You head into her living room, and give her a moment to settle back in her chair.

'There was a letter,' you tell her.

'Letter?'

'In your letterbox. And I'm afraid it's not very nice.'

You read it to her, and she gasps. She presents a happy exterior, does Irene Whitley, but you know she's had more than her fair share of tough times. This is another worry she doesn't need.

'Do you know who could have sent it?'

She looks at you in a way that suggests she feels you've asked a question with a very obvious answer. 'It's only going to be him, isn't it?'

You're inclined to agree. It doesn't strike you that there's a big list of candidates who would regard Irene Whitley as an enemy.

'Has he threatened you before?'

'Only through Sara. I never took him seriously, though. And then . . .'

She loses her composure for a minute, and then gets it back.

'And then poor Sara died. I guess you have to be a bit more wary after that. Especially given' – she pauses – 'given how she was killed.'

You're inclined to agree there. You ask her to tell you anything that might be useful about Hamilton Grainger. She gives you what you can easily glean. One interesting extra fact though: he tends to drive, given that he struggles a little with his leg.

'He can walk okay, though?'

'Yes. But he had an operation or two on his leg a few years ago. It slowed him down. I can't imagine it's getting much better. I bet he still has that slight limp.'

But this poses a question: who just posted the letter? Did you hear a car coming down the street? You can't remember, although you imagine it'd be easy enough to park it around the corner and just walk around.

Maybe you should just check there? Get your
walking boots on at 92.
Perhaps a quick chat with a neighbour?
See if they saw anything? Go to 56.
Or is this the moment to say farewell to Irene Whitley for
now, and head off to the pub to check in on the forensics team?
They're working away at 79.

❖ *133* ❖

You ascend the staircase and arrive at a landing area. Straight away, you spot the difference.

Although the downstairs of Sara McLower's house was perfectly in order, the upstairs? Well, it's nothing that three days of intense cleaning and tidying couldn't make a small dent in. It's a lot more cluttered, and even though there are fewer, bigger rooms up here, they look smaller, given the amount of stuff that Sara had crammed into them.

You have a quick explore. A door opens onto what might just be the largest room, and you head that way. Entering, you see a bed set to the side, and a floor that's absolutely awash with packages, spare lights, decorations and, well, mess. You pity the forensics team who had to give this lot the once over. It's as if Sara McLower had bought half the internet and had it delivered to her upstairs room.

There's no furniture in here outside of the bed, just piles of things she'd bought.

One side of the room is bristling with Christmas decorations and what you presume to be festive gifts. The other, discarded Halloween props and paraphernalia. As if she'd bought as least twice as much as she actually needed when it came to her own decorations, seemingly with the same keenness to put on some kind of show that runs through her sister as well.

While you can't work out who the gifts are for– and you assume they're going to be presents – it does strike you that there's a lot of them.

Why so much stuff, then? Who's she trying to impress?

Or was she simply putting on a show? Giving herself as many options as possible, as she tried to make her house look perfect?

Just as you start to mull that, you hear the noise. A little creak, only for a split second, but definitely something.

What on earth could that be? Is it wind going through the house? Unlikely, given how well the place was modernized, you figure, but still possible. Or – your heart skips a beat as you consider this – might there be somebody else here?

What do you do? Do you play safe, hide and hope whoever or whatever is in here leaves you alone? Or do you seize the initiative and see what the sound was?

Hide, and call it in. Safety first! Go to **16**.
There's no way you're hiding away! Find out what the source of the noise was, if indeed there was one . . . go to **107**.

⇾ *134* ⇽

It's dark when you go to the arranged meeting point. Against your better judgement, you find yourself on the outskirts of Causton, standing in the middle of a secluded field. With just your phone and a warm coat for company.

The condition of the meeting was that nobody was to know. It didn't stop you telling DS Lambie – you can trust him not to run straight to the Chief Inspector – and he does try to talk you out of this. He knows better than to stop you, but he understands if he turns up too, you'll likely be in even more danger. The two of you talk it through, but can't come up with a better plan. You have to head to the field by yourself.

A shadowy figure approaches after a few minutes in the biting Causton winter cold. As he gets closer, you realize you must be looking at Hamilton Grainger. Neither of you quite knows which way this will go.

'Well, Detective,' he says. 'You've been busy.'

'So have you. Sara McLower is dead. Archie Grainger is dead. The Windy Dog is nearly ruined. Your other sister is facing bankruptcy. You must be pleased with yourself.'

You're testing him, and he knows it. You're not completely sure that these events were down to him. In return, he can't fully be aware of what you know and what you don't. Will he cop to any of that? He elects to ignore it as best he can for the minute.

'I'll be gone tomorrow,' he says. 'And I won't be coming back.'

'You need to come to the station with me, and you need to answer some questions.'

'That won't be happening,' he says.

'Then we have a problem.'

'We do.'

'Why did you do it?' you ask.

He's still not admitting anything. 'Archie should never have died,' is the closest he gets. He looks visibly upset as he says this. Maybe the late change-around of the lights at the Windy Dog was an unfortunate accident, you ponder. You'd thought about this already. But still: Archie Grainger was undoubtedly dead, and questions needed to be answered.

'I needed to tell you that,' he adds. 'Archie should never have died.'

You get the message. Presumably, that's why he wanted to meet you. 'I liked him. Always did.'

Duly noted.

'Mr Grainger, you need to come with me.'

'Detective, I'm leaving.'

'You won't even admit to the negative online reviews?'

He pauses. 'You can have that one,' he says.

One last decision, Detective. Now that he's said his piece, do you let him go? Do you have any choice, when you're defenceless in the middle of nowhere?

Do you stay alive, and live to fight another day?
To let him go, head to **118**.
To stop him, go to **9**.

⇒ *135* ⇐

You and DS Lambie head back to your desk, the mug next to your computer screen as good as begging for some caffeine in it. DS Lambie reads the room and takes it to the coffee pot across the office, bringing you a steaming hot drink as you log into your computer. He goes back for his own, and then sits next to you.

The footage from the doorbell camera has been looked at already, of course, and all the basics have long been done and the requisite boxes ticked. Yet nobody's been able to make anything out about the masked figure who called that Halloween night. The person you have to assume has been around town in some capacity for several months at least, if what you've learned of the poisoning adds up.

Whoever it was clearly knew the house, as they were careful to position themselves in a manner than obscured them from the camera's gaze as much as possible. They knew what they were going to the house to do, and they were determined not to be seen.

Hence just a brief, blurred glimpse of their image on the doorbell camera, at an angle that's difficult to make anything out from. As much as anyone stared at the footage, nobody could even approximate a height or age – just that they were looking for a nondescript human being who happened to be wearing black at Halloween. It probably wasn't worth putting out a nationwide search on that basis.

The footage trundles on before you.

'There's hours of this,' moans DS Lambie, as you go through the half hour before and after the attack.

You reach the same conclusion as those who've gone through this material before. This all feels perfunctory. In the weeks since Sara McLower died, there's not been a trace of the murderer. One or two people called it a mercy, certainly, but they meant in the context of how unwell Sara had been. Sara's sister, Betty, has consistently been ringing to see if you've had any breakthroughs, of course.

There's nothing you can really tell her, though, and this feels like a slog now.

What do you think? If you want to keep looking through,
and go back a few days, head to **29**.
Or maybe calling the coroner now might be the better idea.
Go to **213**.

→ *136* ←

Alison Jones is understandably quiet, processing what she's heard. Her eyes are slightly damp, you note, and you're not surprised.

'Tell me who you think could be poisoning you,' you say, trying to be as matter of fact as you can. The pair of them have been really friendly to you – as they are with everyone – since you arrived in the area. Still, to be the most use to them in tracking down what's happened, you think you need to be robust and quite firm. The quicker you get information here, the better.

'I–I genuinely don't know,' she says, and you're inclined to believe her. 'I mean, I've reported a few shoplifters over the years. Not that you lot ever do anything, but you never know. But nothing that would make someone . . . oh my, I can't quite believe this.'

'What about Bob?' you ask.

'What do you mean?'

'Does he know?'

'No,' she says. 'W–we've been having a few troubles,' she admits. 'It just feels like it might tip us over the edge a bit.'

'What kind of troubles?'

She explains that the last few years have been difficult. Not only had they lost their daughter to illness, but they found themselves unexpectedly bringing up their grandson as a result. Teddy has proven a real handful. She's sympathetic to him, and it's hard not to be. Nobody should lose a parent at that age. Bob and Alison had to step into the role of parents again, their bodies and minds notably older than last time they brought up a teenager.

'I thought you all got on?'

She smiles. 'We all care for each other. But I know Teddy wants to move on. He's furiously saving every penny he can get. Taking on any job he can, when he's not on that infernal computer. I–I don't want him knowing about me not being well,' she cautions. 'That boy has had to put up with too much already.'

You agree to keep things secret. But also, you have a case to solve here. And – with two people now feeling the effects of poisoning – Bob and Alison Jones's shop surely has something to do with it.

You need to talk to them both, you conclude.
Best go back to the shop. Go to 197.

⇒ *137* ⇐

You turn to your side, and see the face of an angry-looking man approaching your window. He's quite tall, you place him in his fifties, and you wish you'd tried to take a picture of the screen now.

---

*Move quickly to **163**, and you might still be able to.*

⇒ *138* ⇐

No, you think to yourself. You can't stop now: and why would someone want to stop you anyway? This is going to be opened, and you're going to do it right now.

'Please stop,' comes the voice. There's desperation in their tone now, but you're so in the zone, you don't quite register.

'I think you should stop,' calls Catherine Smart. 'This doesn't feel right.'

The lid loosens and you slip it off the top of the container. You look into it, and see a clear liquid gathered at the bottom of it. 'It looks like water,' you call out across the car park. 'There's just a clear-looking liquid in it. Must have just been a drink after all. We'll get it t–t–tested a–anyway.'

'What's wrong?' shouts Catherine Smart. 'Detective, what is it?'

'N–nothinggggggggg,' you whisper. 'Nottthiiiinnnnnnggggg.'

'Quick!' she shouts back to her officers. 'Get help, and get it fast. Something's not right here.'

'H–help me,' you whisper, the volume draining from your voice the more you try to talk. 'I–I feel a bit . . .'

That's the point when you hit the floor, and lose consciousness.

It's going to take you a long time to come around again, and the only reason you manage to do so at all is that the ambulance for some reason knew the way to the Windy Dog very well. The paramedics still had to take precautions, of course, and even when they got to you, they'd had to put protective gear on first. But still, they were able to get you the care you needed just about in time. Whatever was in that container overwhelmed you, and by the time you came around fully, a vital day of the investigation was gone. Furthermore, Catherine Smart is facing questions on why she didn't stop you, and whoever it was who shouted stop. Well, who knows, Detective?

Not you, that's for sure.

THE END

Go to p.317 to read your performance review.

⇢ *139* ⇠

Your ears prick up when Irene tells you that Hamilton Grainger tends to be around the area quite a lot. He doesn't show himself much, though, if he is.

'He doesn't want to be seen,' she says. 'He knows he's got his fair share of enemies here. But it's that pub, isn't it? The Windy Dog. Susannah – their mother – knew that the children didn't all get on. A lovely woman. She just wanted something that they could come together on. Didn't quite work out, though, did it?'

You agree on that point. Two sisters who get on, one brother who appears to skulk in the shadows.

'Who sees him when he's here?'

'Sara used to. She hated it when he called round. Betty used to, but less so since Archie came out of prison. Archie absolutely hates him.'

'Why?'

'Well, he's very protective of his mother, for a start. But also, I just think he hates him.'

'How often do you think he comes into town?'

'Pretty much every month or so. Sometimes twice. Never stops long, though.'

The door. There's a ring at the door. Who could it be?

You could ignore it and keep talking.
Keep your heads down at **111**.
Or maybe you should answer it. For that, you need **39**.

→ *140* ←

It's not that the two vehicles are going at extremely fast speeds that's the main problem. It's that they're on a collision course on a thin road, and neither of you is backing down.

You mentally brace yourself.

You went out on a limb in the first place leaving the scene of the Windy Dog and pursuing this car. You don't want to go back empty-handed, and potentially face the wrath of the boss for leaving in the first place. Moreover, the car in front of you feels like the only tangible lead you've got at the moment. Whatever the price, you have to see how this pans out.

The gap between the advancing cars closes. You feel like you're at the point of no return now, and you check your seatbelt, close your eyes, brace yourself for impact, and hope your airbags are working.

Your eyes may be shut to what's happening, but your ears aren't. There's a thunderous screech, and a smashing sound just a split second later. The other driver appeared to blink and try to get out of the way at the very last moment. It feels too late, though, and the bump on the side of your car is evidence of that.

But, as you open your eyes, that's all it was. A bump to the passenger door behind you, which is going to take a fair amount of bashing and a good chunk of your credit card to put right. The other car? It's going to need a lot more than the local auto-repair shop.

You brake fast and turn your car around to try and make out just what happened. It looks like it hit the hedge to the side of the road, but at an awkward angle. The car seems to have flipped into the muddy field running alongside the road, but the way it's landed has crushed its panels inwards.

At speed, you safely park your car up and send a message to the station that you urgently need help and – another! – ambulance.

Satisfied from a brief scout of the situation that the car isn't about to explode in the next few minutes, you head to the driver's side, and see it empty. The window is open, and whoever was in there has managed to crawl out.

You panic, and then look around the field. It doesn't take you long to spot a man trying to crawl away, his head bloodied. Even though the results of your last physical left something to be desired, you speedily catch him and read him his rights. You look down. His trousers are ripped, he looks in bad shape.

His wallet is by his side. You pick it up and see his identification.

Hamilton Horace Grainger.

Over the next day or two of questioning, he politely answers questions from you and the Chief Inspector, but gives nothing away. A search of his car reveals some air fresheners, a bottle of a suspicious chemical, and some things that look like they've been hastily brought together in a carrier bag, but nothing that can incriminate him.

Still, Hamilton Grainger is duly charged with dangerous driving and endangering the life of a police officer. You know full well that he was involved with that's been happening in Causton the last month. But for now, you have to content yourself with him being off the streets for a while.

THE END

Go to p.318 to read your performance review.

Northfield Wood might seem to be in the middle of nowhere, but the mobile phone reception hasn't been a problem for some time. The contentious phone mast may have caused unrest when planning permission came in – the protest with the people dressed as hedgehogs made the national news – but it does ensure there are enough bars on your phone to get support.

It takes the best part of an hour for help to arrive, and so you and DS Lambie sit yourselves away from the car. Derek James and Charlie follow suit, and gradually everyone starts to feel a little better. That said, Charlie is taken away to the vet by a relieved Derek, and DS Lambie heads to Causton General Hospital to be checked over. 'Your regular cubicle,' jokes the nurse as she leads him off to be examined. He should be back in action tomorrow.

You've lost a couple of hours in the midst of all of this, you realize, and there's still the matter of the lights switch-on at the Windy Dog.

Meanwhile, a small team examine the car, and report in just as you finish getting ready for the evening's festivities. 'Air fresheners,' DC Stephanie Sterling informs you.

'Air fresheners?'

'Car air fresheners. There was a box in the back of the car. Sara McLower's car boot was leaky, and the cardboard box housing her air fresheners pretty much fell apart. Must have taken a couple of weeks.'

'But still: air fresheners?'

'Yes,' she grimly affirms. 'We're having one of them tested. We fear there may be something wrong with them. Sadly, we won't have the results too quickly.'

No surprise there, on either count.

After a further minute or two of chat, DC Sterling leaves you to ponder. It makes sense that no dogs have found the car before, given that presumably the packaging of the air fresheners would have only just fallen away. The place has been hit by a lot of rain these past few weeks, and it's damp in the woods at the best of times.

But also: was someone trying to kill Sara McLower using – you can't believe you're thinking this – air fresheners? If so, why did they murder her with a pumpkin? Or were these two separate attempts to harm her, possibly even unrelated?

Much to think about, Detective. But now, it's time to get to the lights switch-on. Head over to **201**.

⇸ *142* ⇷

You walk into the Windy Dog, and are instantly glad that you did. The warmth of the old radiators quickly makes its way through to your grateful bones. The vintage radiators may creak, clank and groan, but they do a fine job of spreading heat.

It's quite a large pub, yet with the historical village paraphernalia on the wall and the worn carpet, it still somehow feels like an intimate local hostelry.

The whole place radiates a very real sense that even if everybody doesn't quite know everyone, they'll get a friendly welcome.

There's a concession or two to contemporary times, though. The pub seems to make as much out of its delicious coffee as it does its local craft beers these days. The menu has theme nights, even.

But then these are difficult days for the Windy Dog. You're aware that Betty's made several complaints about reviews that have been left for the pub on the internet. As much as you and your colleagues have explained that there's not much you can do, she's been insistent that they're not fair and not right. Not that she has a computer to read them on – her son Finn keeps her up to date on what's being written.

Betty smiles from behind the bar as she sees you, and you greet her in turn. She looks very different from the woman you saw this morning, and she's managed to switch from mourning her sister to being at the heart of all of this seemingly effortlessly. She seems much brighter, much happier.

Looking around, you recognize faces you saw earlier at Sara McLower's wake. Some haven't even bothered to change clothes, you note. Reverend Martins has, though, a snazzy pink shirt replacing his traditional dog collar, and you see him making polite conversation by the back door, his six-foot frame towering over most of the room. Ralph Maddock, Jack Linus, Bob Jones, Isabel Belvedere . . . well, they might not all get on, but everyone's making an effort. The area needs a lift after the events of the last month.

You approach Betty at the bar. 'You on duty?' she enquires.

'Guess so,' you smile. 'You got one of your coffees ready?'

She heads to the immense-looking machine behind the bar, and it whirs into action. The smell of fresh coffee isn't far behind as she warms the milk and prepares you a very welcome hot drink.

'Has it been okay today?'

'Just the usual argument over the lights,' she sighs. 'My Finn and my Archie still don't get on,' she adds. Is that a tear forming in her eye? You always figured she preferred Archie to Finn, but you know very well she'll defend and fight for the pair of them.

You take a swig of the coffee and let it work its magic. Bliss. Betty turns her attention to the next customer in the growing queue as you pick the cup up, leaving you to decide what you want to do next.

---

*To ask about the argument, go to **200**.*
Or why not take your coffee and go and mingle?
*If you want to do that, go to **193**.*

⇒ 143 ⇐

You offer brief condolences – again – to Betty Grainger, leaving her with Bob and Alison as you head to your car and attempt to follow Teddy. But he's fast, and you're – bluntly – not as fast. Bob and Alison follow you out of the shop, brushing past Betty. You look up and down the road and think you can just about make out the back of Teddy Jones's heels as he runs. Then, a car appears. A familiar-looking car, that you've seen once or twice around Causton.

The car accelerates past you and pulls up next to Teddy Jones, who slows as it approaches, his phone to his ear. Has he called someone?

That's just one of the many questions left behind here, as the car door opens, and Teddy – clearly voluntarily – steps inside. He slams the door shut and the car skids away.

You jump into your car, as Bob and Alison catch up with what's happening. Betty is outside the shop now, muttering 'Oh no.'

Fast pursuit was never a strength of yours, though. It was always DS Lambie that was good at that kind of stuff. Your attempts to keep up with the vehicle feel doomed from the start. With every metre you chase up the road, it feels like the other vehicle is pulling further away. Its windows are open, and an air freshener flies out. Once free of the confines of Causton village and out onto the open road, it comfortably heads off, gobbling up the road ahead of it in a way your car can't match. After ten more minutes of this, you give it up. You know in your heart of hearts that you've lost this one, and that Teddy is gone.

Will he return? You don't know. Who is he in the car with? You can hazard a guess, but you don't know.

What are you going to say to Betty, Alison and Bob, waiting for you back outside the shop, where you now must head?

You don't know.

After this case, what do your career prospects look like?

Well, you don't know that either. What is clear is that any reasonable chance you had of making progress in this case has just zoomed up the road, in a car you've no chance of catching. You're heading back to your desk empty handed, hoping that the next case goes a lot better than this one . . .

THE END

Go to p.318 to read your performance review.

❧ *144* ❧

Dr Elliott's surgery is a very efficient one, especially since he started opening on Saturday mornings. He hates leaving his patients waiting and is careful to limit how many he has on his books. Alison and Bob Jones have been in his care for as long as they've all known each other.

As such, you and Alison are only in the waiting room for a matter of minutes before Mary the receptionist beckons you through. Dr Elliott's office is pristine, unfussy and very much all about the patient. No personal photos or anything of note about the doctor himself. He stands up to greet Alison and warmly greets you, before checking with Alison that she's comfortable with you being in the room. You offer to step outside, but Alison is having none of it.

'You might need to sit down,' says Dr Elliott, his tone going suddenly a lot less warm and a lot more formal.

The colour drains from Alison Jones's face. 'W-what is it?' she asks, fearing the worst. 'Am I dying, Doctor?'

'No,' he says, relaxing her a little as he does so. 'But if you hadn't come to me, it might have been a different story.'

She looks puzzled.

'There's no easy way to say this, Mrs Jones, so I'm just going to have to come straight to the point. As you know, we did a lot of tests last time you were here, and it's taken a while to get all the results back.

We need to do one or two more tests, but the preliminary results I've got suggest, well, they suggest you're being poisoned.'

Alison Jones gasps, and you're not too far behind.

He continues. 'I'm still determining exactly what it is, but when you described your symptoms when you were last in, I did a bit of reading around.'

'And?' you ask, as Alison still sits, dumbstruck.

'A slow poison. I can't determine what it is yet, but I think it's worth checking what you've been eating and drinking. Have you been eating anything outside of your usual diet?'

Even if Alison Jones hasn't worked it out, you certainly have. Sara McLower's plums. It has to be. You need to get hold of any of her old plums and get them tested – and then you need to work out just who had access to them.

Dr Elliott writes a prescription. 'Stick to food that you're familiar with,' he tells Alison, 'and make sure you take the medication I'm prescribing. It'll take a week or so, but you should be back to your usual self by Christmas.'

Alison looks relieved, but your head is working out just what's happened here. Might it be worth having a quick chat with Dr Elliott before you take Alison back?

She doesn't mind, so you need to head to **219**.

⇢ *145* ⇠

Finn Grainger's been training to be a doctor for years now at university. He might not have fully qualified yet, but he's quickly on the floor giving his brother treatment. Theirs has been a difficult bond: two very different siblings, both fiercely protective of their mother but rarely getting on with each other. Still, when it matters, Finn's there, fighting with everything he's got to keep breath in his brother's lungs.

There's not much you can do, short of being alongside him and supporting him. Tears are streaming down his face now, as he contemplates Archie not pulling through.

'I'm so sorry,' he sobs towards his brother. 'I'm sorry, sorry, sorry.'

He continues his lifesaving efforts. 'I know he shouldn't have gone to prison,' he says, through his tears. 'I know that really.'

You feel that he needs someone to tell all this to.

'He was only protecting Mum. He was only trying to close up the pub. One drunken brawl later . . .'

You can hear Betty nearby, almost hysterical. The voice of Reverend Martins is trying to calm her as she says something that registers above the noise of what's going on: that she'd just give them the pub if it meant her Archie was okay.

You look back at Finn, trickles of sweat forming on his brow, as if they're deciding whether to drop to the ground or not.

You both know full well that Archie Grainger went to prison on a short sentence at first, for Actual Bodily Harm. But offences inside – more brawls – led to him serving longer than he was supposed to. All the while, Betty Grainger was getting more and more upset with him, and missing him more and more. It was Finn who had to try and keep her going, even while he was at university.

It's not too long before the ambulance arrives, and Finn steps back, letting the paramedics take over. They quickly get down to work, and you stand up as Betty joins you and Finn. Eventually, they load Archie into the vehicle, keeping treatment going, and Finn goes to the hospital with him.

That leaves Betty standing there, looking shellshocked. Might be a good opportunity for a chat. Go to **99**.

✧ *146* ✧

'You'd better know what you're doing,' says the Chief Inspector when you tell her your plan. She's not keen on this at all, but you tell her that Betty Grainger now has some questions to answer. That you'd rather not ask them alone.

She's still at the hospital, of course. Sitting in a relatives' room, quietly weeping. Her beloved son, gone. Her beloved sister, gone. Her remaining son, driven off.

And then you and the Chief Inspector walk in, check that the three of you have the room to yourselves, and ask if you can have a word. You know this is a terrible time for her, but you also know you have to ask the difficult questions sometimes when they're at their freshest. You need answers.

The Chief Inspector gives you a look as if to ask you if you're sure about this. You take a deep breath, and lay out a few facts for Betty Grainger.

You tell her that you know that she and the Windy Dog are in deep financial trouble. You tell her that you know she's the beneficiary of Sara McLower's will. Then you build to it.

'We've ... well, we've had some information.'

She looks puzzled. 'Have you caught a killer?' she asks, forlornly.

'Your sister was being poisoned,' you reiterate to her. 'We now think that it was via her food, and also that someone has put a chemical or some kind of substance in her air fresheners. We're following that up now.'

She takes this all in. 'W-who do you think it is?' she asks. 'Have you any leads?'

'We need to eliminate you from our enquiries,' you say quietly. To a woman who lost her son but an hour or two ago.

The penny doesn't instantly drop, but when it does, you've comfortably made an enemy for life. Betty Grainger doesn't answer your allegation verbally at first. Instead, she does something you've never seen her do: she screams, and screams loudly.

'How dare you?' she growls, her emotions like a simmering pan whose lid is about to blow off.

The Chief Inspector tries to calm her.

'Don't you dare,' yells Betty. 'Don't. You. Dare.'

The door opens. Uh-oh. Finn Grainger walks back in, and you fear the situation is not about to improve.

Finn is not a man known for his angry outbursts, but everyone has a tipping point.

'Are you part of this?' he asks the Chief Inspector. She looks at them, then looks at you. Big decision here, Detective.

---

*Tell the Chief Inspector you might just have got this wrong, and try and gently withdraw what you've said. Sheepishly head off to **114** and follow up with Teddy Jones instead. No. Why are they reacting like this? Tell the Chief Inspector that you think Betty has questions to answer. Confidently stick it out at **194**.*

→ *147* ←

'It's too risky,' you say, after looking at the phone for a moment. You're tempted, you really are. But what if the information on here is valuable, and you interfere with it in some way? What happens if you damage evidence and you can't land a case?

No, you can't do that. You tell Catherine Smart that this needs sending away for proper analysis. That's not going to give you information that you need here and now, but it's the right thing to do, you think.

---

*Instead, you switch your attention back to the bottle. That's at **165**.*

⇢ *148* ⇠

Reluctantly, you realize you're only going to make a difficult situation worse if you run into the house now and try to apprehend whoever you just saw looking out of the top window. At least if you wait out here you can call this in, and maybe the intruder will still be there when your colleagues arrive. Safety in numbers, right?

The Chief Inspector's very clearly not happy with you as you put in the call, but to her credit she at least sees the urgency of the situation, and directs assistance your way. It's a grumpy DS Brian Lambie who arrives on the scene first, complaining that he was just putting on a fresh pot of coffee. He also tells you that the boss isn't happy you came to the house in the first place. She'll have words about that next week when things have calmed down a bit.

Back to the matter in hand.

You're fairly certain that whoever was in the house is still in there, but you can't be totally sure. They definitely didn't come out of the back window, which is where you positioned yourself to close off the most logical exit.

You hear DS Lambie pull up and run around to greet him. It's the moment whoever was in the house has been waiting for. The two of you hear a crash, and a fast, tall figure runs straight past you both, and heads to the road. They appear to be carrying a small bag. More to the point, they appear to be moving at a speed faster than either you or DS Lambie could manage on foot.

'Jump in,' shouts DS Lambie, and revs the engine up on his car. A frustrated stunt driver, there's nothing DS Lambie likes more than a vehicular pursuit, and his foot is soon on the floor as his car growls firmly into life.

'Slow down,' you urge him, as the car closes the distance between the fleeing figure in double-quick time. The way they run: they don't seem too old, you think. Looks to be male. Looks to be scared. DS Lambie, meanwhile, looks like a man very much on a mission. This was what he dreamed of when he did his training: exciting hot pursuits.

Suddenly, the running figure in front of you stops. DS Lambie hits the brakes, and a loud screech of tyres instantly follows. Things seem to move into slow motion as the figure in front of you leaps to the side at the very last moment. DS Lambie brings the car under control, but it takes him a few seconds to do so. That's all the time the mystery person needs to start moving again, but this time they appear to drop whatever they were carrying.

Do you want to continue chasing them, though?
If that's your plan, go to **100**.
Or do you want to go for the bag instead? You need **52** *for that.*

→ *149* ←

You approach the door to the car and look inside. DS Lambie is not in a good state at all. He's doubled up, and seems to be gasping for air. Your own throat and nose are feeling the impact of whatever's in this car: something is very, very off here.

You take a second or two, as tears start to form in your eyes, to assess what's around you. A couple of bush-shaped air fresheners are dangling from the rearview mirror. One or two discarded food and drink wrappers, a receipt for petrol, an empty air-freshener wrapper, a couple of cables, but otherwise nothing that jumps out at you. It's just you and DS Lambie here. Even the glove compartment has nothing more than a bit of documentation in it.

There's a small lever to pop the boot of the car open, and one for the bonnet. You can't imagine there's much under the hood, but the boot might be a different matter. There's going to be something in here, somewhere, you conclude. The boot may be your best bet.

Yet you can't ignore the fact that breathing is starting to get really difficult. The situation looks even worse for DS Lambie. What do you choose to do? Is this the point where you put your own and DS Lambie's health first? Go to 91.
Or do you want to seize the initiative? Maybe this is the point where you open up the boot and see if the car's mystery can be solved there. Click it open by going to 21.
Yet here's an idea: how about grabbing what you can first and then getting DS Lambie out? Go to 72.

⇀ *150* ↼

As friendly as the voice is on the other end of the phone, you can't help but think that the small company which has been supplying Bob and Alison Jones's shop is part of the problem. The opening exchanges as you contact them are cordial enough, but then you have to turn formal. They may be involved, and you have to treat them as such.

'Your produce is poisoned,' you calmly tell the man at the other end of the phone, to his evident shock.

'P–poisoned?'

'Yes. Poisoned to the point where it nearly killed Sara McLower.'

He doesn't quite know what to say, but you make it very plain that he's now a part of your enquiry. You ask for a detailed breakdown of the supply process, and just how his produce makes it to Causton. He explains that he paid someone to make the delivery every Monday, and by the looks of the invoices they send over to Bob and Alison, they charge a good few quid for the privilege as well.

'Who is your driver?'

You're given the name, address and contact details of someone who happens to live in Causton: Trevor Davies. As everyone around the station knows, this is the man who keeps ringing up to report that he's seen a ghost, or people hanging around, or strangers up to no good with his van. You knew he worked in deliveries, and you figure it makes more sense for a Causton delivery driver to do the collection.

You suppose you could have a quick chat with him, and see what he has to say for himself. Or is this a case of a small business passing the buck? Surely you need to focus your attention on them, and pay them a visit?

Visit the supplier by driving all the way to **5**.
See if Trevor Davies can shed any light on this at **46**.

⇒ *151* ⇐

Wearily, you put the twin pieces of paper back in the brown envelope, without properly checking their contents. You tuck the envelope back inside the newspaper, and get back out of your car. Brenda the cat scarpers as you approach, into the garden next door. You knock on the front door again. It takes Ralph Maddock a little longer to open the door this time, and he looks surprised to see you. A little puzzled as well.

'I'm sorry,' you say. 'I'm genuinely sorry. I shouldn't have asked you, it's my fault. I've been told to hand these back.'

'Told?'

'The chief,' you say, passing the newspaper back to an upset-looking

Ralph Maddock. 'And she's said not to share documents without permission again.'

'I–I was trying to help a murder enquiry,' he splutters, his temperature starting to rise. 'You asked me, Detective. You told me you needed this.'

'I'm sorry, Mr Maddock. It's my fault. I'll smooth this over.'

'You'd better,' he snaps, snatching the newspaper out of your hand and abruptly shutting the door. You don't blame him at all for being unhappy, but this is one you're just going to have to take on the chin.

That's one less Christmas card you're going to have to write, at least. This particular lead's gone cold: maybe the forensics team have turned something up from the Windy Dog last night . . .

Go to **155**.

⇢ *152* ⇠

'D–dad,' says Teddy, into the phone. If Hamilton Grainger wasn't driving, and didn't have so much background noise, he might detect that Teddy had put his device onto speakerphone mode. For the minute, though, he's not worked that out. You think.

'Teddy, I need you to delete the accounts. I need to lay low for a bit. I'll come by and get you tomorrow.'

Teddy looks up, at you, at Bob, at Alison. He tries to process the moment, and work out the right thing to do. He takes a deep breath.

'You've got to run, Dad,' he says. 'The police are here. They want you. Run, please. Run.'

Oh no.

Hamilton knows. Hamilton realizes. He says, 'Love you,' which turn out to be the last two words he'll say to his son. He hangs the phone up, leaving Teddy screaming 'Dad!' into the phone. It's a horrible sight, made worse by the fact that you know you have to question Teddy. Even Finn Grainger, after the 24 hours he's had, can't help but have some sympathy for him.

But still: as tough a life as Teddy Jones has undoubtedly had, he knows something, and he admits it, too. Those accounts his father was talking about? Accounts at online review sites. He's been helping his dad, keen to get away from the grandparents he loves but never wanted to live with.

That's all the information you can get out of him, and as closely as Teddy Jones is watched from that moment on, he never gives anything else up. On the plus side, the Graingers finally got their answer as to who was leaving the rotten reviews. As for an explanation for everything else? It wasn't to be.

THE END

Go to p.318 to read your performance review.

Go to p.318 to read your performance review.

→ *153* ←

Finn Grainger is not in the slightest bit surprised that somebody might want to ruin the evening. 'He's been trying to get my mother out of this pub for months,' he blasts, not yet willing to be drawn further. It might be worth laying the facts out for him, as you see them, instead . . .

Go to 93.

You leave the cellar door and continue your perimeter walk around the Windy Dog premises. There's not too much here, you realize, but you want to get a full sense of the pub tonight. It might be a futile idea, but you're trying to be thorough. Even the Chief Inspector, surely, can't argue with that.

You've come here a few times over the last year or two, but it's always been in a social capacity. The leaving drinks for the man who retired from CID was one. He parked his very swish classic car outside the front door, though, and got quite upset when the local airborne wildlife left a deposit on his windscreen. Then there's been the occasional event like this evening, where it's very much the done thing to show your face, even though you might not be particularly keen to do so. But you tend to stay for an hour or so at most at events such as that. It's enough time to get a flavour of the place, though. You're very aware just what a personable host Betty Grainger has been every time you've popped by, and few people are left in much doubt that it's her pub.

You keep looking around the building itself and don't immediately clock anything. Before you head back to the front, you figure you should take a better look at the car park. It'd been filling up for the last half hour or so, and as you find your way back to the front of the pub, you note that the car park is now emptying a little. Hardly a surprise, although you curse yourself for not getting the names of everyone here.

You do one last quick scout, and note that tucked away on the far side of the building is a small door, presumably to some kind of storage cupboard. It's a tiny bit ajar, so you just pull it back and take a quick look.

But what's in there? Remnants of lights and empty Christmas

decoration boxes. Might be something here, or might be something around the other side of the pub?

---

*If you want to take a closer look at the cupboard, you need **28**. But if you're finalizing your look around the perimeter, that's **45**.*

⇒ *155* ⇐

The forensics team have been working overnight at the pub, and you're keen – and hopeful, in truth – that they've uncovered something that might help. One team was working on gathering evidence, another was doing as good a sweep of the pub as it could with the remaining available officers.

You scan the overnight report that's been sent to you.

There were traces of an explosive powder in some of the old Christmas lights. At least one on the tree, but also one or two that were around the outer wall and front door of the pub. The working assumption is that Archie Grainger was smoking a cigarette right next to the door – his mother wouldn't approve – and a light must have exploded with significant force right by him. He then was effectively flung to the ground, the back of his head hitting the concrete, the blast making mincemeat of his unkempt facial hair.

These were lights that usually would have been near the opening to the car park and not close to actual human beings. One of the forensics team is a regular, and instantly saw they weren't all in the usual place. They must have switched positions this year. You vaguely recall mention of working problems with the lights ahead of the big switch-on. Perhaps the explosive lights weren't actually supposed to be next to the door, you consider. Maybe whoever planted them didn't expect them to be swapped? It's the only notable change to the lights arrangement between this year and the previous few.

Further light explosions caught the Christmas tree, hence its branches were swiftly singed. Samples of the powder have been sent over to the lab, but you imagine they're going to confirm what you're reading.

One or two members of the forensics team will be on site this morning, the report notes, and can answer questions directly there.

You can check in with them if you want to?
You'll need to drive over to 79.
Or might it be time to check in with the hospital, and see how Archie Grainger is doing? You'll find the hospital at 101.

⇘ *156* ⇙

You and the Chief Inspector exchange urgent glances, and you decide to take the initiative here. 'What do you mean?' you say to Betty. 'You should have guessed what?'

'T–that car,' she says, still trembling. Is that a trace of fear in her voice? There's something here that's put the chills through her.

'You know it?'

'I don't know the car, but I recognize the bit of the number plate. You've got one or two letters wrong, but I . . . oh, I feared it was him.'

'Who?' demands the Chief Inspector. 'You feared it was who?'

'Hamilton,' she replies.

Wait: who or what is Hamilton? You look puzzled, and Betty picks up on that.

'My brother,' Betty mumbles.

'You have a brother? I thought you just had one sibling: Sara,' you reply.

The Chief Inspector, who's been around Causton longer, has a look that suggests she's a lot more familiar with Hamilton Grainger than you are. Her look also suggests that she's not best pleased to hear his name.

'Two,' Betty grimaces. 'Two siblings. Hamilton left a long time ago now. I think the last time he showed his face around Causton properly was Mum's funeral.'

'How long ago was that?' you ask.

'Coming up to four years now.'

That makes sense. You've been here for three. Surprising, though, that you've never heard the name before, but still, you also recognize that you've not been the most frequent user of the Windy Dog, and nor were you on Sara McLower's sizeable Christmas list.

'All I've ever tried to do is keep the old place going as she wanted it,' says Betty, turning back to look at the pub. 'This was always hers. She told me it always had to be at the heart of the village. I–I know he just wanted to sell it, but I had to keep it going somehow.'

'Did you know your brother – Hamilton? – that he was about? Or that his car was around?'

'No,' she says, softly. 'But I'm not surprised. Whenever Hamilton's around, things, let's just say, tend to go wrong.'

What does she mean by that? Whoa: does she think Hamilton had something to do with the lights? Go to **110** *to quiz her on that.*
Why did he leave? And why's he back? Go to **186** *if that's your line of enquiry.*

'Mind if I take a look inside?' you ask, nodding your head towards the garage door.

'Of course you can,' says Bob.

'Do you need to get the key?'

'I should do,' he admits. But he applies a little force to the door, and it gives way without too much protest. 'There's a technique to it,' he explains, cheekily, although you're not too convinced. From the outside, the door looks locked, certainly. A little force in the right place, though, and there's little doubt it could be opened. Bob is hardly the world's strongest man.

'Haven't you had anyone break in?' you ask.

'Into here? Ah, nobody knows,' Bob smiles, tapping his pimply nose. 'Our secret!'

But is it?

You walk into the neatly organized storage garage, which doubles as the shop's outside stockroom, and everything seems to be in order. Messy, but in order.

There are boxes to the right, arranged on sturdy-looking shelving. Straight ahead of you, a bank of refrigerators, bulging with milk. Then, to the side, a further unit is housing assorted fruit and vegetables, arranged in individual – but open – boxes.

'Not a bad little setup, is it?' says Bob.

'Not at all,' you admit. 'I'm worried about that lock, though. You will get that seen to?'

He nods, but you don't believe him. He's been making his wife the same promise for months, you'd wager.

'How well did you know Sara McLower?' you ask.

'Oh Sara,' sighs Bob. 'I do miss her. Not just because she was a wonderful customer. She was a friend too.

'How long was she a customer for?'

'Well, she only moved in a couple of years ago. It's in the last year really that Teddy started delivering her groceries for her. From January. And then as she got poorly, he started delivering to her every week.'

'What kind of things did she order?'

'She was picky,' Bob admits. 'She was very insistent on organic fruit and vegetables. We had to get them in from the farm where she used to live in the end. They did a roaring trade, thanks to us!'

You look back out of the garage and towards the shop itself.
Might your time be better spent there? Head to **41**.
Or maybe another question or two about the produce Sara
McLower bought wouldn't hurt. Go to **198**.

→ *158* ←

The voice isn't coming from the direction of the pub. It's coming from the very back of the car park. Seemingly hidden back there, a figure emerges from the bushes and urgently comes scurrying towards you.

You see them start to approach, gathering pace, genuine concern etched into the lines of their haggard face. In fact, they're looking panicked now. 'Stop!' they shout. 'Whatever you do, don't take that lid off.'

You take your hand off the container and stand, edging towards Catherine Smart to give yourself a little extra protective cover. You're unsure at the moment if you need it.

Breathlessly, they come closer to you.

'Who are you, and why are you telling me to stop?' you ask firmly.

'I'm telling you to stop,' they reply, 'because what's in that container is dangerous. And if you took the lid off that, you might end up in serious trouble, and fast.'

'How do you know that?' you retort, your eyes narrowing. You're not daft: you've worked out what the answer to the question is likely to be, but you need to hear them say it.

'It's mine,' the male figure replies, meekly.

'And you are?' you enquire.

'That's Hamilton Grainger,' says one of the officers from across the car park. 'I'd remember that face anywhere.'

'Mr Grainger?' you say, turning back to face him.

He nods. 'Yes,' he confirms, barely audibly.

'What exactly is in that container?' you ask. He stops for a second, but his thinking is as fast as yours. He's outnumbered here, so if he makes a run for it now, the odds are hardly in his favour. Also, he knows that whatever he says could potentially incriminate him.

Still, he's taken the next jump. There's enough evidence here to affirm that he knows of the container and its contents, and he knows full well that you'll be sending it off for analysis. As well as possible, he needs to get ahead of this.

He figures he has to give you something. 'It's a poison, a toxin,' he says. 'Well, more than one.'

'And why would you have that, Mr Grainger?'

'I think I need to call my solicitor before we go any further,' he eventually offers. With that, you figure you've got enough to at least put Hamilton Grainger under caution, and you arrest him, and take him back to the station.

You'll find it at **23**.

➤ *159* ➤

It's all smiles as you head over to the seven-strong choir, who've been practising for their performance over the last few weeks. You were tempted to join yourself once when you transferred in to Causton, but it'd be fair to say that the auditions were on the rigorous side. The polite suggestion that you might want to 'practise more' still stings.

They're going through their warm-ups as the two friendliest members of the choir – Irene Whitley, leaning on her stick, and Alison Jones, looking pale – wave and greet you.

'How are you, ladies?' you smile, as you return their wave.

'Oh, you know. All a bit frantic as always, but think we're just about there. Still feeling a bit under the weather, but I wasn't going to miss this,' Alison says.

'Under the weather?'

'Nothing serious. Everyone gets a bug this time of year, don't they, Detective?'

You think about asking more about this, but Alison Jones has got a point. It's very much sniffle season in Causton.

'Who's minding your shop tonight?' you enquire.

'We shut early,' she giggles, as if she's done something naughty. 'Teddy's been up here helping with the lights, so couldn't do any deliveries this afternoon. We certainly couldn't go and do them. Even Bob said in the end we could call it a day.'

Alison and Robert – known to everyone as Bob – had run their shop in the village for long before you arrived, and the chances are they'll be running it long after you're gone, too. Teddy, their 15-year-old grandson, does the deliveries for them now, but other than that they're very much going strong, and pride themselves on having no other staff. They continue to show that they can do pretty much everything themselves.

'And how are you doing?' you turn to Irene, mirroring her smile.

'Oh, you know me,' she grins. 'Just nice to get out of the house these days!'

'You been here long tonight? It's a bit nippy out, isn't it?'

'Long enough to hear that lot arguing about their lights again,' she laughs. 'Honestly, every year, they seem to mislay some part of the display, or some bulb or other! You'd think that one year it might all go smoothly.'

Maybe it will. But not this year.

'Good luck tonight, like you need it,' you say to Irene. She thanks you, and gets back to her preparation.

Meanwhile, you observe from across the car park Archie Grainger attaching the last of the lights, and figure it's best you get inside and make yourself seen.

Head through the doors at 142.

→*160*←

Now you think you've worked out exactly what happened, you have the small matter of apprehending your chief suspect. You've gone bold here: you head to your desk, pick up the landline phone, and slowly dial your number. The Chief Inspector watches, with a trace put on the call, and spots your finger shaking with nerves. This is a big moment, and you know it.

The phone rings several times, but nothing. No answer. 'It'll come up with number withheld,' you say, 'and he's not going to answer a mystery number. W–we're going to have to use your phone, ma'am,' you say to the Chief Inspector.

You're thankful you didn't save her number with any kind of insulting name. When she calls your phone from hers, what Hamilton Grainger sees on screen are two words: 'The Chief.'

This time, he answers. The Chief Inspector puts her phone on speak mode, and you tell Hamilton Grainger that it's time to come in.

He lets out a small laugh. 'Why on earth would I do that?'

'Because we've worked it out,' you say.

'I'm all ears,' he says, as you hear the noise of a car starting.

'We don't think you deliberately meant to kill Archie Grainger, for one thing,' you say. 'But Sara McLower? That was you.'

He's listening, but not talking.

'We've traced payments via the phone that we found. We know about the chemicals. We know about the hotel rooms. Mr Grainger, we just know.'

He stops and thinks for a second.

'But you don't have me.'

That's the moment when you realize this isn't going to work. You hear the noise of his car engine, the unmistakable sound of a vehicle going at speed.

'Detective?' he says.

'Yes?'

'You know that bus shelter, just past Sara's house?'

You do. Around 15 minutes from where you're sitting.

'Yes?'

'Look in the bin there. That's where you'll find your phone.'

You hear his car slowing, the buzz of an electrical window lowering, and then a thump, presumably as he throws the phone.

As it turns out, exactly where he said he would, capturing the noise of his car speeding away from Causton one last time.

It's a while before you hang up the phone, but you know deep down you've taken this case as far as you can. You can't help feeling you got agonizingly close to making an arrest. But when it came to the key moment? The person you needed back in that interview room at the station was heading far, far away.

THE END

Go to p.318 to read your performance review.

Go to p.318 to read your performance review.

⇒ *161* ⇐

Sitting in the corner of the room, Irene Whitley has been chatting since the moment she got here. She doesn't spend much time out and about these days, not now she can't drive anymore. That doesn't mean she's not aware of who's doing what in Causton, though.

Her face lights up into a beaming smile when she sees you. She greets you warmly, and tells you to sit down. You take the opportunity to ask her a bit about her friendship with Sara. Turns out, geographically at least, it was a little more distant than she'd have liked.

'I'd not seen her in person since before Easter,' she tells you, as she dunks her biscuit into her coffee. Even as the biscuit surrenders and crumbles into the cup, she doesn't blink. 'Betty at the pub talks to her a fair bit, but you could probably guess that,' she giggles. 'But Sara was a bit like me: spending most of her time at home. Neither of us has been in the best of health, really. Even getting here today, it was only because Bob and Alison Jones offered to give me a lift. Bless them. Especially as Alison seems to be struggling a bit these days too.'

'Are you going to the lights switch-on tonight?' you ask.

She nods enthusiastically. 'Of course! I can't miss a party like that,' Irene grins. 'Reverend Martins is giving me a lift: I think I might have myself a boyfriend there! I'll get my fancy outfit on and go disco dancing into the night.' She's laughing now, and it's infectious. You can't help but smile when chatting to her.

'Who else are you going with tonight?' you ask.

'After from the nice young vicar? Well, me and Sara were talking about going, about finally getting to see each other again,' she tells you, a little sadness creeping into her eyes. 'I do miss her.'

She tells you that even though she didn't see Sara face to face these days, they spoke several times a week. Even as Sara was getting a little poorly, they'd still chat, although their conversations were getting shorter and shorter.

'If she wasn't well, why was she planning to go tonight?'

'Well, I think she realized her health wasn't what it was, and she'd been building up to one big outing,' Irene admits.

'Are you a Christmas person?' you ask.

A huge grin appears on Irene Whitley's face.

'Oh yes,' she beams. 'My decorations were up weeks ago! I'm up to 34 Santas around the house'

'At the start of November?'

'I'd put them up earlier if I could!'

You believe her. Fearing you're going down a spiral of early festive chat, you decide it's best to make your excuses and head back to the station . . .
Go to **128**.

162

Betty Grainger waits until exactly 7.30pm before she gets things going by ringing the bell in the bar.

The brutal clanging of Betty's bell means everyone gathered knows what's going to happen next. At first a cheer, and then a silence gradually falls. A few introductory words, and the difficulties of the day – no, the difficulties of the last month – can be put aside for a few precious hours.

The lights to the pub are switched off, and the patrons of the place stand around in darkness, save for the occasional mobile phone light.

Betty starts to address the gathered crowd, with the pub door open so people outside can hear what she has to say. Not that anyone outside can hear: the inside door may be open, but the thicker outer door remains shut. Ah well.

Some people might need a microphone to reach everyone inside of the pub. Not Betty. This is her 29th festive lights switch-on ceremony by her reckoning, and her booming voice is as much a part of it all as the switch-on itself.

'As always,' she says, 'I want to start by toasting my much-missed late mother, Susannah McLower.' The assembled attendees warmly cheer her name. 'It was her idea, one particularly difficult year three decades ago, to introduce the Windy Dog Christmas lights ceremony, and here we are, all these decades later . . . I miss you, Mum,' she says warmly, raising her glass. A smattering of applause.

'And, of course, this is the first time I've done this without my sister, Sara. She'd been looking forward to this especially this year, and I miss her dearly.' Louder applause and appreciation from the gathered crowd.

She thanks them, gulping a little, trying to keep her emotions in check. Then she resets herself, and asks the question: 'Are you ready?'

The further cheer in return confirms that yes, the crowd here is very much ready to party. Tables are banged as they mimic a drumroll. It's surprising how much noise a village inn full of people can make, you think to yourself as you gulp a bit more coffee down.

'Three!' the crowd gamely shouts, greedily guzzling their drinks, and getting into the spirit of the evening. 'Two!' they continue, a few bystanders watching, chomping on their nuts as they wait to see things unfold. 'One!'

And with that, Betty Grainger does what she's done every year for the last thirty. She flicks the switch behind her well-tended bar, and the assorted strings of light burst into life. Autumn is over. Winter is here. Party season is underway.

A loud roar of delight greets the eruption of lights, both the insides and outsides of the Windy Dog now filled with seasonal cheer. The people inside can't hear the people outside, and vice versa. If they could, what happens next may just have taken a different course.

Betty smiles as she takes it all in. She loves it here. This is her favourite time of the year, and it feels especially poignant this year, and not just because of Sara. She fights it, but a tiny tear forms in the corner of her eye. Nobody notices. If they hadn't spotted the signs over the past year, then they certainly weren't going to see them now.

'Come on then,' she roars. 'Anyone want another drink?'

The door to the Windy Dog swings open. 'Betty,' comes the distinctive tone of choir lead John Summers, his unsubtle hairpiece looking characteristically awful. 'What about the lights out here?'

Betty curses under her breath and switches the lights off to try and reset everything.

The one job she'd given her son: to check the outside lights. Why couldn't he even do that?

'Hang on, the plug's come out,' John Summers adds. Betty breathes out, and curses herself for blaming her son.

John Summers heads back outside and now the inner door also swings shut behind him.

Betty opts not to bother with a countdown this time. Instead, she crosses her fingers and hopes it'll work a little better than it did a few minutes ago. She flicks the large switch and the Windy Dog promptly . . . plunges into darkness.

What do you do?

Your phone! It's got a light on it! Switch that on for a start.
Go to **6**.
Or why not go outside, where the streetlights
will surely still be working? You need **58**.

⇾ *163* ⇽

Aware that there's someone next to you, you decide to pretend that you haven't noticed them for a few seconds: that's enough time to get your phone off the passenger seat and try awkwardly to take a few photos with it: photos of what's contained on the screen of the mysterious device.

Never have you been more grateful that you bought a second-hand car that happened to have tinted windows: the person outside the car may not have realized what you were doing. At least you hope they don't know: you dread to think what they may do if they did.

Slight flaw in the plan, though: the inside of your car is relatively dark. Your phone's camera function has a built-in flash facility, and in all the haste you don't even think about switching it off.

It's when the flash goes off that it becomes hard *not* to notice what you've been up to. Reading the signs of what happens next, you determine that the person to the side of you might not be best pleased. The significant clue? A large hand suddenly crashes through your driver-side window, as whoever's next to you has suddenly panicked: and they're not happy.

What do you want to do here? Do you want to see if you can start the car and drive away? Or do you need to fight back? You've got a split second to make your mind up, Detective, and you're in very real danger.

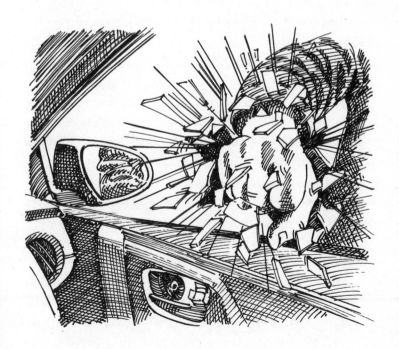

*Turn the ignition and hit the accelerator: you need to get away
from here, surely? Try and escape over at* **61**.
*No! Fight back! You've got a chance of capturing someone here!
Go to* **57**.

⇒ *164* ⇐

'Excuse me a minute,' you say, ignoring for the moment the words that Teddy Jones has just dropped into the conversation. Teddy plays with his phone as Alison and Bob look towards you, curious as to what you're doing. They see you unlock the door and head towards the car that's parked outside.

The driver looks at you and presses a button on the dashboard of their car. Bob and Alison move closer to the window, and can't quite make out the conversation that's going on. Having spent the last period of time with you, though, they correctly guess that you're asking a fair few questions. In this case, the person answering them, who they can't quite make out, doesn't seem to be engaging at all. They work this out as they wind their window up and start their car up, revving the engine. Everyone in the vicinity will be able to hear that.

It's not the only thing that they can hear, either. As you try to stop the mystery person driving away, they hear your scream of pain. You stood in front of the car to try and block its escape, but this did not deter the driver from trying to make a getaway. Your body was hit at speed as they thudded down on the accelerator. They watched as you flew up over the bonnet of the car, and crashed down to the ground behind.

As the car sped off, unlikely to be seen again, Alison and Bob rushed to attend to you. Thankfully, a pulse. The ambulance took a little time, but the paramedics managed to quickly stabilize you.

Still, the hit on your head as you landed needed some care, and it'd be a good week or so before you properly came round, unable to remember what happened in the hours leading up to the impact.

In time, you'll return to work, thankfully. Unfortunately for the people of Causton, this particular case is one that's destined to remain unsolved.

THE END

Go to p.319 to read your performance review.

165

You briefly consider examining the phone – but it's the bottle that's taken your interest here. It's more a really tight container than a bottle, and not a see-through one either. It's metallic, and the lid has been screwed on with some force. Opening this up is going to take some effort, you conclude, as you gently push against the top of it through the clear plastic evidence bag.

'What do you think?' you ask Catherine Smart. 'Any ideas?'

'Not really,' she muses. 'We had a quick chat about it, but didn't want to risk opening it. There's as good a chance as anything that it's just a drink. Given what's been going on around here the last few weeks, though, we're erring on the side of caution. We were going to send it straight off so that someone could open it in safer conditions than out here.'

'It might be an important clue,' you admit. At the forefront of your mind is Betty Grainger's brother, Hamilton. The bag shows every sign of being part of the toolkit of someone up to no good, and if it is Hamilton Grainger, you can't imagine he's going to be hanging around the area too long now things have started to go awry. If he's really in this for the money, then surely all he has to do now is sit back and wait. You look at the container and press on. Time is not on your side, and there might be a clue here that lets you get to him that little bit quicker.

Start opening the container over at **17**.

⇒ *166* ⇐

Well, if you're going to properly examine the two wills you have in front of you, you're going to have to bite the bullet.

This isn't going to be an easy call. You drop a quick message to the station, and they send you Betty Grainger's contact number. It's a landline, though: does she seriously not have a mobile phone? Surely she's at the hospital this morning, with Archie?

You give the number a try anyway. Heck, if she still has a landline, it might even have one of those answerphones with a cassette tape in it.

To your considerable surprise, Betty Grainger picks up the phone on the third ring. You introduce yourself quickly, and ask for an update on Archie.

'I'm heading back to the hospital in a minute, you've caught me on my way out of the door,' she says, efficiently and not too coldly. 'I just had to pop back here for a change of clothes and to give myself a bit of headspace.'

You don't bother with the small talk, given time is short here.

'I need to talk to you about your sister,' you say.

Her tone changes.

'What about her?' she asks. 'What is it?'

'I'll come straight to the point, Betty: I need permission from you to look at her wills.'

'Wills?' she says, noting the plural.

'Yes, wills. She changed her will less than a month before she died, and I'm not entirely sure why. I know that Mr Maddock holds the documents. Her final will and testament I've got access to: I know you got grant of probate to handle it for her. But as her representative, you need to consent for me to see the earlier version of her will. I need to see what changed, and I can't do it unless you let me.'

She's not happy with your questions, and you didn't expect her to be. Surely her son, in critical care, is more important than having to put up with trivial questions like these.

'Why? What are you expecting to find?' she asks, tersely.

'I don't know,' you answer, honestly. 'Might be something, might be nothing. But your son nearly died last night, and your sister was murdered a month ago. I feel we're no closer to finding out who did it. I'm following up every clue I can find.'

A long pause. A cold sweat on the back of your head. 'Fine,' goes the voice at the other end of the line. 'If that's what you need to do, you have my consent. Now if you don't mind, I need to get to the hospital, and my lift is here.'

Her answer takes you by surprise. 'Thank you,' you quickly mumble, as Betty Grainger puts the receiver down. It's time to compare the wills.

Go to **122**.

→ *167* ←

The Chief Inspector calls for one of her other officers and tells them to get a trace on the credit cards. They note down the details and head off to get that sorted. It might take a little while, but if you can get hold of a statement or something you might be able to get a clearer idea of what Hamilton Grainger has been up to.

In the meantime, you and the Chief Inspector try and puzzle out just what's been happening here. Hamilton Grainger seemed to be storing a bag at the Windy Dog and hiding it until he needed it, you reason. What else was in the bag, though?

The masonry saw was suspicious, certainly. That's a very precise tool, and perfect for cutting bricks down to size. 'The bricks in the pumpkin,' you say out loud. 'They had to be chopped down so that they could be hidden in there.' It seems to fit, certainly.

Encouraged, you consider what else. Air fresheners? You wonder if there's something more to do with them. That, or someone somewhere got a very fetching deal on a job lot of them. And then there was a container of liquid. You've not pursued that urgently yet, but neither of you is expecting that to come back clean.

'You think it was just him?' you wonder.

'Probably,' says the Chief Inspector. 'If we assume he sabotaged the lights at the Windy Dog, all he'd have had to do there is lace a few of the bulbs with the explosive.'

'But why would he kill Archie?'

'Not sure that was deliberate. You know how frail and fragile those lights are, and they did change some around at the last minute, remember. Think it might just have been bad luck that a stretch of them had to be swapped over to leave them by the front door.'

'Is that your working theory?' you ask the Chief Inspector.

'At the moment, it feels like the one that best fits.'

'And Sara McLower?'

'Well, that gets more difficult, doesn't it? She was very clearly murdered, and it's also very clear how. The masonry saw puts Hamilton Grainger firmly in the picture.'

'He had the motive, too,' you agree. 'But what about Sara McLower getting ill? Something wasn't right there.'

She ponders this. 'I know. But the problem with that was that she got ill over many, many months. And Hamilton Grainger hasn't been seen in and around the village very much at all. If he was poisoning her, then he'd have needed some help somewhere along the line.'

You've been weighing this up for around half an hour when the uniformed officer returns with the credit card details you were after. The card statements show payments for the mobile phone accounts. Further payments to a company that seems to sell some kind of chemicals. And a few hotel rooms on the outskirts of the area pop up as well.

You've got the evidence here to at least get an arrest done. But what you don't have is the man himself. How are you going to get him?

Well, you could ring him: he's got your phone. Try **160**.
Or you know he's likely to be heading to your house. That might be where you intercept him. Get moving to **88**.

➤ *168* ➤

You look around to see what's happened to Finn and Betty Grainger. You've been examining the lights and their surroundings for a good 15 minutes or so now, and you're concerned about what you've found.

Just what happened with the lights today? Finn and Betty are likely to be able to throw some, well, light on things.

You find them indoors, sitting next to each other, Finn awkwardly comforting his mother, both of them looking a little lost and unsure. Betty is scared she's just lost her son. As for Finn, he's worried about his brother, and protective of his mum, so he's checking on her before heading off to the hospital himself: this was supposed to be a special night for Betty after a horrible few weeks. Now things have got worse.

'I'm sorry to interrupt,' you say earnestly. 'I need to ask a few questions about the lights, if you don't mind.'

They look at you in silence, but don't stop you.

'Who put the lights up that were near the front entrance?' you ask, not waiting for them to offer a yes or no in return.

Betty looks up. 'That'd be my Archie,' she whispers. 'He had to replace them this morning.'

'Replace them?'

'We tested them first thing, before Sara's . . .'

'Before the funeral?'

She nods. 'The ones above the door weren't working. H–he swapped them for the lights by the sign while I was saying goodbye to Sara.'

You look at Finn. 'I think there's been foul play,' you say to him. 'I know this is difficult to hear, and I know you don't want to hear it now. But I need to catch who did this, and I need to move quickly.'

'Foul play?' he asks. 'Tell me what you mean by foul play?'

That's a good question, Detective. Where do you want to go with this?

Tell Finn you think the lights were tampered with, and lay out the facts as you see them. Go to **93**.
Go the other way. Tell him you think somebody wanted to ruin tonight, and you want to know why. Head to **153**.

→ 169 ←

The time for talking is over. Asking nicely hasn't worked. Hopefully, threatening the figure opposite you with a Santa Stop Here sign will unlock the situation you've found yourself in.

'I told you,' you snarl. 'Put the tinsel down.'

You take a step, and the figure in front of you unfreezes and lurches forward. You swing the sign, but while it may be useful for attracting passing present-givers, a Santa sign is too big and too slow for the situation you find yourself in now. Your attack is very comfortably dodged, as your opponent barrels into you, knocking the wind out of you and leaving you stumbling backwards.

You try to regain your footing. You attempt to swing the sign again, but again, it's comfortably dodged. The mysterious figure has now dropped the bag they were carrying, but you appreciate that this is not good news. You anticipate that they're about to properly start fighting back, and when it comes to brute strength, the force they hit you with suggests they have the upper hand.

You need to be nimble here, and so you abandon the sign. Instead, you attempt to tackle the intruder's legs and destabilize them. They certainly weren't expecting that, but it doesn't take them long to get over the surprise. They move in for another attack, and this time they've changed tactics too.

Two sensations hit your neck. The first is a surprising one: a slight tickling feeling. Then you realize what's happening. The string of tinsel is being wound around your neck, and it's tightening. You find yourself struggling to breathe, as you attempt to fight back.

'S–stop,' you splutter. 'I–I can't breathe.'

Your head starts to get lighter and your strength seems to seep away. Eventually, darkness comes, as the tinsel closes tighter and tighter around your neck. As you slump to the floor, the intruder grabs the bag and exits the property, their identity never to be discovered.

You're discovered a few hours later. Nobody knew that you were going to Sara McLower's house, as you neglected to tell them. When they find you, you're just about alive, but it's days before you come around properly. When your eyes flicker open you're a patient at Causton General Hospital, waiting to find out exactly what long-term damage has been done. Meanwhile, a lot has happened in Causton while you've been here. Your jaw drops as you're eventually told, and yet you were powerless to stop it.

THE END

Go to p.319 to read your performance review.

⇒ *170* ⇐

'When you say you've got his number: you mean his phone number?'

'Yes,' she beams, looking at you as if she's been entirely clear about this.

'How have you got his phone number?'

'He used to ring Sara. Well, usually he hid his number, but one time he didn't, and she wrote it down. She gave me a copy.'

'Why would she do that?'

'I guess she was worried. I don't know. But I've got it here somewhere.'

'Have you ever rung it?'

'No. I've no intention of speaking to him, thank you very much.'

She gives you the number and you jot it down. At the very least, if the phone has been active, the station will be able to find out roughly where it is. It's something.

You thank Irene Whitley for her time, after gleaning what else you can from her: she's certainly not a fan of Hamilton Grainger.

You head back outside, get in the car and call to relay the details back to the station. You're driving when they call back: it's vague news, but it's news. There's only a very rough trace on the phone number, but it's been active in the last 30 days. What's more, it's been active roughly around the Causton area. Hamilton Grainger – or whoever's using his phone – may be closer than you think.

You're not going to get a specific trace, you fear. But you're more encouraged than ever to get to the forensics team at the Windy Dog. That's at **79**.
Or Irene Whitley did also say he'd been around the area. Get more details on what she means at **139**.

→ *171* ←

'You're saying that you think Betty Grainger killed Sara McLower? Her own sister?'

Hamilton Grainger's expression doesn't change. He simply nods.

'I've met Betty. I don't think she's capable of lifting a heavy, brick-filled pumpkin and then hitting Sara with it. Not with the force necessary to do so much damage, anyway.'

'I don't think she is, either. But you've met that convict son of hers. And you're not telling me he doesn't have the strength.'

He has a point there.

He continues. 'You knew she wasn't well? That Sara had been struggling for months?'

You did.

'Ask yourself why,' Hamilton adds.

'Okay, I'll bite. Why wasn't Sara well?'

'Because Betty was poisoning her.'

'Poisoning her? How?'

'Two ways, as it happens. Through the fruit that was being delivered to her home every week from Alison and Robert Jones's shop. And through the air fresheners in her car. Sara always did like things looking proper and smelling nice. Well, at least on the surface.'

'Are you seriously telling me that Betty Grainger tried to kill Sara McLower with a poisoned air freshener?'

'Among other methods.'

'Why?'

'The pub's struggling, Detective. She needed money. She needed Sara's house.'

There's logic to what he says – but also, why would Sara McLower change her will to specifically exclude Hamilton? Surely she'd be more likely to exclude Betty?

'Do you have any evidence to support all of this?'

'Well, have you spoken to young Teddy Jones? He's the one who delivers all the groceries to people from the shop. You might want to find out where he gets his fruit from . . .'

There's a lot to take in here. And some big, big decisions to make.

Maybe you should pay a visit to the shop? Go to **114**.
Betty Grainger: do you put these allegations to her? Steel yourself, and go to **146**.
No: this is clearly rubbish. Arrest him. At the very least, for wasting police time. Go to **220**.

→ *172* ←

With Finn Grainger now attending to his brother – and let's face it, his years of medical training trump the few courses that you've been on – you head back into the Windy Dog to find his mother. You switch on the light on your phone.

Word has spread and people know what's happening. There's a cloud of shock over the place, and as you shine your light to the bar, you see there's nobody behind it.

Any impression of holding things together is gone as soon as you locate Betty Grainger. You can hear her loud cries from the back room of the pub, and you head straight there, via the small hallway and the crusty floor. Someone has told her just what's happened.

'M-my Archie,' she screams as she sees you. You instinctively try to comfort her, but you know your efforts will be futile. She's facing what no mother should, and she fears it. 'I–I can't go out there. Tell me he's okay. Tell me he's okay,' she weeps, grabbing your arm.

You can't, you know that. You need to do this as gently as possible, but you can't hide the truth from her. Archie Grainger's life is in the balance.

'Finn is with him, there's an ambulance on its way. It's looking quite serious, I'm afraid, but he's getting care now.'

'Tell me he's not going to die, Detective. Tell me. Please.'

Again, you know you can't. You've never seen Betty anything close to like this before. 'Finn is with him. It looks serious, but . . .'

She interrupts. 'He has to save my Archie. He has to.' The gravitas of what's happening is hitting her hard, and – understandably – she's struggling to cope. You figure if she'd wanted to be outside, she'd have gone, and wouldn't be sat here.

Glancing back into the pub, you spot Reverend Martins looking concerned at the bar, and call to him. He joins you in the room, and sits next to Betty Grainger, just as you see the flashing blue lights through the window. 'If I knew this was going to happen, I'd have given them the pub,' she sobs.

You thank the ambulance crew under your breath for getting here so quickly. 'They're here,' you tell Betty. You get up to go and see them, but the look on Finn's face as you head back outside tells you what you need to know.

'I–I tried,' he says. 'I r–really tried.'

'Is he not responding?' you ask, getting the facts.

'On and off,' he says. 'The blast must have hit him hard. And when he hit the ground, the back of his head hit the paving slab at some speed.'

The ambulance crew move quickly, and seem confident that they've found at least a slight pulse. The next 24 hours are going to be vital. They need to move him, and set to work. Within five minutes, Archie Grainger is heading to Causton General Accident and Emergency department, fighting for his life.

You need to ascertain what happened here, Detective. And you need to make sure that Betty and Finn Grainger are attended to as well. Betty first, though: what's this about giving someone the pub?

You need to find out more from Betty. Go to 99.

→ *173* ←

As the small, dark car pulls off the Windy Dog car park, you note that it makes a right turn. Even as it slides onto the road, it's still going quite slowly, and you think you see the driver turn to take a look at the Windy Dog as they motor past it. Right, you think: I need to see who that driver is.

Hurriedly, you head to your own vehicle. You start it quickly and make for the exit, leaving the commotion of the Windy Dog behind. You hope the Chief Inspector understands, but you figure Archie Grainger is being cared for, and that you need to follow the lead in front of you. Or, in this case, driving away from you.

For two miles, you head along the windy road out of Causton, past Sara McLower's sorry-looking house, trying to keep tabs on the small vehicle. Given the paucity of traffic around, you can't imagine that the driver doesn't know he's being followed – you're pretty sure the driver is male – but you go through the motions anyway and hang back a little.

You keep the vehicle in view, while not attracting attention to yourself by going too fast. Your hope here is that the man driving the other car either doesn't care that you're lagging behind them, or that they don't perceive you as any kind of threat.

As you continue your modestly paced pursuit, though, your head comprehends what you've done. You've left what looks to be a crime scene, and you've also left Archie Grainger fighting for his life in the Windy Dog's car park. Have you done the right thing here, you wonder?

This had better be worth it, you say to yourself, as you look up to check the car you're pursuing is still in view.

Oh no: it isn't. It's nowhere to be seen.

You accelerate slowly, looking for side roads or anything the car could have slipped down. The road in front of you seems empty and you gasp for a minute. Then, from further up the road you see headlights coming towards you. A random passer-by? Or has the driver turned around, and decided to face you?

Do you keep motoring forward here? Or is it time to turn back?

Go back! Play safe! Motor back to **54** *and at least you'll keep your job.*
No! This is your chance. In for a penny, Detective: keep going forward at **123**.

❖ *174* ❖

Teddy bolts out of the shop and you briefly consider going after him, but decide better of it. He just needs to let off steam, you suspect. He's a teenager who's been through a lot. You don't really want to be in the way of that, and you figure you'll talk to him when he returns.

Only you won't.

While you and Bob exchange glances, you hear the front door of the shop lock and the blind being pulled down. The customer who slipped into the shop. The pair of you were oblivious to them as Teddy made his hasty exit.

But this customer knows that you were getting closer and closer to the truth, and didn't like it. Remedies were thus enacted.

When Alison Jones returns, it's not a pretty sight. Bob, for his part, is lying unconscious. As he attempted to fight back against the mystery attacker, he slipped, his head bashing the shop counter, and – for good measure – the charity-shop collection box then tumbling

onto his head. It was his bad fortune that the locals had been so generous this year.

Your bad fortune was to be in the wrong place at the wrong time. That you let your guard down, and failed to notice another person in the room. That other person duly picked up a big jar of instant coffee and hit you on the back of the head with it from behind. Then, for good measure, another hit. An extra shot, if you will.

It'd been a running joke from DS Lambie that it'd be your addiction to coffee that would ultimately kill you. Sadly, Detective, it pretty much proved to be the case. Out of respect for you and the manner of your death, they opted to serve tea at your wake instead . . .

THE END

Go to p.319 to read your performance review.

⇒ *175* ⇐

The online reviews for the Windy Dog have been bothering you: the kind of job that's permanently on the to-do list to take a look at, but there always tends to be something more pressing. Still, thinking you need to head over the forensics team at the pub, you do want to get a flavour of them.

It makes you wish you'd taken a better look before.

A real pattern has developed over the last year, with some hostile feedback as to the quality of the food and drink at the pub, and the friendliness of the landlady. None of these reflect the reputation of the pub in the village itself, where it's hard to find someone who doesn't have a nice word to say about it. Yet for passers-by, there's enough here to make you give the place a very, very wide berth.

You don't have time – again – for a deeper analysis, but you are clear now why Betty Grainger was so concerned. You'll try and make them a priority at some point, you pledge to yourself, as you make your way over to the forensics team at the pub.

Go to **79**.

⇒ *176* ⇐

With a rush of urgency, you show Catherine Smart what you found, and she instantly appreciates the need to get answers, and fast. 'You really should be letting the tech team do this,' she cautions. 'They're the ones who'll be able to get you proper, thorough information.'

'But that'll take them days. And we don't have days.'

Catherine Smart nods. 'There's no internet here, though,' she tells you. You need to get a connection somewhere. Somewhere where you won't get caught for using it.

'Any suggestions?'

She leaves a long pause. As much as she's the kind of person who wants to do the right thing and follow a process, Catherine Smart is also results-driven.

'Take it to the station,' she suggests. 'But pull over just outside Causton first, and see if you can hook it up to your own phone's internet connection. Do you know how to do that?'

You nod. You're not a tech expert, but as one of the younger members of Causton CID, you're used to being the go-to problem solver when the computer is on the blink.

'You sure?' you double-check.

'I'll ring the station and tell them you're bringing it over to get it sent for an urgent tech check,' she nods.

You don't need asking again. You thank her, head briskly to your car and start the engine. Are you doing the right thing? Well, you're committed now, you figure, and drive to the edges of the village. There, you pull your car in at the side of the road, and start trying to connect it to your phone's data connection. This should just take you a minute or two.

Deep in concentration, your usually alert senses have, however, let you down. When you look up after connecting the two phones, you see something alarming in your rearview mirror. Another car has pulled up – and the driver doesn't appear to be behind its wheel . . .

Do you carry on? You don't have much time, you recognize.
Go to **44**.
Maybe you should secure the area first, though?
Try that, at **190**.

≫ *177* ≪

You know this next part of the conversation isn't going to be easy. You steel yourself with a swig of coffee, look at Ralph Maddock and ask him directly: 'What did Sara McLower change in her will?'

The mood of the room changes, as things suddenly get a lot more formal.

'You know I can't talk about things like that, Detective,' says Ralph Maddock, a little affronted by the question. He quickly recomposes himself and adopts his more familiar friendly demeanour. The more he thinks about it, the more he understands why you had to ask, at the very least.

'Mr Maddock,' you say, your own tone becoming more formal. 'It's my suspicion that, at the very worst, sabotage was at play last night at the Windy Dog. Or that there was something just a little off. I also know that Sara McLower was murdered. I have to wonder if the two incidents are linked.'

He's taking this information in, at a crossroads between his professional responsibility and his desire to help the police with their enquiries.

'And, Mr Maddock, you're not a practising solicitor anymore,' you add. 'I respect you guarding the privacy of your clients, but this might just be – and I don't mean this as a pun – life or death.'

This hasn't worked. After a short pause, Ralph Maddock gets up, and takes the coffee cups away, loading them into his expensive-looking dishwasher. Neither of you had finished your drink, but he took it away anyway. 'You are asking me for information I am not allowed to give,' he says, steely.

'I'm asking you to help me stop a killer,' you reply.

Any pleasantries have long since drained out of this room, but neither of you is budging. There's an empty pause that seems to go on for some time. After two minutes that feel like ten, Ralph Maddock announces that 'I think you should go Detective.'

He leaves the room, returning a minute or so later, handing you your coat and the local newspaper. 'If you want tittle tattle, you're best off looking in there,' he adds, gesturing at the thin tabloid.

And with that, he bids you farewell, beckoning you in the direction of the front door. You thank him for his time and head for your car.

What now?

Might as well see what's in the local paper?
Give it a read at **181**.
Should you go to the hospital, though, and
check in on the Graingers? That's at **70**.

⇒ *178* ⇐

'What's wrong with him?' you ask Derek James, pointing at his suffering pooch.

'I don't know. He was okay earlier. I don't think he ate anything, but he's not looking too good.'

You don't know too much about veterinary matters, but you assume that Charlie's downturn is related to the car in front of you. It's lovely that you stopped to check how he is, and you're clearly an animal lover, but it might be time to get to DS Lambie. He might be in deep trouble, and you don't want to explain to the Chief Inspector that you were tickling a dog's tummy when your colleague was suffering.

*Head to **184**! And don't tell DS Lambie you went
to check the dog out first . . .*

⇒*179*⇐

You know this isn't going to go down well, but you also can't ignore
the fact that the produce Sara McLower was consuming came via one
shop. You need to get things on record. Your next words might just
end any friendship that you, Bob and Alison Jones had enjoyed. You
know that, but you need to do your job.

'I'm sorry,' you say, clearing your throat and trying to hide the
butterflies that have sprung up in your stomach. 'But I need to
take you to the station. I need to ask you formally to help with my
enquiry.'

Bob's friendly face drops, and he looks at you with some degree of
disbelief. 'You've got to be kidding me. What have we done?'

'I need to find out exactly what happened. I believe that
Sara McLower was poisoned by items that she bought from your
shop. And that she was poisoned continually over a long period
of time.'

Tears well up in Alison Jones's eyes. 'You can't seriously believe we
did that, can you?' she says, aghast.

You compose yourself. 'I can't rule anything out. I need to make
sure I've got everything down on record.'

Alison struggles to stand, and the pair reluctantly get in your car.

It's around 25 minutes before you all reconvene at Causton police
station. The ice in the car on the way there could freeze a human body
in minutes.

Sergeant Draper is shocked when they walk in. He drops his

cherry cake in surprise. 'Hello, Bob,' he says. 'What are you and Alison doing here?'

'Ask the Detective,' he says. Draper shoots you a confused look, but does his job and leads the pair to an interview room, fetching them a not particularly palatable hot beverage each.

Word has gone around, and the Chief Inspector catches you as you head towards the interview room with a drink of your own. She's not going to stop you, but she's concerned. 'I hope you know what you're doing, Detective,' she says.

'So do I,' you admit.

Are you really going ahead with this? If so, go to **60**.
Or if it's time to issue an apology and take them
back to the shop, go to **202**.

➳ *180* ➳

You step into the middle of the room to take charge of this. 'What's going on?' you demand.

Bob goes to talk, but you tell him to leave it to you. He tries to calm himself and, not wishing to have a second visit to Causton police station today, lets you carry on.

Nobody is very keen to talk. You ask what the argument was about, but it just leaves Teddy and Hamilton staring at each other. Both look angry, both look as though they want to go for the other.

'Do you have permission to be in here?' you ask of Hamilton, starting with the most obvious offence. He knows you might have him there, so he stays quiet. You turn to Teddy, and ask if he's okay. He starts to calm and steps towards Bob.

'Did you invite him here?' you ask.

Teddy mumbles that he didn't. Hamilton Grainger steams, but still stays quiet.

'If you don't tell me something, I'm going to have to take you to the station for trespassing,' you say. The silent face-off continues, with nobody wanting to surrender information to you. You don't feel you can step away from the middle of the room either, in case things kick off here. After several minutes of trying to prise information from three people who've suddenly gone very tongue-tied, you decide you have no option but to make an arrest.

You read Hamilton Grainger his rights, and he realizes he's not in a position of strength here. Without complaint, he heads to the car.

'Are you all going to be okay?' you ask of Bob, Alison and Teddy.

Bob and Alison looked ready to never talk to you again half an hour ago. Now, they look appreciative. 'We'll be okay,' Alison says, quietly. 'We have to be, don't we?'

You take Hamilton Grainger to the station and question him for some time. You have suspicions surrounding him and his activities, but the only charge the Chief Inspector says you can realistically levy against him is to do with trespassing. You know at best he's going to face a brief sentence, more likely a fine. You also know that you've not landed a murder charge on anyone. But at least you feel you've taken someone – of whom you have deep suspicions – off the streets, for a little while.

Hopefully in your next case you can make a bigger charge stick.

THE END

Go to p.320 to read your performance review.

➤ *181* ➤

Sitting in your car, you can't help but feel you've hit a dead end here. At heart, you respect what Ralph Maddock said. You knew you were pushing your luck asking him to disclose what you needed to know, but still: there's a killer out there, and you're not getting any closer to working out who it is, and why they did it. Nobody seems to be coming forward, and it's hard to find anything close to a tangible lead.

You leaf through the local paper. It's a lot thinner than it used to be, and most of the news in it isn't local anymore. Rather than stories of the local community, most of it feels like nonsense about celebrities and television dramas.

There's still three or four pages written by someone who appears to at least visit the area from time to time. The way of the modern world, you sigh. It's not what it used to be.

It's last week's edition that Ralph Maddock has given to you. A story about the lights switch-on at the Windy Dog on page three, with a picture of Betty Grainger smiling in front of the pub sign. Elsewhere, a bit of unrest over some planned roadworks, a full-page advert for Midsomer Blue Cheese, and a note that a classic-car show is being organized for the spring. That's bound to attract one or two who used to work in your office, you think.

But there's something else. The paper doesn't feel as flimsy as you remember it, and sure enough, just before you get to the sports coverage, you realize there's a little extra something inside.

A brown envelope.

You lift the newspaper, and a sealed envelope drops out onto the floor of your car. You look back at Ralph Maddock's house, but the door is firmly shut. Just Brenda the cat prowling the lawn, looking for food.

Opening the envelope, you find two slim pieces of A4 paper.

Both are copies, rather than originals. Ralph Maddock must have gone and run them off for you. Both bear the introduction that they're the last will and testament of Sara Mildred McLower. Yet crucially, with two different dates, a couple of years apart.

You don't read further down the piece of paper while you ponder your options.

Decision time: you know that Ralph Maddock shouldn't have done this, but do you need to bring the Chief Inspector in on it?

Or should you drive somewhere quiet, and keep the secret? If you compare the documents that way, Ralph Maddock should be safe too.

Get in touch with the Chief Inspector at **18**.
Or if you're going to compare the two pieces of paper, go to **122**.

❧ *182* ❧

Having attended the wake of Sara McLower while DS Lambie stayed in the office, you gently suggest that it might be your turn to stay at the station while he goes on the away trip. He's about to argue, but reluctantly gets his coat, and tells you he'll be in touch if he finds anything.

You give it ten minutes, just to check that he's not changed his mind, and you head to your desk. Taking the little key out of your pocket, you unlock the top drawer. With cat-like precision, you target your prey and find it as the drawer slowly slides open: a packet of chocolate biscuits. You know you can't trust DS Lambie with these, and you chomp through a couple, being sure to leave no crumbs behind. He's no fool, is Lambie, and a fine detective.

You secure the biscuits back in their dark prison, treat yourself to a coffee, and think ahead to the lights ceremony that you've got to go to tonight. You know you can't ask DS Lambie to go in your place after he's just done this run for you. He'll be one of the few from the village who won't make an appearance. You imagine by now that Betty Grainger will have the Windy Dog licked into shape, the lights tested, and an evening to kick off the local festivities planned with her usual precision.

You still can't wrap your head around this murder, though. From what you can tell, whoever killed Sara McLower – and you're assuming it's one person, but it could be more – was trying different techniques of increasing severity to do so, leading right up to the particularly severe smashing of a brick-filled pumpkin into her face. While she lay in hospital after the attack, she was never conscious enough to offer any clues, and her sister, Betty, said she'd never let anyone be left to hang on so long again.

You fill the Chief Inspector in on the call log, but there's nothing there that alerts her. Nor you, really.

After an hour or so, a shrill alert from your phone. It's DS Lambie. 'Seems to be her car all right,' he confirms. 'It's just me and the guy who found it here. Oh, and his dog. Have given it a quick visual check, and nothing obvious inside. Just a bit of a smell. Nothing bad. Bit of air freshener, if anything.'

DS Lambie tells you he's going to get the man and his dog back safely, and then a team will tow the car to safety later. If there's nothing obviously wrong, they'll probably check it in detail on Monday now.

'Can't tempt you to go to this thing tonight in my place?' you ask, trying your luck. DS Lambie chuckles, and hangs the phone up.

You'd best head off and get ready. Go to **201**.

✦ *183* ✦

Given his background, some people in the village tend to give Archie Grainger short shrift. After all, he's only been out of prison for ten months, and this is his first Causton Christmas for several years. You've always felt that he's done his time, and you have to at least be seen to be courteous. Not everyone feels the same, his brother included.

Still, Archie doesn't see you as anything close to friendly. He knows exactly who you are, and his relationship with law enforcement has been on the challenging side during his life. He's a little wary as he clocks you approaching, but also appreciates that he's probably best not getting on your wrong side. Also, it's a big day for his mum, and there are lots of people about.

'You need a hand?' you offer, trying to break the ice.

'I've just about done it,' he gruffly replies. He's not hostile, but he's hardly nipping inside to get the red carpet out for you. He'd like the conversation to end quickly, but you've no intention of taking that particular hint.

'Your mum's done a good job,' you continue, unabashed. 'I can't believe she still got all of this done, in spite of her loss.'

'You think she did this?' Archie chuckles, almost dismissively. 'It was me and Teddy Jones who did most of it. The lights by the front door weren't working, so we've swapped them out with the ones on the sign.' That's as much detail as he's willing to give you, and you take the hint.

You've not seen Teddy yet, but you know he'll be hard to miss: the busiest 15-year-old in town, and when he's not out riding his bike delivering groceries he's always on the lookout for other ways he can make a bit of money. His grandparents, Alison and Bob Jones, hardly pay him well.

'Did your brother help?'

Archie chuckles again. 'Finn?' There's a long pause. If the pair are on speaking terms now, they're hardly rushing to demonstrate it. 'His head's in his books as usual. Telling us what we're doing wrong, and then going back in the warm to do a bit more reading.'

Finn's in his final year at university, coming to the end of a six-year course. Once he's graduated, nobody thinks he's going to be sticking around. He's never hidden the fact that he wants out, with ambitions to be a doctor in the big city. Mind you, since their dad left when they were much younger, their mum's not really been the same anyway. Finn has little patience for her, and Archie in turn has little patience for Finn.

Archie fixes the final string of lights, looks at you with no intention of making any further small talk, acknowledges you, and heads inside. He does not wait for you to wrap things up – he just goes.

Perhaps that's what you should do too, you figure.
Head to **142**.

➤ *184* ➤

You spring into action quickly, leaving Derek James and his dog by themselves as Charlie continues to grumble. Priority one here: you hotfoot it towards the car. It's quite easy to access the vehicle once you actually know where it is, and you note that the passenger-side door to it is wide open already.

There doesn't appear to be anyone else about, though, so what on earth could be causing the commotion? What was the thump you heard?

You call out to DS Lambie, and he responds with a hacking cough, the noise of someone who seems to be struggling to get breath in their lungs. You have a horrible feeling you know what the noise was now: a human being slumping, and slumping fast.

As you hear DS Lambie struggle, a slight worry: the closer you get to the car, the more a small tickle is developing in your own throat. Sure, the climb here didn't help, but even so: it seems to be developing very quickly. That's not usual, and you know it.

'Are you okay?' you call out to DS Lambie, and you're met by more coughing that seems to be getting louder.

You can't really see inside the car, and if you want to check it out properly you're going to have to get much, much closer to it. As you consider that, you feel your own nose and throat starting to burn a little. There's a strong, recognizable smell in the air, and it's only increasing. Car air fresheners: but they don't usually make you feel like this.

You need to make a snap decision here, Detective. DS Lambie is clearly in trouble, but you quickly begin to think that you might be as well. Do you save him, or do you see if there's a clue here?

If you want to rush in and get DS Lambie out of there, then go to **14**.
If you want to examine the car yourself, then take a deep breath and step forward to **149**.

⇒ *185* ⇐

Pamela Peters, it turns out, didn't buy the latest model of doorbell, or the top brand. Her hobby is making things, and she'd far rather spend her funds on fabrics and materials. Still, she got a fairly decent model, but it's an unfamiliar make, and she's never had to try and get footage off it before.

After playing with her phone for a couple of minutes – and with a few furious jabs at the screen and slightly sweary words from her mouth – she gets some success. As it turns out, you get a tiny bit of success, too. There's no sign of the car you were hoping to see, but you can at least identify one other person who was on Irene Whitley's street: Teddy Jones on his bike, no doubt making his deliveries.

Nothing out of the ordinary there, but it might be worth going to the shop that belongs to his grandparents – Alison and Bob – and seeing if you can find him there? If you want to try that, go to 25.
But hang on: what about looking back a bit further through the footage? That might be worth a try. Go to 127.

⇒ *186* ⇐

Betty Grainger is, understandably, now keen to get to the hospital. She wants to see her boys. She's doing her best with your questions, but is getting a little frustrated at the delays.

'Hamilton,' you say. 'Why did he leave? Why do you think he might be back?'

'My brother left the minute there was nothing left here for him,' says Betty.

More tears form. 'When Mum died, we all went round her house and tried to split her possessions up fairly. He kept insisting on taking things that we wanted. We let him. We thought they meant something to him. He was just taking the higher value things to sell,' she sobs. 'It's all been about money for him. Always has been, and Mum never saw it.'

That doesn't explain why he left, you point out.

'He left when he realized he wasn't getting the pub. He thought he'd be given the lot, and instead Mum split the majority share between me and Sara. She knew I'd run it, and she knew Sara wouldn't sell it. He demanded we sell the place. We'd be set up for life, he said. But I wanted to do what Mum wanted, and Sara sided with me.'

'Why do you think he'd be coming back now, though?' you wonder.

'He's presumably out of money again,' Betty tells you. 'He'd asked Sara for a loan last year and she said no. He knows better than to ask me. She was always the soft touch, always trying to fit in, always trying to please people. Just look at all those presents she used to buy for people who didn't care in the slightest about her.'

'Had she given him any money?'

'I think she did at some point, but I can't be sure. She never had much money herself. I know she went to Ralph Maddock to get her will changed a little while back, though.'

'But what's that got to do with tonight?'

'Tonight's the most lucrative night of the year for the Windy Dog. Always has been. A good switch-on event can pay the bills for three months. Without it . . .'

She trails off, but she doesn't need to add any more. The pub is in financial trouble, and if she now has to sell it, then Hamilton Grainger is in for a windfall . . .

You need to get to the station first thing tomorrow and gather all the information you can about Hamilton.

Detective, you might just have a suspect. Go to **76**.

⇒ *187* ⇐

Detective, it's known that some people will try and read where they shouldn't, in an attempt to get a sly upper hand in the solving of a particular case. As such, they stumble upon something they perhaps shouldn't. It's a good job your moral fibre would never allow you to do such a thing.

Anyway, air fresheners are important.

⇒ *188* ⇐

You do a double take as you absorb what Finn Grainger has just said. He's still got rage in his eyes, but seems to understand that he's said something of interest to you. The red mist talking.

'What do you mean?' you ask, feeling a chill cross your body. Why would anyone sabotage Christmas lights? Why would someone want to ruin something? And for who?

'Who has sabotaged what? And who is the "her"? Is that your mother?'

He nods, trying to calm himself, but not having an awful lot of luck.

'They couldn't let my mother have just one last happy Christmas in this pub, could they?' Finn snaps. 'Just one more. Her last lights ceremony, after all she's done for this area. And they had to screw it up for her.'

This is a fair amount of new information you're getting here. Betty Grainger wasn't going to be doing the lights at the Windy Dog anymore? Or was she leaving altogether?

And then there's the matter of sabotage: who's doing the sabotaging? What are they looking to gain?

A cry comes from outside to attract Finn's attention. You've got a chance to get one more question in before he needs to run outside.

---

*Dig into this more by going to **64**.*
*Or head outside, and go to **214**.*

⤖ *189* ⤖

You need to put personal safety first, and you fear what – or who – will be waiting for you when you get back to your flat. You request some support, and a uniformed officer is sent along with you.

The instruction: get what you need, and sit tight. It's a marked police car, so it'll be very clear to anyone passing by that there's a police presence. If Hamilton Grainger is trying to get you, he's not going to while there's an active police officer sitting outside your front door.

You nervously go inside the flat, and curse yourself: you spot your little security camera, which will have sent a ping alert to your phone. Hamilton Grainger will now know exactly where you are.

But he's in no rush. You sit down for an hour, nursing a coffee that you barely take a sip out of. You check in with the uniformed officer, Sergeant Draper, but all you succeed in doing is disturbing him as he sucks on his grapes. There's a distinct lack of activity. As night falls, you eventually get a message.

'Thank you for your phone. Very interesting. Watch your back.'

It even ends with one of those cursed emojis, a little wink.

Sergeant Draper is relieved by a colleague, and you awake after a difficult, interrupted sleep to: more silence. More nothing. You come to realize what Hamilton Grainger has done. He's gone. He doesn't need anything now in Causton, he can just wait. He knows where you live. He knows how to find you. He knows who your friends are. He knows how to get to your family.

Even though you don't see him, you appreciate soon enough that you're in a new normal – one where you'll never be entirely safe. One where you'll constantly be looking over your shoulder.

One where you didn't solve the crime, either . . .

THE END

Go to p.320 to read your performance review.

190

Even though you're keen to explore the contents of the phone as quickly as possible, you're also very aware that you're vulnerable here. You don't like mysterious cars pulling up behind you, and you'd far rather be speeding away from them than seeing where the driver has gone.

You turn the ignition and start your car, swiftly moving it a little way up the road. You can't quite make out any figure behind you, and the other car stays where it is. After about half a mile, you risk pulling over and you wait again. Once again, the same car pulls up behind you. That should answer that for you: whoever it was who pulled their car up before was not there by accident. They're interested in you.

You need to move quickly, Detective. Get back to trying to sort through the phone, and move fast: you need **44***.*

You check in again with the team working diligently around the front of the Windy Dog as Finn Grainger heads to his car, which is parked near the entrance. You go around to the back to the more secluded spot where you left yours. You're tempted to follow Finn, to see if he's going to see his mother. Your worry there is you'll probably be quite easy to spot. But you're also curious to know if he's got plans other than the one he's telling you about.

The reviews are in your head, though: you feel you've been ignoring them until now. Is there anyone back at the station who can help there? Has anyone properly looked into them? Head back and find out.

Follow Finn! But do it carefully, over at **75**.
Back to the station: is there anything on these online reviews?
Did anyone bother to investigate? Head to **19**.

While other people head outside to see what's happened, you lift the counter and move behind the bar. You make your way down the small hallway to the back room, and you're greeted by the sight of both Finn and Betty Grainger. Betty looks almost static, as if preserved in an instant of time. She's sitting in a chair, just looking at the wall. Motionless.

Finn is the opposite. He's looking panicked now. 'She won't say anything,' he says to you, as he sees you enter the room. 'I've never seen her like this.' There's a growing noise from outside, and things don't sound too good there. But you're also all too aware that Finn Grainger's concern is moving at some speed towards anger.

Betty looks around, and snaps back into the room. She tries to calm her son down. 'Finn,' she whispers. 'It's okay. It's over.' She gets up, and heads upstairs.

'No!' yells Finn, jumping to his feet. 'You can't give this place up.'

She doesn't really listen. Instead, she turns to him sadly and says, 'You knew this was going to be the last one. Just wish it had gone better. But we've had a good run.'

And with that, she disappears into the maze of rooms at the Windy Dog.

'What's going on here?' you ask, puzzled.

'They couldn't do it, could they? They couldn't let my mother have a final farewell, a last happy Christmas in this pub, could they?'

He looks at you, as you try to process this all.

'This was it, Detective. Keep up,' he snarls. 'She's giving the place up. And they've gone and ruined her lights. Sabotaged it for her.'

Hang on: Betty's leaving? Go to **124**.
Who's sabotaged it? Go to **120**.

→ *193* ←

For the second time today, you're mingling with a warm drink in your hand, making polite-ish conversation with an assortment of Causton residents. You have to admit, though: the coffee's better here. Just the right bitter bite to it, not unlike yourself.

This evening's event is a happier event than this morning's, and the mood is convivial if anything. A toast is raised for Sara McLower, a gesture that Betty Grainger clearly appreciates from across the bar, greeted by a cheer for a woman that it sounds like not too many people went out of their way for. That's the problem of being the newcomer to the village: you're deemed new until you've been there about ten years, from what you can tell. Only then do you get treated like a proper local. That, or you have to die, which strikes you as a drastic course of action.

You make your way around the room, and listen in on bits of gossip as you do so. People are having to talk to each other, because this is usually the part of the evening when residents exchange Secret Santa gifts. Still, after the incident with the novelty sausages two years ago, the idea was retired. All concerned decided they didn't want a repeat of *that* particular evening.

The gossip you hear is the usual village chitter-chatter. Jack Linus bemoaning the fact that the world has gone mad, vowing to stand in next year's local elections. A few murmurings about how Alison Jones isn't looking as well as she once did. A rumour that Irene Whitley has been seen talking to Ralph Maddock. All nonsense, you figure. Although you are temporarily distracted by – and you can't quite place who was saying it – the person chatting about how much trouble Betty Grainger was having with the lights this year.

The conversation got whispered from that point – after all, who wants to be overheard by Betty, and thus get on her bad side? – but there seemed to be a feeling in the room that the lights display is looking a little tired after all these years. Might it be time to invest in some new ones? Then there wouldn't have been the need to swap over the lights from the far side of the car park this morning.

Betty's well-liked around here, though, so it's a supportive more than a critical chat they seem to be having. Still: the evening, even you have to admit, feels just slightly less special than it once was.

After making a little bit more small talk around the place, Betty Grainger calls the Windy Dog to order. It's time for the lights switch-on!

You need to head over to **162.**

You need to head over to **162.**

→*194*←

It wasn't, in the end, the eventual complaint that Betty and Finn Grainger put in that ended your time in Causton. It wasn't their unhappiness that led to you almost resigning from the force altogether, rather than accepting a transfer. Instead, it was when the story of what you'd done started spreading.

The local paper ran it first. Even with one working journalist and just a handful of pages per issue that weren't given over to national news to save money, it mustered up a front-page splash about the police detective who accused the much-loved Betty Grainger of murdering her child and sister, even as her son's body hadn't yet gone cold in the morgue.

The enterprising journalist from said local paper decided to try and sell the story elsewhere, too, and when a national outlet picked it up, then the story exploded, pretty much taking your detective career with it. Not just you: the Chief Inspector decided that this would be a perfect moment for early retirement, albeit with some encouragement from her own superiors.

You quickly had to move out of your flat. People looked at you with horror and disgust, as if you'd been murdering people rather than trying to work out who was actually responsible. In the end, the only transfer that seemed workable was to a small island off the coast. Even then, you still get looks. You know very well that a conversation explaining you were just doing your job is unlikely to be appreciated.

This, of course, is the end of the case for you, Detective. It'll be a long time before you're assigned another . . .

THE END

Go to p. 320 to read your performance review.

⇢ *195* ⇠

You walk around the outside of the Windy Dog. As always, the far side of the building is a lot quieter: given the fact that it has a big car park and isn't directly set on the road, it tends to be the front rather than the back of the Windy Dog that gets really busy.

You decide to move over to its quieter side, where one or two people are milling around. The building is sturdy enough, you note, as you take a look at the pub itself. It clearly could use some time spent on it, and it's getting to the point where a sprucing up really wouldn't hurt. You carefully navigate the hedge that runs around the exterior, too.

There are a few doors to the building as you move your way around. One leads to the large lounge set at the back of the Windy Dog. Another leads, presumably, to the storage and office area. There's a pair of doors slightly ajar that you assume head down to the cellar area. The sizeable tyre tracks next to it certainly hint that this is where the delivery trucks pull up and drop off the beer supply.

You suppose – if you were feeling nosy – that you could take
a look in the cellar, but you'll need to make sure nobody's
watching. They might want to know why you're poking your
nose in there. If you want to try, go to **217**.
Or you could keep working your way around the rest of the
building's perimeter, to see if you can spot anything else.
Trudge quietly to **154**.

→ 196 ←

You decide the logical thing here is to retrace your path back through
the house and make a swift exit – but not before checking out the
front of the garage itself.

You creep your way back up the stairs, through the building and
back to the open window. You've got an uneasy feeling about this
place. It might have been a mistake to venture over here on your own,
you tell yourself.

Still, you have to do things properly, and try to keep safe. You
double-check to see if anything has been disturbed or if there's
anything out of place as you head back the way you came. There's
nothing, but you very definitely have the niggling sense that you're
not alone here. Are you being watched, somehow?

As you walk through the lounge, you spot the place where
Sara McLower presumably spent most of her time sitting: on a
chair positioned perfectly facing the television screen, boxsets of
long-running detective drama shows neatly arranged on shelves
underneath. You look at them with scorn. Not like real life, are they,
you chuckle to yourself.

Then you spot, on a little table next to her chair, a little screen,
and you figure that's the link to the video on the doorbell system.

Maybe that's what's making you feel somebody is watching. Has someone videoed you in the house? If they have, there's nothing you can do about it now.

No matter. You exit the house through the window you came through, and firstly you check the front door. The camera doorbell system is still there, so you figure that it's a false alarm on the video front. Then you check the front of the garage.

Just how much of a long shot it was is hammered home to you when you stand in front of the bright white garage door, a few Halloween decorations still limply clinging to it. 31 October had brought with it a downpour. That, combined with the gravel of the drive, means there's precious little in the way of a clue here. You see that the stones have been pressed down slightly, so there's likely been a car on the drive at some point. For all you know, it was one of the forensics team. A dead end, Detective, and time to head back to the station.

You take one look back at the house as you walk down the drive to get to your own car. This time, there's no doubting yourself. Set a little bit back from the window: a head. You gasp in shock, and realize too: you've been seen. But what do you do?

---

*To head back into the house, go to **3**.*
*Or if this is the moment you call it in and wait, then you need **148**.*

It's not too long before you've made your way back to the shop. Alison Jones stumbles a little as she heads inside. Bob is behind the counter of the shop when you walk in, and does a reasonable impression of someone managing to hold the fort. He looks at Alison with genuine concern. Hang on, though. Bob appears to have a tear in his eye, and Alison hasn't told him anything yet.

Alison soon notices this too. 'Archie Grainger died,' Bob says. Alison doesn't appear to have heard this news and, as it turns out, Teddy Jones certainly hadn't heard it. 'I told Teddy, and he stormed out. I–I tried to stop him, but . . .'

Oh heck.

Choices, then. Are you off looking for Teddy? He's bound to have a phone on him, you can at least try and get him on that. Alison, worried, gives you his number.

And then, at the door, a figure you're not expecting to see at all. The bell above the door clangs, and in walks Betty Grainger. 'I think we need to have a chat about my nephew,' she says.

You need to find Teddy, don't you? Get in your car and try to contact him. Go to **143**.
Nephew? What's Betty on about? Go to **211**.

→ *198* ←

You ask for a bit more information on where Sara's vegetables came from. Bob patiently explains to you that Sara struggled a little when she moved to the area, and needed some more familiar things to help her feel settled. She'd always been picky when it came to food. The Jones's shop was happy to help, particularly someone relatively new to the area. Now all villagers are instantly welcoming.

They came to an agreement where produce would be shipped in to Causton for her, and Teddy would deliver it. Sara didn't balk at the extra charges involved, either. It wasn't bank-breaking, but it all adds up.

You probe further. Bob explains that a selection of fresh produce would arrive especially for her every other Monday, usually. The order had dwindled a little as she got more poorly, and Teddy had to collect the money when Sara was less able to get to the shop herself. But the arrangement was a good one.

'How could you ensure things didn't get mixed up?'

'We kept her stuff separate. Marked it in the fridge at the very end.'

You start to put things together as he speaks.

'What time do you shut on a Monday?' you ask, wondering how long the shop is open for on the day her order is likely to be delivered.

'Ah, Monday is our bridge night at the Windy Dog,' Bob smiles. 'We're done by 6.30pm on a Monday!'

Monday evenings, then. A brief window of opportunity. If someone wanted to mess with Sara McLower's plums, that was their chance. It's not as if the lock on the door was going to stop them.

You have a think. You know it's a long shot even as you're saying it, but might the Joneses have some security footage somewhere?
*Ask at **116**.*
Teddy Jones, meanwhile. You've not met him.
*Worth a chat? Find him at **84**.*

⇾ *199* ⇽

There's a reason this doesn't feel like a particularly even fight, and that's – well – because it isn't one. You don't stop, but you know you're going to have to do something special to win this battle. Their arm may be injured, but you're seated, they're stronger, and they're reaching for your keys.

Your immediate aim is to stop that. This does not go well. They reach for your keys, and you hammer down on their hand.

The temporary advantage you gain is then heavily negated by the swinging fist that connects with the side of your head. You scream as you feel the crunch of a bone inside you, which if anything encourages this person, who's seemingly not keen to make friends. A further punch deflates you, but you're determined to land something in return. You try to push their arm back down against the glass, a tactic that worked last time. This time they see it coming, move their arm in time, and your fist smashes straight down into the glass.

They take their opportunity as you scream louder, by grabbing your keys and throwing them into the foliage to the side of the ride. Then, they've opened the passenger door of your car, retrieved their phone and kept yours for good measure.

Blood drips heavily from your arm as they return to their vehicle, bloodied but victorious, and head away. They've managed to get a crucial piece of evidence back, they've managed to get your unlocked phone, with all your personal details. Finally, they've managed to leave you in serious need of medical attention.

It would be fair to say that your investigation here has come to an end. It has not been successful.

THE END

Go to p.320 to read your performance review.

Go to p.320 to read your performance review.

⇾ *200* ⇽

You wait until Betty has served a few more customers, and then you attract her attention again.

'Everything all right, Detective?' she asks, a little bit of curiosity in her narrowing eyes.

'What were they arguing about?' you ask as casually as you can muster. You know you need to sound friendly: you, like most of Causton, don't want to get on the wrong side of Betty Grainger's ferocious temper. But Archie and Finn must have been upset about something.

Thankfully, Betty's in her element tonight: putting on a show in her pub. It's her safe space, and you calculate she won't want anything to risk things going wrong. You also get a feeling that she wants to talk, that she's relieved someone is actually asking her about this.

'The lights, really, but it could have been anything these days. Those two have been even worse since Archie got out of pr . . . since Archie came home.'

The Grainger family, you're well aware, doesn't enjoy conversations about Archie's imprisonment.

She turns her attention back to today's disagreement. 'We always seem to lose the last part of the display. Something always seems to have gone wrong, there's always something that we've missed. Should have checked everything fully yesterday. Swore that everything was done, but Finn said we'd missed a bit and the lights weren't properly working this morning. He tested them before we left.'

'Why did that cause an argument, though?'

'Ah, you know. The usual. Finn telling Archie what to do. Telling him to fix everything while I was at the funeral and wake. Archie telling Finn what he could do with his instructions. Me stuck in the middle, having to sort the boys out, on the day I'm burying my sister. Just today, they could have given me a break.'

Her face creases a little as she opens up, but she quickly tries to correct that. She's still trying to put on her best show.

'They're hardly boys,' you smile, trying to edge the conversation to where Betty might be a little more comfortable. Nobody's called the 26-year-old non-identical twins 'boys' for years.

'Want me to talk to them?' you offer.

'No offence, Detective, but I doubt Archie will want to talk to you.'

Of course. Not that you're going to be sending him back to prison just by chatting to him, but every interaction you have with Archie Grainger, as you well know, is a frosty one. He's not suddenly going to be buying you a fancy Christmas card.

'Finn's in the back if you want to see him. But be quick: I've got to do the lights in ten minutes,' she offers. She's clearly keen to move the conversation on: but are you?

Go to **33** *if you want to pick things up with Finn.*
Or do you reckon Betty has more to say?
Keep chatting to her at **13** . . .

⇢ *201* ⇠

It's been a long day, and you're well aware there's still some way to go. After all you've been through to get this far, you now have to get your head straight, ready for whatever's thrown at you next – after a quick stop to smarten yourself up and get ready. A swift wash never hurt anyone, you tell yourself. You throw a thick blanket on the back seat of your car in case it gets cold, and get moving. You cut your arrival fine, but on the upside, you do smell quite nice.

You arrive at the Windy Dog to find the evening's festivities already getting underway. You've not been in Causton too many years, but during the time you've been here you've been made very aware of just what a big deal the festive lights switch-on is. Furthermore, how central the Windy Dog pub is for kicking off the area's Christmas build-up.

Not that you mind all of this. On the moments when your head isn't on the job, you enjoy taking the area in, and there's something warm, charming and traditional about seeing such a picturesque place decorated with old-style twinkling lights.

It's still chilly, but at least it's not raining as you step out of the car. You look at the pub building itself, a traditional large black-and-white construction that has very much – architecturally, at least – stood the test of time. The big car park is rarely short of space, but most gravitate to leaving their vehicles near the main entrance.

The old place is coated in unlit lights, and as you look back you see that the twisty lane leading up to the pub itself is similarly decorated. It's a lot of work, and Betty Grainger has been at the heart of it for as long as you've been in the area. Even as she was dealing with personal grief from the loss of her sister, she wouldn't let the village down.

It's not quite no expense spared, though, as some of the lights look like they've put in a fair amount of service. In fact, some of the decorations and lights looked past their sell-by date last year, too. There's been no fresh money spent this time around that you can see. There seem to be no lights around the pub sign that sits at the entrance to the car park either. That's unusual.

People are milling around outside the pub already. Archie Grainger, Betty's son, appears to be double-checking a few light arrangements on the outside of the pub building. The village choir is assembling, ready to sing in the festive season around a princely looking Christmas tree. Its lights, too, are waiting to be switched on as part of the big event.

It's just the kind of occasion that Causton is good at, and as you look around you're half-tempted to take a photograph. Even unlit, the place looks beautiful.

Still, as much as you want to enjoy the evening, you're aware there's work to be done. It's a long shot, you realize, that Sara McLower's murderer is still in the area, but you need to make sure you cover all bases anyway. Best get talking to a few people. You have a small window of time before things get under way, so what do you want to do?

Do you want to go straight into the pub? If so, head to **142***.
Archie Grainger looks like he could use a hand. You can offer,
at least, by going to* **183***.
Maybe you should mill with the choir for a moment, and find
out what treats they have in store? You need* **159***.*

➤ *202* ⬅

'I'm sorry,' you say. 'I had to be certain. I don't think you're something to do with this. I'm just hitting a dead end trying to uncover what's going on. Someone must have poisoned what Sara McLower was eating.'

They're angry at first, but they do soften. Sara was a good customer. Even though you've hardly got on their good side here, ultimately you all want the same thing.

'I really don't know what to tell you, Detective,' says Bob, helping Alison to her feet. 'I trust news of us being here won't be leaking out?'

'Even if it does, I'll just say I needed your help with something. Which is true.'

They seem comforted by this. 'We really didn't know, you know. We're not just saying it. This has come as much of a surprise to us as it has to you.'

You offer the pair a lift back to the shop, and they begrudgingly accept it. At least you can keep talking on the way. It's small talk, and you detect that the relationship between the three of you is likely

the
Windy
Dog

forever changed. As polite as everyone is, you did just haul them over to the police station.

Pulling up outside the shop, you see that the door is – of course – closed, and any interested customers have realized that it's not opening straightaway. There's no queue outside.

You get out of the car, and go to help Alison do the same. She rejects your offer. 'I think it's best I do that myself, Detective, don't you?' she says curtly.

The awkwardness is quickly interrupted, though, by a noise. In fact, something of a commotion. Bob gets out of the car quickly, and moves to the storage garage. Alison heads to the shop to unlock it.

'It's you,' you hear him exclaim. 'What on earth are you doing here?'

You rush to the garage, catching up with him. Two people are standing facing each other, both angry.

Teddy Jones is one. Hamilton Grainger is the other. What on earth has been going on?

Let Bob do the talking here? Go to **87**.
You do the talking. Take control at **180**.

→ *203* ←

'Teddy, stop!' you yell, chasing him as best you can out of the shop. He's fast, though, and he races off down the road a small way before sitting down on the kerb and all but crumpling.

You sit down. What this young man has been through in his life is a lot for anyone to bear, and you take that into account when he says what he's about to say.

'It's my fault,' he starts to sob. 'It's my fault.'

Hold on a minute: what's your fault?

'I know what's been going on. I've heard what you've all been talking about. I delivered the food to her. Now my nan isn't well too.'

He cries more. 'The lights,' he says. 'The lights. They weren't supposed to go off there. T-they were just supposed to mess the evening up. They weren't supposed to kill anyone. A-am I going to have to go to prison?'

Wait: Teddy sabotaged the lights? Teddy delivered the food? Was this him all along, a teenager lashing back at the world? It seems so out of character, even though parts of it, at least, make sense.

He's given you no choice here, and you know it. After a few minutes, the pair of you stand up and walk towards your car. When Alison finally makes it home around an hour later, she'll find her husband sitting in the middle of the shop in tears, explaining that their grandson was part of what's been going on. That their grandson is now sitting in Causton police station being charged with a crime.

It's an arrest that gives you no pleasure at all, but his confession is pretty straightforward. It doesn't answer every part of the puzzle, and you're convinced there's more to it. But for Teddy Jones, an already difficult life is about to get a lot harder, as he prepares for time behind bars. As for his grandparents, they still can't wrap their head around everything. They still don't think it makes sense.

At heart, nor do you. But you've got your arrest, and you're sure another difficult case can't be too far away.

THE END

Go to p.321 to read your performance review.

➤ *204* ➤

You know that Alison and Bob are going to be devastated with what you're about to tell them – but ultimately, what choice do you have?

You explain what you think has happened. That somewhere along their supply chain, the supplies they've ordered in for Sara McLower have been contaminated. That somebody has been deliberately poisoning her plums, and this has contributed to her illness. It obviously wasn't what killed her, you confirm, but it still could have done.

The pair of them are on the verge of tears as you tell them this. You're sure that they had no knowledge of this, but even so. They can't help but feel responsible.

They take a minute to try and recompose themselves, and Bob makes the unusual decision to close the shop, putting up a sign saying that they'll be back in an hour.

When they're certain nobody is going to disturb them, then the tears start to flow. Teddy Jones, hearing the upset, detaches himself from his games machine and comes down the stairs. 'It's okay,' you say to him. 'You go back upstairs. They just need a minute.'

He looks at them, and starts to get upset himself.

'I think it's my dad,' he whispers.

Which is just the moment when you notice the car that's parked outside. With someone in the driver's seat, looking straight through the shop window.

His dad? What did he mean by that? Go to **71**.
The car? A distraction, or something you should investigate?
Go to **164**.

⤐ *205* ⤐

You walk into Teddy's room, and he does what any good teenager does the second they see an authority figure: he deletes his internet history and tries to look a little less flustered. You try not to smile as you greet him.

He nervously smiles back, but it's not often he has a police detective in his room, and even though he won't say it, he wants to know why you're there.

'Have you got a minute?' you ask, politely. 'Your nan said I could come up.'

'Have I done something wrong?' he asks.

'No, no. Nothing like that,' you smile. You must have spoken to Teddy but one or two times over the last couple of years. You both know of each other, but you've never really had a reason to chat.

You take a look at the computer that's teetering on the edge of a desk at the side of his room. It's a bit of a beast, and the discarded food and drink cartons around said desk suggest that Teddy doesn't move from here unless he has to.

'I want to ask about you delivering groceries,' you say softly.

'I only do it because they make me,' he complains in response. 'But I suppose they pay me for it, at least.'

'I'd imagine it helps fund that,' you say, smiling as you nod at his computer.

'Well, yeah.'

'You used to deliver groceries to Sara McLower?'

He nods, but isn't offering anything. Talking about people who are no longer here isn't on Teddy's list of favourite things to do.

'Can you just take me through what you used to do?'

He looks a little puzzled. Surely that's a basic question?

'What I always do. I take the order that Grandad has bagged up, and I deliver it.' He leaves a pause. 'That's about it, really.'

'How was Sara?'

'Just like most of the others. They smile, take the bags, sometimes ask me to carry them into the house, and then I go. Although she did used to buy everyone nice Christmas presents . . .'

'You ever do odd jobs for her, or anything like that?'

'No,' he says. 'A few people asked me, but not her. I'd rather just be back here, though. I work a lot as it is.'

You thank Teddy for his time, then head back down the stairs and through the shop.

'Was he okay?' asks Alison. 'You know teenagers: he doesn't really talk to me. Only when it's payday.'

'He was fine,' you say. But now you want to find out more about that security footage. You head down into the shop, steeling yourself to ask about it . . .

Go to **116**.

➤ *206* ➤

Fearing the worst, with a dose of panic, you opt for cutting your losses, jerking the steering wheel violently to the left and veering off the road. Your car hits the bush that separates the road from the field, and you violently bash the brakes with all your might. Ahead of you is a scarecrow left over from the autumn, and the expression on its face indicates that it wasn't really expecting to see you.

You try and swerve to avoid it as your car's speed decreases, the impact of the force with which you hit the brakes jolting, while the muddy field happily chews up any grip your tyres had. You hear the sound of the other car scooting off in the other direction and swing your wheel around, trying to turn to follow them.

Your car comes down to a manageable speed, and the scarecrow now looks a little relieved that you didn't hit it. But you have a different problem to negotiate. Your tyres are struggling to get traction in the muddy field, and as you put your foot back on the floor, all they seem to be doing is spinning and redistributing mud.

Thankfully, the mud isn't too thick, so your car doesn't come to a total standstill. But it still takes a few minutes to manoeuvre your way out of the field, inch back through the bush and out onto the road. The car you were following is, of course, long gone, and there's little chance of tracking it down now.

You sigh, but you're intact at least. Your car is dirty, your pride beaten down a little bit, but the investigation goes on. You make the slow drive back to the Windy Dog, and you're not expecting the Chief Inspector to be in the best of moods when she hears about this . . .

Motor on back to **54.**

207

Not wishing to cross the Chief Inspector, you get up early the following morning and head straight to the station. There's no update overnight about Archie Grainger, which is the first thing you ask. For the minute, it sounds like no news is good news.

You get a quick check done on the envelope to ensure that it's safe to open. You do worry you're being over-cautious here, but then have to remind yourself that a Christmas light blew up in someone's face earlier.

You open up the envelope and unfold the sheet of A4 paper that's within it. Like the envelope, the letter itself is handwritten. Sara McLower has signed it.

It reads:

Dearest Betty,

I know we're had our ups and downs over the years, but I wanted to tell you that you've always been special to me, and I've always been proud to be your sister. Mum would be so proud too at how you've kept the pub going. Especially with everything's that gone on this year. I'm so sorry about the all the trouble you've been having with the reviews, and I'm sorry that the police aren't taking it seriously.

I'm still not feeling my best. I've not been feeling well all year, and I fear it's getting worse. If I end up ill or in hospital over Christmas, I've bought all my Christmas presents, and please make sure they are sent around the village. I still don't know if they appreciate them, but I want to send them something for all the support they gave us after Mum died.

I've not heard from him for a little while. Hopefully we've seen the last of him after last Christmas. But if he does come back, and I'm not around, don't give in. You deserve that pub, and you deserve so much for all the good you've done for everyone. You're a good person, Betty, and I love you so much.

Much love,

Sara.

So many questions there, and you don't quite know where to turn.

You need to confer with the Chief Inspector, really. She might have some light on all of this. Go to **36**.
Perhaps, though, it's time someone took a closer look at those online reviews. Go to **175**.

A pause. You shoot Teddy Jones a glare that tells him not to utter a word. Finn Grainger looks at you, in stony silence. Bob and Alison Jones look concerned for their grandson, knowing that there are questions that may need to be answered.

You? You want Hamilton Grainger.

'I think we should meet, Mr Grainger,' you tell him.

He leaves a further long pause. You give him your number.

'Call me,' you say.

The Chief Inspector isn't best pleased when she hears you've arranged to meet him, but it buys you the space to calm Finn Grainger down, and send him back to his mother. To talk to Bob, Alison and Teddy, and temper the situation there.

And then you wait. It's agonizing, and it's a gamble. If he doesn't call, what will you do? What will the Chief Inspector do?

But also: you're hoping the death of Archie Grainger has hit him hard. You're hoping he'll call. You need him to call.

He calls.

You arrange a meeting. One hour from now. But you've got to go alone.

Good luck . . .

Go to **134**.

209

You know you're going to have to head back to the station fairly sharpish, but also you recognize that a lot of Sara McLower's friends are here. Well, friends and people who knew her, or received one of her Christmas gifts and smiled in appreciation. There are one or two family members here as well: you can certainly spot her sister, Betty Grainger, from across the room. This is a busy day for her, you appreciate. Her sister's funeral and wake in the morning, and then the festive lights switch-on at the Windy Dog later on today.

You look around. Irene Whitley is also smiling, and could comfortably hold a long conversation with a stranger without even blinking. One of the loveliest people in the village, you know she was friendly with Sara. You wonder if it might be worth just checking in with her.

Reverend Martins, meanwhile, is trying valiantly to circulate and fit in, despite barely knowing a single person in the room. You could go and save him, and see how he feels everything has gone today?

Take your pick, Detective.

If you want to talk to Betty and pay your respects,
then walk over to 4.
If the idea of a natter with Irene Whitley is more tempting,
then try 161.
To take comfort in a man of the cloth, thanks to a chat with
Reverend Martins, go to 50.

You're not stopping. You're adamant you're not stopping. Teddy Jones's safety is at stake and you need to move fast, no matter what a mystery voice is telling you.

Not that the voice remains a mystery for very long. You hadn't noticed a figure under the blanket on your back seat, but now they've sat upright with a protective face mask on. You rushed to your car so quickly you didn't do the basic checks, and now you're on a country lane with an intruder in your vehicle.

You know there's not another house on this part of the road for about a mile. You look at your speedometer. The speed limit here is 30mph. Even if you sped up, you're two minutes away from safety.

'I'm not stopping,' you state, as assertively as you can muster.

'I won't ask again,' says the male voice, muffled under the mask.

'I'm not stopping.'

Only you are. Quick as a flash, the figure behind you presses something up against your face.

'Stop the car,' they urge you as you realize what it is. A car air freshener, but one with an overpowering smell. The figure next to you yanks on the handbrake, and the car's rear wheels lock, sending you into a spin neither of you can control. You can't see straight and your head is feeling lighter and lighter: whatever you've just breathed in isn't a regular air freshener, and you feel real fear. The car swerves towards the edge of the road and crashes through the hedge that lines it. As it does so, your head hits the steering wheel and the airbags deploy. The person behind you has locked their seatbelt just in time, and is better prepared for the impact.

They find you on the side of the road. DS Lambie, as it turns out,

was ten minutes behind you, and thank goodness he was. But as you come around, and start to recall what happened, the news isn't good.

Your car? It's gone, you're grimly informed.

Teddy Jones? He's also gone. Nobody knows where, nobody quite knows why.

Oh, and your chances of ever solving this case? They appear to be gone too. Bad luck, Detective. But don't worry: on this occasion, you'll make a full recovery.

THE END

Go to p.321 to read your performance review.

Teddy rockets out of the door while you take in what you just heard: the word 'nephew'. As surprised as you are to see Betty Grainger – after all, she lost her son earlier today – you're even more surprised to hear her utter that word.

'Nephew?' you ask.

It's as if a secret that's been locked away has just wriggled free.

'Nephew,' she says. 'Teddy is my brother's son. And I want to see my brother.'

'Wait,' you say, absorbing this. 'Are you telling me that Teddy's actual father is Hamilton?'

You look around the room. You're the only person here who didn't know. Everyone else did.

'Oh, don't worry about not knowing,' says Betty. 'He abandoned the boy before he was born. And he presumably only gets in touch with him when he wants something. But I guessed if anybody around here knew where I could find my brother, it'd be Teddy.'

It's pin-drop silence in the shop, as the door opens once more. You all turn, and there he is: Hamilton Grainger. Right in front of you. He locks the door shut behind him. Suddenly, you're glad that Teddy isn't here, although you assume that Hamilton, from wherever he's been hiding, watched him run.

'Detective,' he says. He walks with a slight limp, and gestures an unwelcome hello towards Betty, Alison and Bob.

'I'm sorry about Archie,' he says to Betty, 'truly.'

She gives him a look that words haven't yet been invented to describe.

'I'm leaving,' he says. 'Don't worry. I'm not coming back. I just wanted to say goodbye to Teddy before I went.'

Silence.

He turns to his sister. 'When you sell the Windy Dog,' he says, 'I want half of my share to go to Teddy. He's always deserved better than me.'

No disagreement there.

'Will you arrange that with Alison and Bob?' he asks. She grunts, a nod. She's not happy, but she knows she's lost the pub now. At least if Hamilton is putting some money towards Teddy, it's something. But it feels like there are no winners here.

'Unless the Detective wants something from me, I'll make my way out,' he says, after another awkward minute. You suppose you could arrest him, you think, but you've got no hard evidence to go with. Nothing tangible, and you know the Chief Inspector would need something substantive.

You stop for a minute, and then step back, letting him out of the way. You feel powerless. Betty feels powerless. Hamilton unlocks the door, steps into his car, never to be seen in Causton again. By the new year, Betty will be gone too. By the following summer, Bob and Alison will follow suit.

As for you? You just wish you had that magic piece of evidence. Without it, you have to consign this case to the unsolved pile. You'd best come back on Monday morning and see what else Causton has in store for you . . .

THE END

Go to p.321 to read your performance review.

⇒ *212* ⇐

It feels odd having to break into your own house, but you simply can't take the risk. You need an element of surprise or, at the very least, you don't want anyone to be alerted to where you'll be.

You park around five minutes from your ground-floor flat, but the walk there takes ten, as you go the back way and keep away from the lit areas. Then you head straight towards the back of your building, thankful that you picked a place with a back door to it. You know that your interior camera isn't quite pointing at it – you only bought two, and you put one facing the front door and the other one just inside your bedroom. It means there are only two places in your flat you can go, realistically, without risking triggering the cameras and sending an alert to your phone.

Those two places? The lounge and kitchen area, and the toilet. You opt for the loo.

The toilet itself sits next to a modern shower cubicle, and you elect to leave the door open, but hide yourself. Then? It's a waiting game. You only have half an hour to wait.

You're unsure exactly what Hamilton Grainger's plan is: presumably he was going to sit in your flat and wait for you? He makes quick work of the lock on the front door, though, and is soon in your building. You tense up, hearing him. You grab the metal object next to you and hold it close, as you hear him head to your lounge area.

He waits there for around ten minutes or so. You can't see him, but you can hear him. He sounds like he's getting fidgety. Then you realize why: he needs to use the facilities.

Who knew it would come down to this?

Some things in life, though, are hard to predict. In the rich history of Causton, there's only one known example of a suspect having to attend to the call of nature, and then being confronted with a police detective leaping out of an adjacent shower, hitting them hard with a metal toilet brush.

Then hitting them again, and again.

One more time for good measure. Heavy blows to the head that send Hamilton Grainger to the floor, and not entirely with everything in place.

The Chief Inspector is annoyed at first that you've put yourself at such risk. She can't, however, argue with the result. Realizing at the very least he's facing a breaking and entering charge that'll put him away, and suspecting you've got more evidence on him, Hamilton Grainger cuts a deal. He confesses to the murder of Sara McLower. In doing so, he dodges involvement in the death of Archie Grainger, even

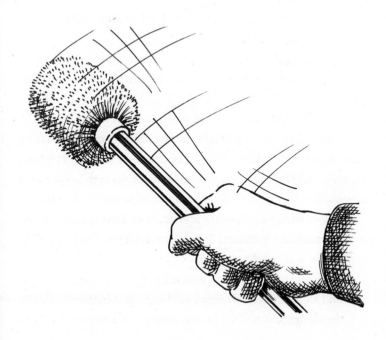

though there's a suspicion he was integral to it. The online reviews? Well, after the severity of the sentence that'll be handed down to Hamilton Grainger for premeditated murder, the courts agree to let those slide.

For Betty Grainger there's some rare good news to end the year, as the villagers rally around her – not least when they realize just how tough things have been for her. She can hold on to the Windy Dog for at least a little while longer.

And as for you, Detective? The Chief Inspector is so impressed that the word 'promotion' is briefly mentioned. Right now, though? You figure you've earned yourself a nice glass of wine, and a good DVD boxset to relax with.

Well done.

THE END

Go to p.322 to read your performance review.

⇒ *213* ⇐

You head back to your desk and make a valiant attempt to drink your coffee. Worse luck: the coroner answers quickly. Deborah Cottrill is efficient, and is interested in wasting as little as your time as possible.

'Hello, Detective,' she says. 'Sara McLower, I'm guessing.'

She recognized the number. Pleasantries are over.

'The poisons?'

'Ah, you've spoken to the Chief Inspector. She's got the details, yes. But I'd suggest that Sara McLower had been dying for some time.'

'How long?'

'Well, one of them could have been in her system for months. I didn't know her, I'm afraid, but you can assume she would have been feeling unwell for some time.'

'How much longer would that poison have taken to kill her?'

'Well, it seems that she's been taking it for most of the year by my estimate, and I'd imagine you'll find traces of it in her food. If she carried on like that, it's feasible that she could have passed at the end of this year, early next?'

'What about the other poison?'

'Well, this one worked quicker, but still weeks, rather than days. I'd ordinarily recommend checking her house for air fresheners or pot pourri, something like that. But the Chief Inspector said several officers have been through her house and – while they smelt nice – they hadn't found anything of concern. It does seem like something she'd breathe in through her nose, though.'

'How long would that one have taken?'

'Like I said' – this is not a woman who likes to repeat herself, you realize – 'a few more weeks at the rate she seemed to be taking it in.'

'Would she have known she was being poisoned?'

'Almost certainly not. Just that she was gradually feeling more and more ill.'

This could, then, have been an invisible murder. But why wasn't it allowed to play out? What caused the killer to hasten their attack on Sara McLower? What caused the fresh urgency?

Good question. But you see another call coming in, and thank Deborah Cottrill for her time. Turns out that someone's gone and found Sara McLower's car – and you need to go and check it out.

Pop over to 7 to do just that.

⇢ *214* ⇠

You head outside to see what's going on. It's trouble, and lots of it.

It's quite the scene that greets you and Finn Grainger, as he also takes it all in. The once-impressive Windy Dog Christmas tree, which had been erected next to the main door into the pub, looks like it's had part of its body blasted away. The green pine needles are now smoking and have lost their colour. Shards of glass from the Christmas lights litter the floor.

Alison Jones, from the local shop, approaches you straight away. 'We've called an ambulance, Detective,' she tells you. 'They said they were going to be here as quickly as they could.'

Hang on: an ambulance?

'What for?' you ask.

'For him,' she replies, pointing at the prone body of Archie Grainger, lying a foot or two from the base of the Christmas tree. A jolt of shock hits you, but nothing like the jolt that presumably has hit Archie Grainger. Before you can do anything, Finn Grainger is by his brother's side, pushing past everyone and giving him urgent emergency care. Within seconds, it looks like he's doing chest compressions and mouth-to-mouth resuscitation. This is clearly very, very serious.

'Why didn't you call me?' you ask, giving Finn space, but checking to see if Archie Grainger has a pulse. He does, but it's a very faint one.

Betty Grainger remains inside the pub, but there's no doubt by now that she'll have an idea of what's going on.

'How long's the ambulance going to be?' Finn bellows. 'I'm losing him!'

'We called it a few minutes ago. They said there's a unit not far away, but it'll still take a couple of minutes,' says Alison. You hope under your breath that it doesn't even take that long to get here. Archie might not have much time left.

You look around. It's the lights on the Christmas tree. It seems like some of them have – surely not? They can't have *exploded*? You knew the lights were old, but even so: they're not going to simply blow up like that. Something isn't right here. Sabotage. The word lingers in your brain. It's certainly possible: just like Sara McLower's pumpkins, whoever's done this could have prepared it anytime.

But why would they want to attack Archie Grainger? True, he's been in prison, and may have made a few enemies over the last few years, but even so: how could they know he'd be standing under the tree when the lights were turned on?

Then it dawns on you. They couldn't, unless the person who rigged all of this was nearby. Or unless they prepared it days ago, and Archie just got in the way.

You stand in the car park of the Windy Dog, wondering just what you next move should be.

Do you want to look at the lights, to see what might have ignited them? Go to **68**.
Or do you want to see if – gulp – there may be someone suspicious about? You need to go to **83**.

→*215*←

Alison Jones is a little taken by surprise at your suggestion of going to the doctor with her. Still, when you offer to drive her over to see Dr Elliott she softens, and admits it's not a bad idea. After all, Bob can't take her, can he? He has the shop to look after.

In all your time in Causton, you've not spent much time actually talking to Alison. You see her regularly enough, of course, but it's very transactional: she talks to you on the rare occasion there's a shoplifter at the store, you talk to her when you're popping into the shop to get a few bits and pieces.

She tells you that the shop is as busy as she's ever known it, and how she and Bob would be lost without Teddy doing all their deliveries. He's thinking of going to university, though, in a couple of years, and they're both resigned to shutting up shop when he finally goes.

She admits, too, that the pace of trade hasn't been matched by her own health. That these last few weeks in particular, she's started to feel her age. You ask how old she is. 'Sixty-three,' she smiles, and had you guessed, you'd have gone a good six or seven years younger.

It was Bob who persuaded her to book an appointment with Dr Elliott. He'd noticed she was slowing down and, given Alison's energy levels were usually sky high, it wasn't tricky to spot when she was flagging a bit.

'I've not told him,' you say.

'Told him what?'

'That this is my second appointment, not my first.'

'When was the first? Why didn't you tell him?'

'Oh, you know Bob. He'll just worry.'

'You must be worried, though, to have booked in the first place, and not told him?'

For once, Alison goes quiet. 'I-I just hope the tests come back okay.'

Tests? What tests?

Head into the appointment with her:
you can do that by going to **144**.
Or should you go back and try and talk to Bob when she's not
there? You could drop her off, and then head back to him.
Do that at **112**.

≫ *216* ≪

'Tell me more about the reviews,' you ask, regretting your words as soon as you've said them.

'We've been reporting them all year,' she says, almost smiling with despair. 'Nobody's talked to us about them properly. Just fobbed us off and didn't really take any notice.'

'When did you first notice there was a problem?'

She's a bit irritated about this, even though it's not the most important thing on her mind at the moment.

'Trade was down over Easter,' she tells you. 'Things are always a bit tight in the pub trade at the start of the year, but it picks up for Mother's Day and Easter. This year, though, we didn't get anywhere near as many bookings as we were expecting. We just figured people were tightening their belts. Then Finn told me what was happening.'

Technology and Betty Grainger never really got on too well, you knew that. It was, she explains, Finn who showed her the review sites on the internet, with scathing words about the quality of the Windy Dog. For years until that point, it'd been a much-loved and hugely popular pub, and was always mentioned in local visitor guides and such like. But while locals had stuck with the Windy Dog, passing trade had declined, and declined fast.

'Did you try and do anything about them?' you ask, once again regretting the question.

She just gives you a look. This is one of those moments when silence speaks volumes, Detective.

You quickly work out the rest. That the pub – and Betty – began to run out of money. She'd spent her savings on legal representation for Archie when he had his court case, not that it did much good. Now her bank account is drained and the business is in trouble.

'I told Sara, of course,' she says. 'She would have given me the money, but she'd spent all hers buying her house in the first place. Still, she was going to let me move in with her. But . . .'

She breaks down in tears again. You see the Chief Inspector approaching, having arrived a few minutes earlier. She comes over and offers to take Betty to the hospital, an offer that's readily accepted.

Maybe it's worth seeing if there's anything else she can tell you?
She seems to be sharing things with you now. Go to **121**.
Or it might just be time to let the forensics team gather what
they can. You might want to go to the station first thing to find
out more about Hamilton Grainger. Go to **76**.

⇒*217*⇐

You approach the unlocked cellar doors, but stop yourself for a minute when you think you hear people approaching from the other side of the car park. False alarm: they're just walking hand in hand away from the building, and towards their car.

You take the opportunity to open up the cellar door properly, and it swings open as you pull it towards you. A small ladder leads down, and you note a light switch on the right as you descend. You wonder whether you should leave the light off, so as to attract less attention. Then you remind yourself: you're a police detective, and you're trying to, well, detect. It's not as if you don't have a reason for being here.

You flick the light, and then chuckle to yourself. That was a waste of time – clearly it's on the circuit that also connects the outside lights. Bottom line here: it's not working, so you opt for the trusty torch function on your phone. It takes a few seconds of fumbling for you to get the light on, and it's soon beaming as best it can into the dank and dark cellar.

It's clean, though. Betty Grainger, whether you like her or not, is clearly very well schooled in the art of keeping a pub tidy, organized and well run. You see the cask-ale metal barrels to the left of you. A barrel of what looks like Bob Jones's homemade cider is to the right. A nice bit of homebrew, that, and it's been a real hit since Betty added it to the Windy Dog's offerings at the start of the year.

You scout around to see if you can find anything of use, but seem to be coming up short. There's no clue that you can spot here.

That's the least of your worries, though.

You hear the door of the cellar start to close, as a figure walks down the short steps. Their face is covered, and that doesn't make you feel any safer. No wonder, too: whoever it is grabs a barrel of Bob Jones's cider, and promptly throws it hard and fast in your direction.

They're a good shot. It catches you straight in the midriff and throws you back into the wall. You let out a yelp, and this seems to anger the person who's in here with you. They reach for another barrel – a metal one this time – and you realize you've got virtually no wiggle room to get out of the way.

You breathe a sigh of relief, though, when it appears to be just a little too heavy for whoever this other person is, and they can't get the lift or thrust required to throw it with any great force. You stumble to your feet, and try and get yourself a foothold. But while you're working on that, the other person has grabbed the barrel of Bob's produce and is halfway through flinging it your way again.

As the Chief Inspector would mournfully tell your colleagues the following day, your death was, ultimately, down to a medium-sized barrel of cider hitting you directly on the head and taking you out cold. Killed by the drink, as it were.

The force of the impact, and the subsequent bleed on the brain, could have been treated, had you been found quickly. But whoever your attacker was decided to shut the doors behind them as they left the cellar, heading off for a life of freedom.

You? You're heading, sadly, to the ground.

THE END

Go to p.322 to read your performance review.

❧ *218* ❧

While you're waiting for assistance to arrive, you dial the number of the filling station. You know the one: it's a tiny garage just off the main road. After a little wait, a happy-sounding man answers the phone.

You quickly get to the point, and he turns out to be rather helpful. Yes, that certainly sounds like the sandwiches he sells in the shop, and yes, your assumption that the sandwich's sell-by date is within 48 hours of it being sold is correct as well.

So far so good.

His filling station doesn't do too much trade, and he admits that the profit comes from the little workshop he has next to it, where he undertakes car repairs. Even then, he sounds very relaxed, and as if he's on his fifth cup of coffee and not had a customer for an hour or two.

On the matter in hand: you mention the rough date, and the purchase of nourishment. Unsurprisingly, he comes up blank there, and can't recall the exact customer. You push him a little on this, and describe Sara McLower to him. It doesn't register with him at all. You reel through everything you can think of: petrol, sandwiches, air fresheners, drinks?

'Air fresheners?'

Oh, hello.

'Odd you should say that,' he says. 'There was a guy here a month or two ago who bought a box of them.'

A box? The bush-shaped air fresheners that dangle from your mirror?

He confirms those, indeed, were the ones. As a bonus, this has jogged his memory too. Definitely a man, definitely not Sara McLower. A tall man, too, around six feet. Specifics are difficult as it was weeks ago, and there's a chance the person's face was all but covered up. People have been reaching for their scarves a lot of late, to keep the cold away. An officer will go and visit the filling station later to try and glean more, not with any real success.

Still, you've got something tangible. It was a man in Sara McLower's car, and given that she lived pretty much alone, you have to assume that whoever was driving the vehicle is a suspect in her death. You also note the air fresheners. Someone seems to have bought a lot of those, and it's worth keeping an eye out for more. That'll be a signifier that you're on a good path, you figure.

Finally, a rumbling engine sound from afar indicates that help has probably arrived. A message to your phone confirms so, and the process of getting everyone to safety and the car towed for further examination gets underway. Which leaves you free to get ready for the shindig at the Windy Dog.

Let the festivities begin. Head over to **201**.

Alison heads off to talk to Mary on reception. You close the door and turn to Dr Elliott.

'Poison?' you say.

He nods. 'I'm afraid so,' he confirms. 'Nowhere near a fatal amount, but I'd imagine when we get more detail back, it'll corroborate what I think. That whatever's poisoned her, it was over weeks, not days. Just small doses, nothing you'd detect when you were taking it. But enough to do some serious damage over time.'

'Over how much time, Doctor?'

'It's hard to put a number on it, really. I've not had too much experience in this department, I'm afraid. From what I've read up, she'd have needed to take whatever it was for many months for it to do really significant damage, but just a couple of weeks was enough for her to start feeling very much under the weather.'

'Sara McLower,' you say. 'Did she ever have the same tests done?'

'I know where you're going with this,' admits Dr Elliott, 'and I had the same thought myself. I can't give you anything 100 per cent cast iron, and there may be other theories that fit. But I do believe that it's a possibility at the very least that Sara McLower was taking whatever was making Alison Jones unwell too.'

'Do you know what it could have been?'

'Something they've breathed in. Something they've eaten. I'm sorry, Detective, but with the information I've got, all I can give you is a best guess. And that's my best guess.'

You head outside to find Alison on the phone. You open up the car and she sits down, looking shellshocked. Your head is awash with questions.

'I could really use some thinking time,' she says to you. Can you go back to Bob, and let me walk home?' You take a little persuading, but you're inclined to agree. Do you want to ask her another question before you go, though?

Has she any idea what was poisoning her?
Ask her, by going to 136.
Or head back to Bob at 112.

220

The more Hamilton Grainger talks, the less and less you believe of what he's saying. You don't like him, and you don't like the way that he's firing accusations around. Isn't he a person of interest, too? You can't shake the fact that he seems to know everyone, and he seems to have a theory for each of them. But what about him? He's the one who appears to be acting in the shadows.

You open up your phone, and he doesn't look happy about it.

'What are you doing?' he says.

You move quickly, with the Chief Inspector on the line in a matter of seconds. You switch it to speakerphone so she can hear him, and he can hear her. In the back of your mind, it gives you a little extra safety: if he is actually dangerous, then it'll be very obvious that he's attacked you.

But – and you're not disappointed about this – he doesn't want to attack you. He seems quite placid, if anything, the calm one more in charge of the situation. You ask him to reiterate everything that he's just told you, and he does. He has no qualms about that.

You type a message to the Chief Inspector, that she can see and Hamilton Grainger can't. 'I don't buy it,' you write.

'Nor do I,' she responds, as the conversation continues.

'Can I bring him in?'

There's a long pause, and Hamilton Grainger has guessed that something is going on.

'Your call,' she types.

You have to follow your gut here. You caution him, but the best you've got is wasting police time. Hamilton Grainger seems to know the way to play this too, being a model of cooperation. Even as you interrogate him back at the station, he's sticking to his guns. You attempt to make the wasting police time charge stick. You know it's a maximum of six months in prison in serious cases.

You also know this isn't a serious case. When it eventually comes to court, Hamilton Grainger pleads guilty, gets a ticking off and leaves you with the sense that you might not have made the right choice. Still, a minor conviction. Not an awful day at the office . . .

THE END
———

Go to p.322 to read your performance review.

YOUR PERFORMANCE REVIEW

5: AWOL

At a pivotal point in the investigation, the Detective left the scene. Well, not just the scene, but the entire area.

....

Recommended course of action: Reassign them to a job that involves them not leaving their seat. Certainly not detective material. Go to **epilogue three**.

9: OH DEAR

The detective's ability to solve the case was severely compromised by the fact that they are now dead.

....

Recommended course of action: Get the job advert out. And send some flowers.

11: AND THEY'RE OFF

Mild promise was shown by the detective in this investigation, but severe misgivings about their ability to conclude a case.

....

Recommended course of action: Let them try another case. May need closer monitoring.

22: CLOSE, BUT NOT CLOSE ENOUGH

Were it not for a sloppy mistake, the detective may very well have made an arrest here. A lot of promise, though.

....

Recommended course of action: Send them off for a day of training, and we'll see them again on Monday morning.

23: A MINOR SUCCESS

The detective made substantial progress and managed to land a conviction. The murder cases remain open.

. . . .

Recommended course of action: They've done enough to secure another murder case. At least we've got someone off the streets. Go to **epilogue one**.

40: GNOME ALONE

On the bright side, the detective will make a full recovery. Less impressively, they didn't solve the case, and Irene Whitley's gnomes are looking lonelier.

. . . .

Recommended course of action: Send for a gnome, and make the detective personally deliver it. Go to **epilogue three**.

42: THIS DID NOT GO WELL AT ALL

Where do we actually get these people from? Arrested the wrong people, caused lots of bad will, damaged reputation of upstanding citizens.

. . . .

Recommended course of action: Suggest they do anything but police work. Go to **epilogue three**.

51: WAS BARELY WORTH THEM TURNING UP

Had they not died, this report would have been very damning. As it is, they died, and died quickly. Eradicate all mention of their poor detective skills from their file.

. . . .

Recommended course of action: Flowers, a whip-round and better recruitment.

54: WENT MISSING WHEN IT MATTERED

The detective's idea of actually detecting a case involves leaving an active crime scene and indulging in a car chase.

....

Recommended course of action: Clear their desk and send them estate agent listings for properties at least 100 miles away. If not further.

61: WHERE DO WE GET THESE PEOPLE FROM?

No arrest, no tangible leads, a very bad headache, and the need for some new car keys? Smashing.

....

Recommended course of action: Memo to HR about sharpening the quality of our recruitment.

71: A MILD DISCONNECT BETWEEN THEIR BRAIN AND THEIR ACTIONS

The detective did manage to make progress and do some good detecting, but failed to turn it into actions to resolve the case. Still, at least Causton seems a little bit safer.

....

Recommended course of action: Give them a patronizing pat on the back, let them keep their job and talk about them behind their back a bit. Go to **epilogue one**.

85: JOB DONE!

A tremendous result. An arrest, a full cracking of the case, and it's hard to see how their performance could be improved upon.

....

Recommended course of action: Promotion, and a really nice swivel chair. Go to **epilogue two**.

94: THE AIR IS NOT FRESH

On the bright side, the detective will clearly make a full recovery. On the less bright side, they've managed to add nothing of substance or use to the enquiry.

. . . .

Recommended course of action: They can keep their job. They make decent coffee.

113: IN THE BALLPARK, BUT STILL NOT GOOD ENOUGH

The detective showed real promise, and had they managed to get a result from the interview with the prime suspect, this would be a very different report. They didn't, though, so it's this report.

. . . .

Recommended course of action: Not sure this line of work is for them, but let them carry on. Go to **epilogue one**.

118: A GOOD WINTER'S WORK

Really impressive performance. Estimated that they cracked pretty much – if not quite all – of the case. But hard to argue with the result: a conviction, and a lengthy sentence.

. . . .

Recommended course of action: Send the file over for promotion consideration. Open the extra-special packet of biscuits, too. Go to **epilogue two**.

119: OUTSTANDING

This is what we want. An arrest, a conviction and a completely solved case! Where did we get this detective from, and where can we find more like them?

....

Recommended course of action: A commendation, a promotion and a warmer seat in the office.

129: SITUATION VACANT

Had it not been for the intervention of the detective, we may have ended up with fewer dead bodies.

....

Recommended course of action: Make sure they spend the rest of their life doing anything other than police work. Go to **epilogue three**.

138: NOT THE BRIGHTEST LIGHTBULB IN THE BOX

A rookie error, and one of our best officers too having to answer questions? Sigh.

....

Recommended course of action: Give them back their uniform, and get them out of CID.

140: WILL HAVE TO DO

A conviction was secured, even if the murder cases remain unsolved. Still, heading off on a car chase wasn't the wisest of moves.

....

Recommended course of action: Consider them for another case, take their 'Fast & Furious' DVDs off them. Go to **epilogue one**.

143: CAREER CHANGE

A very disappointing detective, this one. The kind that makes a bit of progress, but messes things up when it really matters. They, and the department, can do better.

....

Recommended course of action: Are we allowed to quietly encourage them to leave? If not, give them easier cases for the foreseeable future. Go to **epilogue one**.

152: NOT ONE OF OUR FINEST

The detective managed to resolve arguably the least important part of the case, and did not manage to resolve, well, the murders.

....

Recommended course of action: They're not without use, but detecting cases is not their future. Go to **epilogue one**.

160: DIDN'T QUITE GET THE MEMO

It's all very well detecting a case and coming up with a suspect, but at some point you do actually have to apprehend them.

....

Recommended course of action: Training. A lot of training.

164: WELL, THEY'RE NOT DEAD

This report can easily conclude that the detective is willing to put their body on the line. If they could engage their brain a bit more, that'd be more useful.

....

Recommended course of action: Let's just give them desk duties for a bit. And make sure they send a thank-you card to the paramedics. Go to **epilogue one**.

169: DONE UP LIKE A CHRISTMAS TREE

In all the history of writing these reports, there's never been a case of a detective allowing themselves to be strangled by tinsel. With a bit of luck, these words will never have to be uttered again.

....

Recommended course of action: Reassign elsewhere. Don't put them in charge of the Christmas party.

174: CAFFEINATED TO DEATH

A promising detective cut down in their prime. A real pity. And what a way to go: please make sure we come up with a cover story for their relatives.

....

Recommended course of action: Another job advert. Abstaining from coffee for a month as a sign of respect.

180: SOME SUCCESS, BUT NOT MUCH SUCCESS

Job one is to get a dangerous criminal off the streets. The detective appears to have done that. Job two is to actually crack the case. The detective appears to have not done that.

Recommended course of action: The detective has done enough to get another assignment. Go to **epilogue one**.

189: THEY'RE ALIVE. NOT MUCH ELSE, THOUGH

A decent detective who found themselves outthought and outplayed. The prime suspect is gone, and the detective will need security equipment installing at home.

Recommended course of action: Arrange a 50 per cent discount at the security suppliers.

194: GET THEM OUT OF TOWN

Good grief. The detective has brought negative publicity to the department, and not solved the case. Could it have gone much worse?

Recommended course of action: Offer to help write their CV.

199: ALIVE, BUT THAT'S ABOUT IT

An unsuccessful investigation, and an injured detective, expected to be out of action for several weeks.

Recommended course of action: Double-check the department sick-pay policy.

203: AN ARREST, BUT A CONFLICTED ONE

We asked the detective to make a solid arrest and they did. Very much the feeling that the wrong person is behind bars, though.

....

Recommended course of action: Not much we can do. See them again on Monday.

210: THEY'LL BE BACK

Can confirm that the detective's injuries will heal quickly and they'll be back at work shortly. Not that it'll do our crimes solved rate any good.

....

Recommended course of action: Be suitably sympathetic, but give the next big case to someone else. Go to **epilogue one**.

211: UNRESOLVED

The detective managed to work through a fair amount of the case, without actually making an arrest. Not a very good performance.

....

Recommended course of action: Reassert the need to actually land a conviction. Find a new local shop to get the biscuits from. Go to **epilogue one**.

212: GOOD WORK, GOOD WORK

We've got a good one here. The detective's methods may not always have been as we'd like, and a reminder of some safety basics wouldn't hurt. But a welcome arrest, even if some part of the case remained unresolved.

Recommended course of action: We might have to consider this one for promotion. And self-defence classes. Go to **epilogue one**.

217: FACE AND PALM

Killed by a barrel of cider? We might have to come up with something a little more conventional when we put the press release out.

Recommended course of action: Apart from sending flowers and paying our respects, it's probably best to lay off Bob Jones's homebrew for a bit.

220: THAT'LL HAVE TO DO.

The fact that we've had these murders and ended up with the chief suspect getting pinned at best for wasting police time is hardly ideal. Sometimes, we take what we get.

Recommended course of action: We may as well keep the detective in post, and hope that someone better comes along soon. Go to **epilogue one**.

EPILOGUE ONE

At the end of what turned out to be a dramatic year in Causton, you opt for a quiet New Year's Eve. You get up late for a change, take time to enjoy your coffee, and swing by the station for a few hours.

You check the messages that have come in. Jack Linus isn't happy with Ralph Maddock's cat again. Apparently, the feline assassin has deposited two small presents in Jack's back garden, and he wants prompt action.

Trevor Davies? Well, he's insistent that his Christmas was ruined by three spooky sightings on Christmas Eve. He's vowed to mend his ways going forward, and you add his latest stories to your file.

Finally, someone called Martine Moffett has left a message to give DS Lambie the news he was waiting for, that he won the prize cheese in the annual village Christmas raffle. DS Lambie will be thrilled, you smile.

Around 5pm, you grab your coat and head to your car. Time to go home, you figure. You take a drive to Jones's Store and pick up a bottle of wine and a couple of bags of your favourite crisps. Then, you detour to the Windy Dog.

The pub that was supposed to be at the heart of the village's New Year celebrations lies eerily dormant. The lights are off, the doors are locked and the inside is empty. Betty Grainger had shocked the village with the news that she was giving the pub up, and over the coming months you imagine a new owner will come in and make it their own. For now, just quiet. Causton villagers, rather than coming together for New Year, opt to stay at home, and hope for a more peaceful time ahead.

You restart the engine to the car, switch the radio on, and start to make your way out of the otherwise-empty car park. But hang on a minute: was that a figure moving around in the bush at the back of the car park? Was there someone there?

You blink twice, and if there was anything or anyone there, they seem – like Betty Grainger and her family – to be gone. Do you get out and investigate? Or do you go home, put the fire on and crack open your wine?

You smile to yourself. Enough drama for this year, you figure. Your foot presses down on the accelerator and, just this once, you vow to keep your appointment with your sofa . . .

EPILOGUE TWO

You double-check the invitation that you and most of the village had been sent. A party at the Windy Dog, to celebrate New Year's Eve. Betty Grainger is really going to town on the evening too, you smile. She's pushing her luck a bit to suggest a smart dress code, but nonetheless, you figure you might just make an effort after the last month or two she's had.

Just before Christmas, she had the haunting job of burying her son, with Archie Grainger being laid to rest in the crowded churchyard, just a plot or two up from Sara. Reverend Martins officiated the service before returning to the city, and you reflect that it was as nice as anything like that could realistically be.

The village rallied round Betty when the news broke about what she'd gone through. The experience she'd had at the hands of her brother, and how the reviews online had nearly driven the Windy Dog into the ground. It's bittersweet that she lost two people so close to her, of course, so she's struggled to celebrate anything, and she's changed forever. But Betty clung to her Windy Dog as she always had done, and wanted to thank those who'd rallied round her. After the full story of what'd happened appeared in the newspaper, the community came together, and bookings soared.

What's more, Causton CID finally got the online reviews sorted that had plagued the Windy Dog over the last year. The future for the pub is at least looking a lot brighter than it was.

When you arrive, Betty Grainger spots you quickly and greets you. The place only reopened this morning, and she admits that she's not sure now how much longer she wants to carry on. She'll be getting the inheritance from Sara's house coming through, and her financial problems are behind her. But also, as she looks around her beloved Windy Dog, she knows it's a place filled with ghosts now. Her son, her mother, her sister . . . She can see their faces when she closes her eyes, but she knows they're gone.

'I'm just going to enjoy tonight I think', she tells you. 'I have to take each day as it comes. I think I might just go away for a bit after this, though. I've been around this village a long time. I think it can live without me for a couple of months.'

You raise a glass to her and tell her that she might just deserve that. She gives you a warm smile, but her eyes betray that this is a Betty Grainger with part of her life that'll never be what it was.

Still, she's got a party to get going, and what's a party at the Windy Dog without Betty Grainger at the heart of it? One day, probably soon, the villagers here will have to find out. But not tonight: Betty's here, the pub is full, and for once you might even stay longer than an hour, and try and enjoy yourself.

With that, you grab the fresh shandy Betty has poured for you, smile, and head into the middle of the party . . .

EPILOGUE THREE

You wake up late. You reach for your phone, and find out just how late: it's 31 December, and the time has just gone 11. You're supposed to be at the station for 12, and in spite of what Sergeant Draper may sometimes demonstrate, a bit of personal hygiene is required before you head into work. A quick shower later, you jump into your car and make it to your desk with a minute or two to spare.

It's quite quiet today, but there's a sombre feeling about the place. The removal vans came yesterday to the Windy Dog, to transport Betty Grainger's belongings. Finn helped her, of course, but then he was soon off, heading back to university early. You feel sad when you realize that Betty's journey to her new home would have taken her past where her sister used to live. Sara McLower's house was up for sale now, and with Betty given no choice – financially at least – but to move out of Causton, and hope the proceeds of the sale would help cover the debts from the pub. They should do.

Mind you, the repairs to the pub won't be on her watch anyway. After spending an hour or two at your desk, curiosity gets the better of you, and you get in your car and drive over to the Windy Dog. It won't be open tonight, but a freshly-erected sign does promise that it'll be reopening soon, with an 'under new management' placed above the door.

In fact, someone's been busy. Betty only left yesterday morning, and already it looks like a day's hard work has been done to refashion the pub. You notice her name is no longer above the door, either. She's not the licensee here. Instead, there's a different name in her place: Mr H Grainger.

Once he managed to get her out of the pub, it looks like he decided not to sell it after all. At least for the time being. Instead, it looks as if he's going to run it for a bit. You wonder if he's just doing that out of spite, to rub Betty's nose in it. Whatever the reason, you figure he won't be there in a year. He just wants the money now, and keeping the pub alive should keep its value bubbling nicely.

You decide that it's probably for the best to not hang around: it's not bringing back nice memories, and you can't help but think that the wrong person benefitted here. You drive back via the Jones's shop. It's Bob behind the counter again. Alison's struggling now, he tells you. They never could fully reverse what was making her ill, and her health has not been improving. He explains that they'll just get through January, and then see how things are. But he, too, is thinking of moving away from Causton. He'll do whatever it takes to make Alison happier, and to hopefully help her get better too.

It's been a tough few weeks around these parts. You pay for your bottle of wine, and weakly wish Bob a happy new year. Hopefully, you say to yourself, it'll be a calmer and nicer one.

Notes

AND IN CASE YOU DIDN'T KNOW . . .

ISBN 9781788402996 | £12.99